On Two Wings

On Two Wings

Humble Faith
and
Common Sense
at the
American Founding

Expanded Edition

MICHAEL NOVAK

ENCOUNTER BOOKS
New York • London

First paperback edition published in 2003 by Encounter Books, an activity of Encounter for Culture and Education, Inc., a nonprofit tax exempt corporation.

Encounter Books website address: www.encounterbooks.com

Manufactured in the United States and printed on acid-free paper. The paper used in this publication meets the minimum requirements of ANSI/NISO Z39.48-1992 (R 1997)(*Permanence of Paper*).

Library of Congress Cataloging-in-Publication Data

Novak, Michael.
    On two wings : humble faith and common sense at the American founding / Michael Novak.
        p. cm.
    Includes bibliographical references and index.
    ISBN 1-893554-68-6 (alk. paper)
    1. United States—Religion—To 1800. 2. Church and state—United States—History—18th century. 3. Religion and politics—United States—History—18th century. 4. Statesmen—United States—Religious life. 5. United States Constitution—Signers—Religious life. I. Title.
        BL2525.N68 2001
        200'.973'09033—dc21
                                                                        2001040978

10   9   8   7   6   5   4   3   2   1

Dedication

For our forebears who brought us here...

and

For our children and our children's children,

unto

the nth generation...

Tell the Israelites: "I bore you up on eagle wings and brought you here to myself. Therefore, if you hearken to my voice and keep my covenant, you shall be my special possession, dearer to me than all other people."
—Exodus 19:3b-5

I always consider the settlement of America with reverence and wonder, as the opening of a grand scene and design in Providence for the illumination of the ignorant, and the emancipation of the slavish part of mankind all over the earth.
—John Adams (*Works* I.66)

I will insist that the Hebrews have done more to civilize men than any other nation. If I were an atheist, and believed in blind eternal fate, I should still believe that fate had ordained the Jews to be the most essential instrument for civilizing the nations. If I were an atheist of the other sect, who believe or pretend to believe that all is ordered by chance, I should believe that chance had ordered the Jews to preserve and propagate to all mankind the doctrine of a supreme, intelligent, wise, almighty sovereign of the universe, which I believe to be the great essential principle of all morality, and consequently of all civilization.
—John Adams to F. A. Vanderkemp,
16 February 1809

We cannot but acknowledge that God hath graciously patronized our cause and taken us under his special care, as he did his ancient covenant people.
—Samuel Langdon, *The Republic Of The Israelites: An Example To The United States*

Contents

The Forgotten
One Hundred

Most of us grow up these days remarkably ignorant of the hundred men most responsible for leading this country into a War for Independence and writing our nation's Constitution. Benjamin Rush and James Wilson were reputed to be the most learned men amongst them, but what do most of us know about the fundamental beliefs and convictions of either of them? It would be easy to list ninety names from among the top one hundred and defy the reader to describe what they did or stood for; only a handfull are well known.

This is a scandal. How could it have happened?

For one thing, many of the guardians of the nation's memory are secular men, for whom the faith of our fathers is of diminishing importance. The law schools, the jurists, and the history departments show little interest in religion.

One wing of the eagle by which American democracy took flight has been quietly forgotten.

If the words of George Washington in his Farewell Address to the Nation (to be recounted later) are to be credited, this forgetfulness may yet undo the nation.

Although I have wanted to write this book for some forty years, my own ignorance stood in the way. It took me a long time, time spent searching up many byways and neglected paths, and fighting through a great deal of conventional (but mistaken) wisdom, to learn how many erroneous perceptions I had unconsciously drunk in from public discussion.

This book is a record of what I found. It is, perhaps, too filled with concrete stories and vivid anecdotes, and a little too heavily laden with direct quotes and documentary evidence. Yet I had no choice but to produce overwhelming evidence, in order to overcome the prevailing (and complacent) mischaracterizations of our past that predominate in the better circles.

At the end, I append some biographical sketches of a score or more of the "forgotten founders," in order to incite a thirst among others to bring us back yet more of the drama and depth of their lives, so that we might better understand our own obligations.

I offer this book as a token of the love and gratitude I feel for the haven this blessed land has offered to my family and scores of millions of other families. I pray that the American people shall ever keep our end of the Covenant with our Creator, from which our beginnings issued. "*Annuit Coeptis* [He smiled on our Beginnings]," our founders wrote upon the Seal of the United States.

ONE

*The sacred rights of mankind are not to be
rummaged for among old parchments or musty
records. They are written, as with a sunbeam,
in the whole volume of human nature, by the hand
of Divinity itself, and can never be erased
or obscured by mortal power.*

—Alexander Hamilton

FIRST CHAPTER

Jewish Metaphysics
at the Founding

In one key respect, the way the story of the United States has been told for the past one hundred years is wrong.[1] It has cut off one of the two wings by which the American eagle flies, her compact with the God of the Jews – the God of Israel championed by the nation's first Protestants – the God Who prefers the humble and weak things of this world, the small tribe of Israel being one of them; Who brings down the mighty and lifts up the poor; and Who has done so all through history, and will do so till the end of time. Believe that there is such a God or not – the founding generation did, and relied upon this belief. Their faith is an *"indispensable"* part of their story.

By contrast, to read most philosophers and historians of the American polity today is to learn that America is an historical embodiment of secular philosophy, the Enlightenment. Virtually all schools of politics and law today diminish the power of religion in American thought – the conservative as much as the progressive school, the traditionalists as well as the civic republicans, and the followers of such diverse political philosophers as Leo Strauss and John Rawls.

Yes, most admit, the Pilgrims believed in God and covenants, sin and justice, damnation and moral uprightness, but the Constitution privatized religion, neutralized it, and put it on the slow road to extinction under the marching feet of knowledge and prosperity. Religion was deliberately subordinated to secular purposes. "The Constitution was ordained and established to secure liberty and its blessings," one scholar writes, "not to promote faith in God. Officially, religion was subordinate to liberty and was to be fostered only with a view to securing liberty."[2]

This picture of the United States is partly correct and, therefore, wrong in the most dangerous way – it is partly wrong. What is truthful in it makes the rest seductive. The true part is that without the Enlightenment America would not have assumed the beneficent shape it did.[3] The influence of the arguments and formulations pioneered by Locke were both extensive and persuasive to many Americans – so much so as to have become a kind of common sense. Locke had to escape the wrath of the British monarch by fleeing to Holland for a time, as did the first Pilgrims on their way to Massachusetts. Locke's search for a better design of government was analogous to their own. Indeed, Locke may have gleaned many new ideas from reflecting on the early American compacts and declarations.[4]

Like theirs, Locke's prose, too, sometimes moved on two levels at once. In calm phrases exuding a serene common sense, he nonetheless sketched in dark and atomic terms a "state of nature" outside civil society: As if individuals alone and in the state of nature were threatened, vulnerable, selfish, and committed above all else to self-preservation. Although presented in the sunny idiom of reason and common sense, Locke's view of man had a Protestant loneliness in it. Indeed, if any in the founding generation felt incompatibility between Locke and the Protestant tradition (as many writers do today), they did not mention it; and many preachers and writers cited both Locke and the Bible in the same paragraph.[5] The founding generation moved easily between faith and practical, common-sense reasoning,[6] indeed mounted upwards on both those wings in unison.

Professor Donald Lutz counted 3,154 citations in the writings of the founders; of these, nearly 1,100 references (34 percent) are to the Bible, and about 300 each to Montesquieu and Blackstone, followed at a considerable distance by Locke and Hume and Plutarch.[7] No American edition of Locke was available until the nineteenth century, but copies printed in England were available in many law offices and church studies.[8] Those who cited Locke in the writings of the founding period frequently listed him alongside Sidney, Cicero, Aristotle, "and the elementary books of public right," as Jefferson did in describing the sources of the Declaration.[9] Scholars of a secularizing bent rightly point to Lockean phrases and turns of argument in Jefferson's Declaration of Independence, but fail to note the older influence of other authors and, particularly, the Bible. Before Locke was even born, the Pilgrims believed in the consent of the governed, social compacts, the dignity of every child of God, and political equality. As Professor Lutz writes:

> That all men are created equal is a position central to Locke's writing, but for a repetitious insistence upon the point, it is to Sidney we should turn. However, the sentiments, ideas, and commitments found in Locke and Sidney existed also in American colonial writing long before these two English theorists published their great works.[10]

Before Sidney and Locke, Americans had fashioned a political doctrine from the Hebrew Bible, and had acquired historically unparalleled practice in the arts of self-government. It is less true to say that America was Lockean, Lutz writes, than that Locke was American.[11]

Thus, a purely secular interpretation of the founding runs aground on massive evidence. Let me begin with seven factual events that draw attention to the second wing by which the American eagle took flight. I mean by "second wing" a Biblical metaphysics, the Jewish vision of the world outlined in the Jewish Testament.

Practically all American Christians erected their main arguments about political life from materials in the Jewish Testament, and they did so for three reasons. First, the early American Protestants loved the stories of the Jewish Testament, and from them took many names for their children. In addition, in national debates, lest their speech be taken as partisan, Christian leaders usually avoided the idioms of rival denominations – Puritan, Quaker, Congregationalist, Episcopal, Unitarian, Methodist, and Universalist. The idiom of Abraham, Isaac, and Jacob was a religious *lingua franca* for the founding generation. Third, the Christian Testament has little to say about the polity that is not already said in the Torah, and what it does say relies for its plausibility on the rich and complex experiences of nation-building already described in the Jewish Testament. For all these reasons, the language of Judaism came to be the central language of the American metaphysic – the unspoken background to a special American vision of nature, history and the destiny of the human race. Its effect upon the American understanding of law was vast,[12] and also upon its understanding of human sinfulness.[13] Thus John Adams warned Thomas Jefferson – the latter less tethered to the Bible's realism, more tempted to simple rationalism – in these words:

> Power always thinks it has a great soul and vast views beyond the comprehension of the weak; and that it is doing God's service when it is violating all

His laws. Our passions, ambitions, avarice, love and resentment, etc., possess so much metaphysical subtlety and so much overpowering eloquence that they insinuate themselves into the understanding and the conscience and convert both to their party.[14]

Hebrew Metaphysics

It has been often remarked that the people of the United States come nearer to a parallel with Ancient Israel, than any other nation upon the globe. Hence OUR AMERICAN ISRAEL is a term frequently used; and common consent allows it apt and proper.

—Abiel Abbot, *Thanksgiving Sermon*, 1799

"The Bible was the one book that literate Americans in the seventeenth, eighteenth, and nineteenth centuries could be expected to know well," Robert Bellah has written. "Biblical imagery provided the basic framework for imaginative thought in America up until quite recent times and, unconsciously, its control is still formidable."[15] As a design for the Seal of the United States, Jefferson suggested "a representation of the children of Israel in the wilderness, led by a cloud by day and a pillar of fire by night."[16] He later concluded his second inaugural address with this same image: "I shall need... the favor of that Being in whose hands we are, who led our fathers, as Israel of old, from their native land and planted them in a country flowing with all the necessaries and comforts of life." This image of "God's American Israel"[17] made available four fresh perspectives, brought to intense focus by the Americans in a new and historically original way.

The first of these new perspectives was a narrative of purpose and progress. The Gentiles of the ancient world believed in cycles of time as regular (they thought) as the circular movements of the stars. They believed in eternal recurrence. But the Americans of 1770-1799 did *not* believe that time is cyclical, going nowhere, spinning in circles pointlessly. They believed that history had a *beginning* and was guided by Providence for a *purpose*. Thus, John Adams: "I always consider the settlement of America with reverence and wonder, as the opening of a grand scene and design in Providence for the illumination of the ignorant, and the emancipation of the slavish part of mankind all over the earth."[18] Time (in the view of the founders) was created for the *unfolding of human liberty*, for human emancipation. This purpose requires humans to choose for or against building cities worthy of the ideals God

sets before them: liberty, justice, equality, self-government, and brotherhood. The very first paragraph of *The Federalist* stresses this moment
of choice:

> It seems to have been reserved to the people of this country, by their con-
> duct and example, to decide the important question, whether societies of
> men are really capable or not of establishing good government from
> *reflection* and *choice*, or whether they are forever destined to depend for
> their political constitutions on accident and force. If there be any truth in the
> remark, the crisis at which we are arrived may with propriety be regarded as
> the era in which that *decision* is to be made; and a wrong election of the part
> we shall act may, in this view, deserve to be considered as the general mis-
> fortune of mankind.[19]

Time was created by a God who "humbled Himself," reaching down to
dramatize full human potentialities by "providential signs" among the
human beings He had created. Thereafter, "in the course of human
events," human beings are called to learn from their own mistakes and
failures, to put together piece by piece "an improved science of politics,"[20] and slowly work out a design for institutions of liberty in
political economy. History is a record of progress (or decline), measured
by permanent standards, God's standards, as learned from and tested
by long experience.

    History, in this sense – open, purposive, contingent in liberty – is
not a Greek or Roman idea. It is Hebraic; its source springs from the
Biblical historians and prophets. Probably most of the humans who had
ever lived before the arrival of Judaism on the world stage never even
heard of "progress." The literature of Greece and Rome looks backwards, to golden ages of the past; the movement of time is circular. For
Jews and Christians, by contrast, history is heading somewhere new:
toward the New Kingdom of God, a kingdom of justice and love and
peace, a new city on a hill. Humans are impelled by their inmost nature
to seek that new city. This "pilgrim's progress" is not a straight line, and
it is not automatic or inevitable; it is by way of trial and suffering. Here
is *Federalist No. 14*:

> Had no important step been taken by the leaders of the Revolution for
> which a precedent could not be discovered, no government established of
> which an exact model did not present itself, the people of the United States
> might at this moment have been numbered among the melancholy victims of
> misguided councils, must at best have been laboring under the weight of
> some of those forms which have crushed the liberties of the rest of mankind.

Happily for America, happily we trust for the whole human race, they pursued a new and more noble course. They accomplished a revolution which has no parallel in the annals of human society. They reared the fabrics of governments which have no model on the face of the globe. They formed the design of a great Confederacy, which it is incumbent on their successors to improve and perpetuate.[21]

Second, Hebrew metaphysics held that everything in creation in all its workings and purposes is intelligible – suffused with reason, not absurd – in the eyes of a divine and loving Creator, Who created from nothing everything that is, and saw that it was good, and loved it; a Creator Who is more powerful than earthquakes, floods, erupting volcanos, hurricanes or anything else in the world, and different from them. One should not mistake this God for any part of His creation – as the Mayan Indians seem to have done, identifying God with rain and snakes and frogs and jackals (powerful forces in the dark, all of them). On the one hand, the world is not in itself divine. On the other, its Creator cannot be touched, tasted, heard, seen, or smelled. The Creator is independent of the world; therefore, the world can be looked into, investigated, and experimented with without infringing on His divinity. Strictly speaking, the Creator is beyond human categories, cannot be expressed in words that are like other words, imagined from the things of this world, or named as other things are named. He is not part of the material world. Seeking Him, it is better to aim one's mind in the direction of Spirit and Truth rather than matter, toward an Ineffable One Whom we do not name.[22] Instead, we place four letters where a name would normally be: Thus, the Hebrew letters that in English we pronounce *Jahweh*.

Third, cherishing humble and weak things most of all, the Creator made at least two creatures to know Him, to love Him, and in total freedom (and not as slaves) to walk with Him – "male and female, He made them" (Genesis 1:27). "The God Who gave us life gave us liberty at the same time," Jefferson wrote,[23] summarizing the Biblical metaphysic. Liberty is the human condition established by the Bible, nearly every chapter of which turns upon the exercise of that freedom, as a wheel upon its axis. What will Adam, King David, Peter, Saul do next?[24] Liberty is the axis of the universe, the ground of the possibility of love, human and divine. Thus John Adams wrote: "Let us see delineated before us the true map of man. Let us hear the dignity of his nature, and the noble rank he holds among the works of God...and that God Almighty has promulgated from heaven, liberty, peace, and good-will to man!"[25] Moreover, the American tradition clearly distinguishes a false idea of liberty – license – from the true liberty exercised in reflection and deliberate choice.[26] Despite this high calling, men and women fail often, are vulnerable to human weakness, and are in want of checks and balances against their frailties.

Fourth, in Hebrew metaphysics the brief span of a human life is experienced as a time of suffering, testing whether humans can remain faithful to God's purposes in creating them – whether we will (or will not) show grace under pressure. In the Bible, the bright red thread of human history is not just liberty but liberty on trial. God, wrote John Perkins, "deals with mankind as rational beings, in a state of trial and probation."[27] For many generations of Americans, *Pilgrim's Progress* dramatized this time of trial. The young should steel themselves for later suffering. The drama of their lives can be simply stated: Will they exemplify under pressure a noble use of liberty, as their forebears did?

> Let us read and recollect and impress upon our souls the views and ends of our own more immediate forefathers, in exchanging their native country for a dreary, inhospitable wilderness. Let us examine into the nature of that power, and the cruelty of that oppression, which drove them from their homes. Recollect their amazing fortitude, their bitter sufferings, – the hunger, the nakedness, the cold, which they patiently endured, – the severe labors of clearing their grounds, building their houses, raising their provisions, amidst dangers from wild beasts and savage men, before they had time or money or materials for commerce. Recollect the civil and religious principles and hopes and expectations which constantly supported and carried them through all hardships with patience and resignation. Let us recollect it was liberty, the hope of liberty for themselves and us and ours, which conquered all discouragements, dangers, and trials.[28]

This drama of liberty gave birth to two "whig" theories of history, one Protestant and one Catholic.[29] Nowadays, even secular people interpret history in the light of progress, rights, and liberty. Yet unbelievers received these concepts neither from the Greeks and Romans nor from Enlightened Reason, but via the preaching of Jesus Christ, from whom the Gentiles learned the essential outlook of the Hebrews: that the Creator gave humans a special place among all other creatures, and made them free, and endowed them with incomparable responsibility and dignity.

This sequence of related conceptions – that time had a *beginning* and *is measured for progress (or decline)* by God's standards; that everything in the world is intelligible, and that to *inquire, invent,* and *discover* is an *impulse of faith* as well as of reason; that the *Creator endowed us with liberty and inviolable dignity,* while the Divine Judge shows concern for *the weak and the humble;* that life is a *time of duty and trial;* and that history is to be grasped as *the drama of human liberty* – all these are the background that make sense of the Declaration of Independence. America and Israel, the first Israel and the second, shed light on each other:

> The God of heaven hath not indeed visibly displayed the glory of his majesty and power before our eyes, as he came down in the sight of Israel on the burning mount; nor has he written with his own finger the laws of our civil polity. But the signal interpositions of divine providence, in saving us from the vengeance of a powerful irritated nation from which we were unavoidably separated by their inadmissible claim of absolute parliamentary power over us; in giving us a WASHINGTON to be captain-general of our armies; in carrying us through the various distressing scenes of war and desolation, and making us twice triumphant over numerous armies, surrounded and captivated in the midst of their career; and finally giving us peace with a large territory and acknowledged independence; all these laid together fall little short of real miracles and an heavenly charter of liberty for these United-States.... We cannot but acknowledge that God hath graciously patronized our cause and taken us under his special care, as he did his ancient covenant people.[30]

Without this metaphysical background, the founding generation of Americans would have had little heart for the War of Independence. They would have had no ground for believing that their seemingly unlawful rebellion actually fulfilled the will of God – and suited the laws of nature and nature's God. Consider the jeopardy in which their rebellion placed them: When they signed the Declaration, they were committing treason in the King's eyes. If their frail efforts failed, their flagrant betrayal of the solemn oaths of loyalty they had sworn to their King doomed them to a public hanging. Before future generations, their children would be disgraced. To still their trembling, they pled their case before a greater and wholly undeceivable Judge, "appealing to the Supreme Judge of the world for the Rectitude of our Intentions."

In analogous straits, other Christians in other places and times acted differently. Contrast the role given to rebellion (Satan's "*Non serviam!*") in John Milton's *Paradise Lost* with Benjamin Franklin's "Rebellion to Tyrants is Obedience to God." The Bible is not a cut-out book. It is not a pattern book that has been used by all peoples at all times in the same way. Americans took its appeal to the imperishable dignity of each person with uncommon hope and optimism, erecting on it (with the help of Locke and many others) a new structure of rights and covenants. The depths of this metaphysical background gave them unusual moral strength.

Any recounting of the story of the American polity that cuts off this metaphysical background will never fly.

Seven Events that Revealed the Power of the Second Wing

Out of multitudes of incidents that could be cited, let me list but seven events that bared the depth and power of the Hebraic view of reality shared by this nation's founding generation. These vital incidents constitute mighty obstacles to a merely secular interpretation of the founding.

The first event was the first act of the First Continental Congress. During early September 1774, from every region, members of the First Continental Congress were riding dustily toward Philadelphia, where they hoped to remind King George III of the rights due them as Englishmen. As these delegates were gathering, news arrived that Charlestown had been raked by cannonshot, and red-coated landing parties had surged through its streets.

As their first motion, the gathering delegates proposed a public prayer, that they might gain in sobriety and wisdom. Mr. Jay of New York and Mr. Rutledge of South Carolina spoke against this motion, because Americans are so divided in religious sentiments (they said), some Episcopalians, some Quakers, some Anabaptists, some Presbyterians, and some Congregationalists, that all could not join in the same act of worship. Sam Adams arose to say he was no bigot, and could hear a prayer from any gentleman of piety and virtue, who was at the same time a friend to his country. Mr. Adams said he was a stranger in Philadelphia, but had heard that a certain Reverend Duché had earned that character, and moved that the same be asked to read prayers to Congress on the morrow. The motion carried.

Thus, it happened that on September 7, 1774, the first official prayer before the Continental Congress was pronounced by a white-haired Episcopal clergyman dressed in his pontificals, who read Psalm 35 aloud from the *Book of Common Prayer*:

Plead my cause, O Lord, with them that strive with me: fight against them that fight against me.

Take hold of shield and buckler, and stand up for mine help.

Draw out also the spear, and stop the way against them that persecute me: say unto my soul, I am thy salvation.

Let them be confounded and put to shame that seek after my soul: let them be turned back and brought to confusion that devise my hurt.

Let them be as chaff before the wind: and let the angel of the Lord chase them.

Let their way be dark and slippery: and let the angel of the Lord persecute them.

For without cause have they hid for me their net in a pit, which without cause they have digged for my soul.

Let destruction come upon him at unawareness; and let his net that he hath hid catch himself: into that very destruction let him fall.

All my bones shall say, Lord, who is like unto thee, which deliverest the poor from him that is too strong for him, yea, the poor and the needy from him that spoileth him?

Let them be ashamed and brought to confusion together that rejoice at mine hurt: let them be clothed with shame and dishonour that magnify themselves against me. (KJV)

Before the Episcopal priest knelt Washington, Henry, Randolph, Rutledge, Lee, and Jay, and by their side, heads bowed, the Puritan patriots, who could imagine at that moment their homes being bombarded and overrun. Over these bowed heads the Reverend Duché uttered what all testified was an eloquent prayer, "for America, for Congress, for the Province of Massachusetts Bay, and especially for the town of Boston." The emotion in the room was palpable, and John Adams wrote to his wife Abigail that he "had never heard a better prayer, or one so well pronounced. I never saw a greater effect upon an audience. It seemed as if heaven had ordained that Psalm to be read on that morning.... It was enough to melt a heart of stone. I saw tears gush into the eyes of the old, grave pacific Quakers of Philadelphia.... I must beg you to read that Psalm."[31]

The second event was the sermon of John Witherspoon of Princeton on May 17, 1776, in which this president of Princeton, having hitherto opposed the rebelliousness implicit in open revolt, went over to the side of independence, and expounded with a fine Scottish brogue on the meaning of Providence for a young America, in the light of the struggles of the people of Israel against their own kings. Witherspoon was James Madison's teacher, and the latter had spent an extra year at Princeton in a personal tutorial. In all, Witherspoon taught one vice-president, twelve members of the Continental Congress, five delegates to the Constitutional Convention, forty-nine U.S. representatives, and twenty-eight U.S. senators; three Supreme Court justices, eight U.S. district judges, three attorneys general and one secretary of state, two foreign ministers, and scores of officers in the Continental Army.[32] He was the most influential academic in American history. His famous sermon was printed and distributed in over 500 Presbyterian churches throughout the colonies. It helped prepare many consciences for the supreme act of the Declaration of Independence seven weeks later on July 2-4, 1776. Using as his text Psalm 76:10 (*Surely the wrath of Man shall praise thee; the remainder of Wrath shalt thou restrain*), Witherspoon lays out a vision of how Providence actually works in history, which bears comparison with the teaching of Thomas Aquinas on the same subject.[33]

"The doctrine of divine providence," Witherspoon begins, "extends not only to things which we may think of great moment, and therefore worthy of notice, but to things the most indifferent and inconsiderable." Even things that seem harmful and destructive may be turned to our advantage; even the enemies of the law and morality cannot escape being the instruments of Providence. Providence does not manipulate people like puppets on a string or move things and events like a *deus ex machina*. Rather, the hazards and contingencies of nature work their natural effects, as if in a pattern favorable to His purposes. The armies of the enemy, ferocious and irresistible, are rendered irresolute when their commander comes down with dysentery on the eve of the intended assault; rains make the terrain of the final charge impassable; an unforeseen fog brings operations to a halt. Nature affords countless chinks in its regular workings through which the Divine Artist, without bending any law against its nature, or any will against its own choice, can govern events.

Thus it happens that, to apply this doctrine "more particularly to the present state of the American colonies, and the plague of war, the ambition of mistaken princes, the cunning and cruelty of oppressive and corrupt ministers, and even the inhumanity of brutal soldiers, however dreadful, shall finally promote the glory of God." The King of England may huff and puff, and his great fleets may set sail to rage against American ports, but Providence has countless resources by which to tame their pride. "It would be a criminal inattention not to observe the singular interposition of Providence hitherto, in behalf of the American colonies," he concludes.

> The signal advantage we have gained by the evacuation of Boston, and the shameful flight of the army and navy of Britain, was brought about without the loss of a man. To all this we may add, that the counsels of our enemies have been visibly confounded, so that I believe that I may say with truth, that there is hardly any step which they have taken, but it has operated strongly against themselves, and been more in our favor, than if they had followed a contrary course.[34]

Witherspoon's underlying argument is that liberty is God's gift and all of creation has been contrived so that it will sweetly, freely, even out of darkness and despair, come to fruition. He believes that God and civil liberties go together:

> So in times of difficulty and trial, it is in the man of piety and inward principle, that we may expect to find the uncorrupted patriot, the useful citizen, and the invincible soldier. God grant that in America true religion and civil liberty may be inseparable, and that the unjust attempts to destroy the one, may in the issue tend to the support and establishment of both.[35]

In the preaching of the time, Americans learned as follows: Providence does not mean that God works magically. Rather, from all time every detail of the tapestry is known to the one who weaves it. To the Eternal God, there is neither time nor sequence, but every detail of the tapestry is visible to Him as if in one simultaneous moment, each thing acting independently and freely, but cohering as a whole, like characters in a well-wrought novel. Thus, the horseman bearing the secret order of battle takes a wrong turn in the darkness and is captured by those about to be attacked, just in time for them to thwart their more powerful foe. Nothing more common in the affairs of human beings than circumstance and chance, which surprises those who lived through them in time and sequence but seems quite natural to later observers. The very sermon Witherspoon preached on behalf of Independence in April 1776 was a sermon on how Providence acts by contingent and indirect actions – not *foreseen*, because God does not "foresee" anything. He is *present* to everything, in the Jewish and Christian understanding. He is not *before* and *after*; He is present to all things at one time. In one creative vision, He sees the details of what He does, and how they all hook together, without forcing anybody's liberty, without manipulating anything.

As Witherspoon took his text from the Jewish Scriptures, so also did the Reverend Samuel Cooper of Harvard, whose text for the sermon to celebrate the ratification of the Constitution of Massachusetts was Jeremiah 30:20-21. Of the fifty-five printed sermons of the Revolutionary Era collected by Ellis Sandoz, thirty-three took texts from the Jewish Testament for their guiding themes.[36] During the years 1770-1776, the fires of revolution were lit by Protestant divines aflame with the dignity of human conscience. "To the Pulpit, the *Puritan Pulpit*," wrote John Wingate Thornton, "We owe the moral force which won our independence."[37]

The third event was the prayer written as a sub-text of the Declaration itself. The very form of the Declaration was that of a traditional American prayer, a compact not unlike the Mayflower Compact, and only the latest in a long series of local and regional covenants, ratified by Americans as "a public elaboration, almost a celebration, of a people's fundamental values," which "put everyone on notice, legislature, governor, and the people at large,"[38] by solemnizing "their national compact."[39] In that document, Thomas Jefferson at least twice referred to God in Hebrew terms, and before assenting to it, the Congress added two more Hebrew names.[40]

The fifty-six Signers were, mostly, Christians; they represented a mostly Christian people; and it was from Christian traditions that they had learned these Hebrew names. Of names specific to the Christian faith (such as Savior, Trinity, Father, Son, Holy Spirit) the Signers were wisely silent, since it lies not in the competence of Government to adjudicate theological differences beyond those essential for the common good.

Recall the four names that these Americans gave to God: *Lawgiver* (as in "Laws of Nature and Nature's God"); *Creator* ("endowed by their Creator with certain inalienable rights"); *Judge* ("appealing to the Supreme Judge of the World for the Rectitude of our Intentions"); and *Providence* ("with a firm Reliance on the Protection of divine Providence").

Three of these names (Creator, Judge, Providence) unambiguously derive from Judaism and came to America via Protestant Christianity. The fourth name for God, "Lawgiver," could be considered Greek or

Roman as well as Hebraic. But Richard Hooker showed that long tradition had put "Lawgiver," too, in a Biblical context.[41]

If these Hebraic texts of the Declaration were strung together as a
single prayer, the prayer would run as follows:

> *Creator, who has endowed in us our inalienable rights, Maker of nature
> and nature's laws, undeceivable Judge of the rectitude of our intentions, we
> place our firm reliance upon the protection of divine Providence, which
> you have extended over our nation from its beginnings. Amen.*

The fourth event demonstrating that more than the Enlightenment was at work in the Revolutionary War is as follows. Only five
months after the Declaration, as the pinch and suffering of war and the
poor harvest of that year seriously imperilled morale, Congress set aside
December 11, 1776, and decreed that the separate States should orga-
nize on that date a Day of Fasting and Repentance. In part, the Decree
read as follows (it was composed by John Witherspoon, now a key member of the Congress):

> *WHEREAS, the war in which the United States are engaged with Great
> Britain, has not only been prolonged, but is likely to be carried to the great-
> est extremity; and whereas, it becomes all public bodies, as well as private
> persons, to reverence the Providence of God, and look up to him as the
> supreme disposer of all events, and the arbiter of the fate of nations; there-
> fore,*
>
> > *RESOLVED, That it be recommended to all the United States, as
> soon as possible, to appoint a day of solemn fasting and humiliation; to
> implore of Almighty God the forgiveness of the many sins prevailing among
> all ranks, and to beg the countenance as assistance of his Providence in the
> prosecution of the present just and necessary war.*
>
> > *The Congress do also, in the most earnest manner, recommend to all
> the members of the United States, and particularly the officers civil and
> military under them, the exercise of repentance and reformation; and fur-
> ther, require of them the strict observation of the articles of war, and
> particularly, that part of the said articles, which forbids profane swearing,
> and all immorality, of which all such officers are desired to take notice.*[42]

In all moments of imminent danger, as in the first Act of the First Continental Congress, the founding generation turned to prayer. In a kind
of covenant, they pledged to God that the people of America would pursue His will as best they could, confident that He willed for them and for
all men the exercise of natural liberty.[43] They would bear the costs
and the suffering; they pleaded for His mercy and His assistance.

The fifth event occurred when George Washington became commander of the amateurs without uniforms who became the Continental Army, and began immediately to steel them against the adversity to come. To stand with swollen chests in a straight line, beneath snapping flags, to the music of fife and drums is one thing; to hold your place when the British musketballs roar toward you like a wall of blazing lead, and all around you the flesh of screaming friends and brothers is shredded, is another. Washington knew there would be bitter winters and hot summers with no pay and little food, and that some would stay at their posts and some would shirk. He knew that victories would be scarce, and that frontal combat must be as rare as he could make it – the men would have to become inured to retreating, falling back, and evading, maneuvers hard for masculine morale.

Thus, Washington knew his only hope lay in a profound conviction in the hearts and daily actions of all his men that what they did they did for God, and under God's protection. His only hope lay in fashioning a godly corps, whose faith lay not in instant signs of encouragement upon the field of battle, but in total confidence that their Creator willed the ultimate vindication of the rights with which He had endowed them.

Therefore, Washington gave orders that each day begin with formal prayer, to be led by the officers of each unit. He decreed, as well, that all profanity be banned, and all conduct that might offend the citizens upon whose support they utterly depended. He promised dire punishment to any who uttered oaths that would offend God or man. The men of the Continental Army must secure God's blessing on their efforts every day, by every means within their power. Nothing else could guarantee success. There was no other hope. Thus, on July 9, 1776, Washington issued a circular Order that "The Colonels or commanding officers of each regiment are directed to procure Chaplains" according to the decree of the Continental Congress, "persons of good Characters and exemplary lives – To see that all inferior officers and soldiers pay them a suitable respect and attend carefully upon religious exercises."

> *The blessing and protection of Heaven are at all times necessary but especially so in times of public distress and danger – The General hopes and trusts, that every officer and man, will endeavor so to live, and act, as becomes a Christian Soldier defending the dearest Rights and Liberties of his country.*
>
> *The General commands all officers, and soldiers, to pay strict obedience to the Orders of the Continental Congress, and by their unfeigned,*

*and pious observance of their religious duties, incline the Lord, and Giver of
Victory, to prosper our arms.*[44]

In 1783, in a Circular Address to the States, General Washington
later invoked a kind of *"brotherhood* theology," asking God to bind the
nation together and to grant its citizens the social and personal virtues
necessary for the country's survival. These words have often been
reprinted as the Prayer of Washington for this country:

> *I now make it my earnest prayer, that God would have you, and the State
> over which you preside, in his holy protection, that he would incline the
> hearts of the Citizens to cultivate a spirit of subordination and obedience
> to Government, to entertain a brotherly affection and love for one another,
> for their fellow Citizens of the United States at large, and particularly for
> their brethren who have served in the Field, and finally, that he would most
> graciously be pleased to dispose us all, to do Justice, to love mercy, and to
> demean ourselves with that Charity, humility and pacific temper of mind,
> which were the Characteristicks of the Divine Author of our blessed Reli-
> gion, and without an humble imitation of whose example in these things, we
> can never hope to be a happy Nation.*[45]

The sixth event occurred toward the end of the fighting season in
late August, 1776, when George Washington had assembled a main body
of some 12,000 local militiamen of the Continental Army on Long Island.
By sudden naval maneuvers, British Generals Howe, Clinton, Corn-
wallis, and Percy, with the German Major General von Heister, landed
a royal detachment twice as large to the rear of the Continental Army.
The British took up positions to march swiftly toward the East River to
trap Washington's entire army, and put a sudden end to the insurrec-
tion. As night fell, seeing the large force they had assembled and their
high morale, the British were confident of victory the next day. The
Americans, however, knew they might lose everything. Washington desperately sent out the call for every available vessel and began ferrying
his troops by cover of night back to Manhattan. All night the men
scoured for boats, marched in silence, and rowed, but as dawn was rising in the East only a fraction of the Army had made its escape. While
working with frantic speed, the Americans prepared for the worst.[46] As
if in answer to their prayers, a heavy fog rolled in and lasted until noon.

Employing every minute of those extra hours, Washington saw
the last of his men disembark. His entire Army had escaped. Many
thanks to God went heavenward. For many men, the miracle of Long

Island was one of those "signal interventions" of Divine Providence of which both Washington[47] and the author of *Federalist No. 37* made mention. Despite so many reasons for disunity – the delegates had arrived from slave states and free, from small states and large, from rich states and from poor – Publius marveled at the improbable unanimity arrived at in the Constitutional Convention:

> It is impossible for the man of pious reflection not to perceive in it a finger of the Almighty hand which has been so frequently and signally extended to our relief in the critical stages of the revolution.

In two other passages, also, *The Federalist* notes the blessings of Providence upon this country.[48]

The seventh event demonstrating conclusively the Biblical metaphysic appeared at the end of the third year of the war. Congress had many reasons for expressing the nation's thanksgiving to God, and to beseech His continued mercy and assistance. John Witherspoon was deputed to draft a Thanksgiving Day recollection for those events, and the Congress decreed national Days of Thanksgiving on October 20, 1779; October 26, 1781; and October 11, 1782. A sampling of the words set before the whole nation on these occasions testifies to the covenant the people had entered into with the God of liberty. In 1779, the Congress urged the nation "humbly to approach the throne of Almighty God" to ask "that he would establish the independence of these United States upon the basis of religion and virtue."[49] Then followed –

The Congressional Decree of 1781:

> *Whereas, it hath pleased Almighty God, the father of mercies, remarkably to assist and support the United States of America in their important struggle for liberty, against the long continued efforts of a powerful nation: it is the duty of all ranks to observe and thankfully acknowledge the interpositions of his Providence in their behalf. Through the whole of the contest, from its first rise to this time, the influence of Divine Providence may be clearly perceived in many signal instances, of which we mention but a few.[50]*

The Congress then listed seven accomplishments of Providence on behalf of the cause of liberty: in revealing the councils of the British in fortuitous ways; in strengthening the union of states; in heightening the number and zeal of the friends of liberty; in rescuing our forces from certain disasters and blessing us with surprising victories; in bringing the great strength of France to liberty's aid; in leading the British "to pursue such measures as have most directly contributed to frustrate their own desires and expectations;" and, seventh and "above all, in making their extreme cruelty to the inhabitants of these States, when in their power, and their savage devastation of property, the very means of cementing our union, and adding vigor to every effort in opposition to them."

The Continental Congress was so moved in its own retrospection that it urged the people of the United States not to overlook "the goodness of God in the year now drawing to a conclusion," in which they again counted a half-dozen blessings: a year "in which there have been so many instances of prowess and success in our armies; particularly in the Southern States, where, notwithstanding the difficulties with which they had to struggle, they have recovered the whole country which the enemy had overrun, leaving them only a post or two on or near the sea;" and "in which there has been so plentiful a harvest, and so great abundance of the fruits of the earth of every kind, as not only enables us easily to supply the wants of the army, but gives comfort and happiness to the whole people." They are grateful, as well, for "the success of our allies by sea," and because "a General of the first Rank, with his whole army, has been captured by the allied forces under the direction of our Commander in Chief." They express the desire of their constituents:

> with grateful hearts, to celebrate the praise of our gracious Benefactor; to confess our manifold sins; to offer up our most fervent supplications to the God of all grace, that it may please Him to pardon our offences, and incline our hearts for the future to keep all his laws; to comfort and relieve all our brethren who are in distress or captivity; to prosper all husbandmen, and give success to all engaged in lawful commerce; to impart wisdom and integrity to our counsellors, judgment and fortitude to our officers and soldiers; to protect and prosper our illustrious ally, and favor our united exertions for the speedy establishment of a safe, honorable and lasting peace; and bless all seminaries of learning; and cause the knowledge of God to cover the earth, as the water covers the seas. [51]

The Congressional Decree of 1782 (exhibiting its own view of "the separation of church and state"):

> It being the indispensable duty of all nations, not only to offer up their supplications to Almighty God, the giver of all good, for his gracious assistance in a time of distress, but also in a solemn and public manner to give him praise for his goodness in general, and especially for great and signal interpositions of his Providence in their behalf; therefore the United States in Congress assembled,...do hereby recommend...the observation of...a day of

solemn thanksgiving to God for all his mercies; and they do further recommend to all ranks and testify their gratitude of God for his goodness, by a cheerful obedience to his laws, and by protecting, each in his station, and by his influence, the practice of true and undefiled religion, which is the great foundation of public prosperity and national happiness.[52]

Following the wartime precedent of the Congress, Washington issued his first Thanksgiving Day Proclamation shortly after becoming president in 1789. The president did not boast of his own leadership, or even "legacy," but thought backwards to the help of God in the Battle of Long Island and so many battles, including Yorktown.

President Washington's Decree of 1789:

Whereas it is the duty of all Nations to acknowledge the providence of Almighty God, to obey His will, to be grateful for His benefits, and humbly to implore His protection and favor.... Now therefore I do recommend and assign Thursday the 26th day of November next to be devoted by the People of these States to the Service of that great and glorious Being, who is the beneficent Author of all the good that was, that is, or that will be. That we may then all unite in rendering unto Him our sincere and humble thanks, for His kind care and protection of the People of this country previous to their becoming a Nation, for the single and manifold mercies, and the favorable interpositions of His providence, which we experienced in the course and conclusion of the late war.

Washington, speaking for the whole nation as its new president, saw in thanksgiving to God a bond of unity among all citizens, newly emerged from the crucible of war. He also saw in God the deepest and most reliable resource for the insight and habits necessary to a self-governing, law-abiding people:

And also that we may then unite in most humbly offering our prayers and supplications to the Great Lord and Ruler of Nations and beseech Him to pardon our national and other transgressions, to enable us all, whether in public or private stations, to perform our several and relative duties properly and punctually, to render our national government a blessing to all people, by constantly being a government of wise, just and constitutional laws, discreetly and faithfully executed and obeyed.[53]

Later on, Lincoln called Americans "an almost chosen people," just as many before him had seen our nation as a "Second Israel." The first people of Israel, in the Bible's retelling, often turned away from God. Would not Americans do the same thing?

Summation

The record shows beyond the shadow of a doubt that the second wing of the American founding, the wing that reaches to the deepest energies of the human spirit, drew its power from the Hebraic vision of the Bible. Practically to a man, Americans understood that they would meet their Judge at death for an account of how they used their liberty. "I tremble," Jefferson wrote later in the silence of the night, "when I reflect that God is just."[54]

Americans of the founding generation appealed without flinching to the undeceivable Judge of all consciences, precisely because they believed they had formed a covenant with Him, in the name of His most precious gift to the universe, the liberty of the sons of God. The United States was established, in the mind of its founders, to advance the fortunes of that great gift.

> *Our fathers' God! To Thee,*
> *Author of liberty,*
> *To Thee we sing.*
> *Long may our land be bright*
> *With freedom's holy light;*
> *Protect us by thy might,*
> *Great God our king.*[55]

In brief, a mass of evidence demonstrates that what the founding generation did cannot be explained by the Enlightenment alone.

TWO

The belief in a God All Powerful, wise, and good,
is so essential to the moral order of the World and
to the happiness of man, that arguments which
enforce it cannot be drawn from too many sources
nor adapted with too much solicitude to the different
characters and capacities impressed with it.
— James Madison

SECOND CHAPTER

Two Beat as One:
Plain Reason, Humble Faith

O n two wings the American eagle rose into the sky. On plain reason and humble faith. Plain reason is not so hard to
understand. But how did the founders think of faith? And
what, in their minds, did faith add to reason?

What is Faith?

What the founders meant by reason is not far to seek. They meant the
qualities of mind to which the *Federalist* addressed its arguments. These
qualities were quite well known in the ancient and medieval tradition:
sober reflection and calm deliberation; an ability to overcome passion
and self-interest; and a capacity to consider the larger picture, the public good, and the future interests of posterity.[1]

They also meant "common sense:" a due regard for the long experience of mankind, a close observation of concrete facts, a sharp eye
for the newness of the present, and a willingness to try practical experiments. The most important thing is this: the founders saw themselves
laboring within a long community of inquiry, at home simultaneously
in the world of biblical and classical examples and in the practical world
of the eighteenth century. For most of them, the Bible and plain reason
went hand in hand, moral example for moral example. Even for those
few (such as Thomas Paine) for whom common sense and the Bible were
antitheses, plain reason led to belief in God. Paine ridiculed the Bible,
but, as we shall see, he was not an atheist.

For most of the others, the Bible itself drew attention to reason.

27

The God Who made all things understood every detail of what He made. Thus everything, absolutely everything, could be studied with practical profit, from lightning flashes to the way water bubbles in a pot with enough force to gently raise its lid. Everything could be studied for its inner workings and its coherence with everything else. Americans had full confidence that study pays off in practical benefits.

On the other hand, everywhere that reason led, Americans found the Bible. If they read Francis Bacon, they found the Bible. If they read Isaac Newton or John Milton, they found the Bible. In Shakespeare, they found the Bible. In John Locke, they found an attack on Filmer for using the Bible badly to defend monarchy, while Locke claimed successfully to be using it better even when moving beyond it. In the world of the founders, the Bible was an unavoidable and useful rod of measurement, a stimulus to intellectual innovation.

Tom Paine called his attack on the Bible *The Age of Reason*, and many accused him of being an atheist, but in fact he was so hostile to atheism that he sailed to France after 1789 to fight against it, holding it responsible for the bloody massacres of the Terror.[2] Such hostility to atheism was nearly universal in America, on the ground that where there is no omniscient Judge, political power knows no moral check. The highly admired Unitarian preacher of New England, Jonathan Mayhew, articulated this in 1766:

> Power is of a grasping, encroaching nature, in all beings except in Him, to Whom emphatically it "belongeth"; and Who is the only King that, in a *religious* or moral sense, "can do no wrong." Power aims at extending itself, and operating according to mere will, where-ever it meets with no balance, check, control or opposition of any kind.[3]

Each American slaveholder had to be prepared either to wield the lash upon recalcitrant slaves or to order others to do so. From this dreadful master-slave relationship, the early Americans (even those not directly involved in it) knew how bad slavery was, and feared lest something similar might lie in store for them, too. They dreaded stealthy encroachments on their liberty. "For while men *sleep, then the enemy cometh and soweth tares*, which cannot be rooted out till *the end of the world*," Jonathan Mayhew preached. "*Obsta principiis* [*Stop it in its beginnings*]. After a while, all will be too late."[4]

For the founding generation, common sense arises from the traditional wisdom of the ancient philosophers and moralists, and from close personal observation of daily life. But the founders also appealed to a second source of illumination: the Holy Scriptures, read with the eyes of faith. The Scriptures in their hands, American Protestants tried very hard to be teachable. "The philosophy of Jesus is the most sublime and benevolent code of morals ever offered to man," Jefferson wrote. "A more beautiful or precious morsel of ethics I have never seen."[5] America's founders believed that the Bible is the best book on republican principles ever written.[6] They rejected atheism because it was opposed to common sense:

> Atheism is so repugnant to every principle of common sense, that it is not possible it should ever gain much ground, or become very prevalent.... Atheism is a sanctuary of vice, by taking away the motives to virtue arising from the will of God, and the fear of future judgment.[7]

Were atheism widely promulgated, most believed, everyday morals would slide into decadence, and reason would lose its steel. Without a Judge of consciences, men would learn to rationalize away their weaknesses, and do their evil deeds in private chambers, unswayed by moral qualms. Is not all history a witness to the seductions of disorder? First atheism, then astrology, satanic cults, contempt for reason, surrender to tyranny:

> Erase all thought and fear of God from a community, and selfishness and sensuality would absorb the whole man. Appetite knowing no restraint, and poverty and suffering having no solace or hope, man would trample in scorn on the restraints of human laws. Virtue, duty, principle would be mocked and scorned as unmeaning sounds. A sordid self-interest would supplant every other feeling, and man would become...a companion of brutes.[8]

Some atheists were highly moral and responsible, the founders knew. When Washington wrote, "Whatever may be conceded to the influence of refined education on minds of peculiar structure," he was probably thinking of Jefferson and a few others. The famous David Hume, for instance, prided himself on being a secular saint. But a whole people over a long time, Washington concluded later in the same sentence begun above, is a different matter. "Reason and experience both forbid us to expect that National morality can prevail in exclusion of religious principles."[9]

Atheism, the founders thought, undermines republican institutions in four ways. It lifts an important limit to political power, by removing the God Who infuses the rule of law with majesty and sanction that towers over pretending emperors and kings. It erases the Creator Who (the Declaration states as a truth) endowed all individuals with inalienable rights, beyond the power of the state to take away. Third, it weakens the motives of many individuals who observe the law and do their duty day after day. Fourth, it leaves most individuals vulnerable to their own passions and appetites, and without clear direction for acting responsibly. Among philosophers, reason alone is not adequate for posting such directions (philosophers don't agree). Reason is not even adequate for its own defense (many are irrationalists). Among ordinary people, the debility of reason brings despair to many persons of good will, emboldens the immoralists, and herds the weak toward vice. When being reasonable and responsible is burdensome, there is no ringing answer to the taunt, "Who cares?"

By contrast, the founders held faith to be the habit of seeing things through the eyes of God, as they had been taught to see them by a community of reflection on the Bible. Each reader might learn his own lessons from Scripture, but the community as a whole keeps alive certain basic motifs, and renews and reawakens them whenever public consciousness of such matters begins to fade, as it always does. Far from being contrary to reason, faith strengthens reason. To employ a poor analogy, faith is a little like a telescope that magnifies what the naked eye of reason sees unaided.

For the founders, it was evident that faith in the God of Abraham, Isaac, and Jacob magnifies human reason, encourages virtue, and sharpens a zest for liberty. Faith whets the hunger for *Veritas* and nourishes an appetite for building universities. Moreover, a free society demands a higher level of virtue than a tyranny, which no other moral energy has heretofore proven capable of inspiring except Judaism and Christianity. In the case of a few unusual persons, belief may not be needed for virtue, but among a whole people and in the long run, George Washington warned in his "Farewell Address,"

> Of all the dispositions and habits which lead to political prosperity, Religion and morality are indispensable supports...let us with caution indulge the supposition, that morality can be maintained without religion. Whatever may be conceded to the influence of refined education on minds of peculiar structure, reason and experience both forbid us to expect that National morality can prevail in exclusion of religious principle.[10]

By the accounts of some historians, the most religiously detached

of all the signers of the Declaration or the Constitution was probably
Thomas Jefferson. No orthodox Christian, believing neither in the
divinity of Christ nor in the Trinity, and not at all in the miracles
recounted in the Bible, Jefferson nonetheless held firmly that there is a
Creator, Governor of the universe, Providence, and Judge to Whom
all will answer after death.[11] In his days as president, the largest church
service in the United States took place every Sunday in the Capitol
Building, and Thomas Jefferson thought it his duty to attend. One clergyman who lived close by did not hesitate even on the street to chide
Mr. Jefferson about his lack of orthodoxy, as is recorded in the Reverend's handwritten diary, now in the possession of the Library of
Congress:

> President Jefferson was on his way to church of a Sunday morning with his
> large red prayer book under his arm when a friend querying him after their
> mutual good morning said which way are you walking Mr. Jefferson. To
> which he replied to Church Sir. You going to church Mr. J. You do not
> believe a word in it. Sir said Mr. J. No nation has ever yet existed or been
> governed without religion. Nor can be. The Christian religion is the best reli-
> gion that has ever been given to man and I as chief Magistrate of this nation
> am bound to give it the sanction of my example. Good morning Sir.
>
> —The Rev. Ethan Allen[12]

Jefferson, it will be noted, did not *deny* that he didn't "believe a word in
it." What he strenuously affirms is that the Christian religion is necessary for a republic. During his administration, he supported with
government funds the large church services held every Sunday in the
Capitol building and other public buildings.[13]

But *why*? What led Jefferson and his other contemporaries, some
fairly worldly men and some moderately pious, to link the success of
republican government so tightly with religious faith, especially Protestant Christian faith? In this matter of religious faith, the Americans
were altogether different from their contemporaries in Europe. "There
is no country in the world," Alexis de Tocqueville wrote, "in which the
boldest political theories of the eighteenth-century philosophers are put
so effectively into practice as in America. Only their anti-religious doctrines have never made any headway in that country."[14] Indeed,
Tocqueville went further: "For the Americans the ideas of Christianity
and liberty are so completely mingled that it is almost impossible to get
them to conceive of the one without the other."[15] In this, America is not

at all like France. "In France I had seen the spirits of religion and of freedom almost always marching in opposite directions. In America I found them intimately linked together in joint reign over the same land."[16]

More than that, Americans had learned to *think* about liberty from the wisdom of the ancients and the experience of their own lives, as well as from Holy Scripture. In a famous sermon, Jonathan Mayhew pointed to all these sources:

> Having been initiated, in youth, (1) in the doctrines of civil liberty, as they were taught by such men as Plato, Demosthenes, Cicero and other renowned persons among the ancients; and such as Sidney and Milton, Locke and Hoadley, among the moderns, I liked them; they seemed rational. Having, earlier still (2) learnt from the holy scriptures, that wise, brave and vertous [sic] men were always friends to liberty; that God gave the Israelites a king in his anger, because they had not sense and virtue enough to like a free commonwealth, and to have himself for their king; that the Son of God came down from heaven, to make us "free indeed"; and that "where the Spirit of the Lord is, there is liberty"; this made me conclude, that freedom was a great blessing. Having, also, (3) from my childhood up, by the kind of providence of my God, and the tender care of a good parent now at rest with him, been educated to the love of liberty, tho' not of licentiousness; which chaste and virtuous passion was still increased in me, as I advanced towards, and into, manhood; I would not, I cannot now, tho' past my middle age, relinquish the fair object of my youthful affections, liberty; whose charms, instead of decaying with time in my eyes, have daily captivated me more and more. [enumeration added] [17]

There you have it. From the ancients, from Holy Scripture, and from his experiences, Mayhew learned his love for liberty. He was not a Puritan but a Unitarian (as Jefferson was), very nearly a philosophical Universalist; in New England terms, something of a Rationalist. He was almost scholastic in his attachment both to faith and reason. He sang this hymn to *Liberty*:

> Long mayest thou reside among us, the delight of the wise, good and brave, the protectress of innocence from wrongs and oppression, the patroness of learning, arts, eloquence, virtue, rational loyalty, religion! And if any miserable people on the continent or isles of Europe, after being weakened by luxury, debauchery, venality, intestine quarrels, or other vices, should in the rude collisions, or now-uncertain revolutions of kingdoms, be driven, in their extremity, to seek a safe retreat from slavery in some far-distant climate, let them find, O let them find one in America under thy brooding, sacred wings; where our oppressed fathers once found it, and we now enjoy it, by favor of him, whose service is glorious freedom. [18]

In these beliefs, Mayhew was not alone. Virtually all the founders of the American Republic believed mightily that of all philosophies and religions, the Jewish and Christian religion is the best foundation for republican institutions. Here are but a few texts, to whose number scores of others could be added:

- *James Madison:*
The belief in a God All Powerful wise and good, is so essential to the moral order of the world and to the happiness of man, that arguments which enforce it cannot be drawn from too many sources nor adapted with too much solicitude to the different characters and capacities impressed with it. [19]

- *Thomas Jefferson:*
And can the liberties of a nation be thought secure when we have removed their only firm basis, a conviction in the minds of the people that these liberties are the gift of God? That they are not violated but with his wrath? [20]

- *Joseph Story:*
The promulgation of the great doctrines of religion, the being, and attributes, and providence of one Almighty God: the responsibility to him for all our actions, founded upon moral freedom and accountability; a future state of rewards and punishments; the cultivation of all the personal, social, and benevolent virtues—these can never be matters of indifference in any well-ordered community. It is, indeed, difficult to conceive how any civilized society can exist without them. [21]

- *The preamble of the Constitution of North Carolina:*
We, the people of the State of North Carolina, grateful to Almighty God, the Sovereign Ruler of Nations, for the preservation of the American Union and the existence of our civil, political, and religious liberties, and acknowledging our dependence upon Him for the continuance of those blessings to us and our posterity, do, for the more certain security thereof and for the better government of this State, ordain and establish this Constitution. [22]

- *Sir William Blackstone:*
Upon these two foundations, the law of nature and the law of revelation, depend all human laws; that is to say, no human law should be suffered to contradict these. [23]

But let us hear out other, fuller testimonies. John Adams exhorted clergymen to lead the way toward freedom. "Let the pulpit resound with the doctrine and sentiments of religious liberty," he said. *"Let us hear of the dignity of man's nature, and the noble rank he holds among the works of God....* Let it be known that British liberties are not the grants of princes and parliaments."[24] In 1775, Adams bragged that the Philadelphia ministers "thunder and lighten every Sabbath" against George III's despotism, and Jefferson noted that in Virginia "pulpit oratory ran like a shock of electricity through the whole colony."[25] John Wingate Thornton concluded that "To the Pulpit, the Puritan Pulpit, we owe the moral force which won our independence."[26] In America, religion favored the cause of liberty, and political statesmen favored religion. No other institution in America was so responsible for inspiring and motivating the American War of Independence as the Protestant churches – and the few thousand Jews and Catholics of the land along with them.

In Philadelphia, the wise and much revered Dr. Benjamin Rush also anchored republican government in religion:

> The only foundation for a useful education in a republic is to be laid in religion. *Without it there can be no virtue, and without virtue there can be no liberty,* and liberty is the object and life of all republican governments. [emphasis added][27]

This text expresses the essential core of the three-step logic of the founders:

> *Liberty is the object of the Republic.*
> *Liberty needs virtue.*
> *Virtue among the people is impossible without religion.*

From which it followed that there must be education in religion. Otherwise, there will sooner or later be moral weakness, from which will flow yielding to tyrants.

Rush felt so strongly about this that he would sooner see the teachings of Confucius or Mahomet taught in American schools than "see them grow up wholly devoid of a system of religious principles." While he insisted that the religion *he* supported was "that of the New Testament," most of his references are to the Torah. "It is foreign to my purpose," Rush continues,

> to hint at the arguments which establish the truth of Christian doctrine. My only business is to declare, that all its doctrines and precepts are calculated to promote the happiness of society, and the safety and well-being of civil government.

Rush then utters a sentence which he will repeat three times, and so I

add emphasis to it: *"A Christian cannot fail of being a Republican."*
The first of his three arguments for this point is that

> the history of the creation of man, and of the relation of our species to each
> other by birth, which is recorded in the Old Testament, is the best refuta-
> tion that can be given to the divine right of kings, and the strongest
> argument that can be used in favor of the original and natural equality of
> all mankind.[28]

Even if he knows no philosophy, convictions about limited government
and the equality of every individual in the eyes of God are available to
any coppersmith or carpenter who reads his Bible closely. Each citizen, no matter how humble, marveled that God knew his individual
name before the ages, that the mighty will be brought low and the lowly
exalted, and that all are ultimately equal in His sight. Each citizen has
the God-given dignity of being responsible for how he uses his liberty.
Then comes Rush's second argument:

> A Christian, I say again, cannot fail of being a republican, for every precept
> of the Gospel inculcates those degrees of humility, self-denial, and broth-
> erly kindness, which are directly opposed to the pride of monarchy and the
> pageantry of a court.[29]

In emphasizing "brotherly kindness," Rush chooses a different starting place than Locke. Locke begins with a pre-Christian "state of
nature," in which men are certainly not brotherly; his state of nature
is before civil society, before virtue, before religion. Man in the state of
nature is by Locke's definition outside ordinary civil society, outside
grace, outside justification. Locke worries about the transition from
state of nature to civil society. Rush adds a worry about the transition
from civil society to virtue. The two transitions are not unrelated.
Preachers of the time often linked them, interpreting Locke's "state of
nature" as a synonym for, or at least an analog of, "the fall" so much
stressed by Protestant (especially Puritan) theologians.[30] For Rush,
man, whether in the state of nature or in civil society, still needs the simple, plain, brotherly virtues taught by the precepts of Christianity,
especially those virtues so stressed by the Quakers.
Like the term "state of nature," the term "natural law" had been
used by British philosophers such as Thomas Hobbes and John Locke in
ways that could be construed as anti-biblical. The Americans typically
put these terms back in a biblical context, and understood them in ways

consistent with classic Christian thinking. Sometimes they did so in passing, but often they did so expressly, as when Alexander Hamilton rebuked Thomas Hobbes, in order to reclaim "natural law" for the biblical (and more American) point of view:

> Moral obligation, according to [Hobbes], is derived from the introduction of civil society; and there is no virtue but what is purely artificial, the mere contrivance of politicians, for the maintenance of social intercourse. But the reason he ran into this absurd and impious doctrine was that he disbelieved the existence of an intelligent superintending principle, who is the governor and will be the final judge of the universe....
>
> To grant that there is a supreme intelligence who rules the world and has established laws to regulate the actions of his creatures; and still to assert that man, in a state of nature, may be considered as perfectly free from all restraints of law and government, appears to a common understanding altogether irreconcilable. Good and wise men, in all ages, have embraced a very dissimilar theory. They have supposed that the deity, from the relations we stand in to himself and to each other, has constituted an eternal and immutable law, which is indispensably obligatory upon all mankind, prior to any human institution whatever. This is what is called the law of nature.... Upon this law depend the natural rights of mankind.[31]

To generalize this point: When some founders use such terms as "law of nature" and "natural rights of mankind," they are not using them in the same way Hobbes and Locke did. They are not abandoning their Christian beliefs as Hobbes certainly did and Locke may have. On the contrary, they are asserting that "natural law" and "the natural rights of mankind" are harmonious with Christian beliefs, even spring from Christian beliefs. Recall John Adams, as quoted just above: *"Let the pulpit resound...let us hear of the dignity of man's nature, and the noble rank he holds among the works of God."* Thus, the founders use Locke's terms in more traditional ways, consistent with Hooker and Sidney, even Cicero, Seneca, and Aristotle (for the ancients also stressed man's noble rank among the animals).[32] They are not concerned with nice academic arguments, however.[33] They are not acting as philosophers but as nation builders, expressing the will of a religious people.[34]

"And lastly," Benjamin Rush writes in offering his third reason why a Christian cannot fail to be a republican, "his religion teacheth him, in all things to do to others what he would wish, in like circumstances, they should do to him."[35] This is a good teaching for a society whose desperate struggle is to maintain the union and whose deepest wish is to build a brotherly city.

The physician of Philadelphia is not the only one to hold that biblical religion is particularly linked to republican government. John Adams wrote to Rush in 1807: "The Bible contains the most profound philosophy, the most perfect morality, and the most refined policy, that ever was conceived upon earth. It is the most republican book in the world."[36] Noah Webster repeated this theme in 1834, eight years after the deaths of Jefferson and Adams:

> The Christian religion ought to be received, and maintained with firm and cordial support. *It is the real source of all genuine republican principles.* It teaches the equality of men as to rights and duties; and while it forbids all oppression, it commands due subordination to law and rulers. It requires the young to yield obedience to their parents, and enjoins upon men the duty of selecting their rulers from their fellow citizens of mature age, sound wisdom, and real religion. [emphasis added]

Lest this admonition sound merely theoretical, Webster, as becomes the author of a dictionary, makes the point in unmistakenly practical terms:

> Never cease then to give to religion, to its institutions, and to its ministers, your strenuous support.... Those who destroy the influence and authority of the Christian religion, sap the foundations of public order, of liberty, and of republican government.[37]

Because the principle we are tracking here seems so alien to contemporary secular scholars, it is useful to provide two more texts, the more precisely to stress the convergence between common sense and faith. A native of Scotland and later a justice on the Supreme Court, Pennsylvania's James Wilson wrote in "The Laws of Nature" in 1790,

> How shall we, in particular cases, discover the will of God? We discover it by our conscience, our reason, and by the Holy Scriptures. The law of nature and the law of revelation are both divine; they flow, though in different channels, from the same adorable source. It is, indeed, preposterous to separate them from each other. The object of both is – to discover the will of God – and both are necessary for the accomplishment of that end.[38]

The same idea appears in a sermon from a New England divine, Samuel Cooper, D.D., preached before Governor John Hancock and the Senate and the House of Representatives of Massachusetts on October 5, 1780, for the Commencement of the Constitution of Massachusetts and the Inauguration of the New Government. Cooper had received his doctorate at Edinburgh after graduation from Harvard, served as a member of the Harvard Corporation, and turned down the presidency of Harvard. He began his sermon (which was anthologized in Holland and elsewhere in Europe as an archetypal American political sermon) that October day with an extended parallel between the people of Israel and "our own circumstances" in 1780, based on the thirtieth chapter of Jeremiah which dwells on the groaning of the Israelites in captivity, desolation, and conquest. Not hesitating to link George III to Nebuchadnezzar, Cooper noted that the Hebrew government, "tho' a theocracy, was yet...a free republic, and that the sovereignty resided in the people," and in that way he rooted republican liberty in biblical religion. "Such a constitution," he proceeded, "twice established by the hand of heaven in that nation, so far as it respects civil and religious liberty in general, ought to be regarded as a solemn recognition from the Supreme Ruler himself of the rights of human nature." Setting aside the circumstances peculiar to the situation of the Jews at that time, he adds, you may discern "in general what kind of government infinite wisdom and goodness would establish among mankind."[39]

Then Dr. Cooper marvels how the humble dictates of common sense beat in unison with "a special revelation from heaven":

> We want not, indeed, a special revelation from heaven to teach us that men are born equal and free; that no man has a natural claim of dominion over his neighbours, nor one nation any such claim upon another.... These are the plain dictates of that reason and common sense with which the common parent of men has informed the human bosom. *It is, however, a satisfaction to observe such everlasting maxims of equity confirmed, and impressed upon the consciences of men, by the instructions, precepts, and examples given us in the sacred oracles.*[40]

Having made the case for liberty, independence, and republican government from biblical examples, Cooper goes back to an argument from reason and common sense:

> [A]s piety and virtue support the honour and happiness of every community, they are peculiarly required in a free government. Virtue is the spirit of a republic; for where all power is derived from the people, all depends on their good disposition. If they are impious, factious and selfish; if they are abandoned to idleness, dissipation, luxury, and extravagance; if they are lost to the fear of God, and the love of their country, all is lost.[41]

Members of the new House and Senate of Massachusetts, in the middle of a dangerous war, had reason to feel much strengthened by the artillery of philosophy and religion that Dr. Cooper rolled up to support them on that October day. What faith taught, reason supported. What reason taught, revelation reinforced.[42]

As Tocqueville pointed out, it is impossible to establish convictions such as these on the premises of reason alone, as the Continental Enlightenment tried to do. Regarding religion, Europe and America took different paths. As the nineteenth century dawned, Europe put its trust in reason alone, America in both faith and common sense. In their depths the two civilizations went in different directions.

The Added Lift of Faith

In recent generations, many writers on the American Experiment have shown painfully little knowledge of detailed discussions of faith and reason that had taken place among learned Christians since the third century A.D. By contrast, most of the nation's founders knew the meaning of such classic terms as "sentiment," "opinion," "conviction," and "evidence" in their original Latin and Greek and (in Madison's case) Hebrew. From the generally high intellectual level of preaching in many American churches (ministers often being the best educated of all citizens), they had also learned to draw classic distinctions and to deploy traditional terms. The "Commencement Theses" required of graduating students by Columbia, Harvard, Yale, Princeton, and William and Mary, for instance, were still in the language and forms of medieval scholasticism.[43]

But what, we may ask, did these learned men think that the lamp of faith *added* to the lamp of reason and experience? What did faith provide that reason itself did not supply? The founders mentioned at least seven contributions.

First, faith adds to reason a cosmic *stage*; a *drama* of the free exercise of personal responsibility in history; and an acute awareness of a *climactic judgment* on "the last day," in which no thought, word, or deed will escape scrutiny. In these ways, faith enlarges the human horizon, lifts the eyes. Humans come to see themselves as among all creatures "the free and the brave" – free, because unlike all the other animals they must make choices, and brave because they will have to do battle, against themselves first of all, but also against cosmic forces of evil and darkness that may sometimes overwhelm them. The fact that men and women alone of all creatures are contrived with reason and understanding, not brute instinct alone, proved to the founders that they are ordained for self-government and self-control.[44]

Second, faith stimulates and enlivens the *conscience*, making it aware of small nuances of temptation, inclination, and resistance. When a young man asked Thomas Jefferson how to prepare for a life of freedom, Jefferson replied:

> Give up money, give up fame, give up science, give the earth itself and all it contains, rather than do an immoral act. And never suppose, that in any possible situation, or under any circumstance, it is best for you to do a dishonorable thing, however slightly so it may appear to you. Whenever you do a thing, though it can be known only but to yourself, ask yourself how you would act were all the world looking at you, and act accordingly. Encourage all your virtuous dispositions, and that exercise will make them habitual.

Then, as if predicting exactly what could happen to a future leader, Jefferson adds:

> Nothing is so mistaken as the supposition, that a person is to extricate himself from a difficulty, by intrigue, by chicanery, by dissimulation, by trimming, by an untruth, by an injustice. This increases the difficulties ten fold; and those who pursue these methods, get themselves so involved at length that they can turn no way but their infamy becomes more exposed. It is of great importance to set a resolution, not to be shaken, never to tell an untruth. There is no vice so mean, so pitiful, so contemptible; and he who permits himself to tell a lie once, finds it much easier to do it a second and a third time, till at length it becomes habitual; he tells lies without attending to it, and truths without the world's believing him. This falsehood of the tongue leads to that of the heart, and in time depraves all its good dispositions.[45]

Faith, in short, lifts one's eyes to goals beyond those of fame, advancement, science, and any of the goods of the earth. Faith teaches us that some deeds, even if unknown to others, and even if utilitarian, are contemptible in themselves. All this from Jefferson, perhaps the least religious of the major founders.

Third, as an ill-fated bill in the Virginia Assembly put it in 1784, "The general diffusion of Christian knowledge hath a tendency to correct the morals of men, restrain their vices, and preserve the peace of society."[46] Although Americans are bold and enterprising in making their fortunes, Tocqueville writes:

> American revolutionaries are obliged ostensibly to profess a certain respect for Christian morality and equity, and that does not allow them easily to break the laws when those are opposed to the executions of their designs; nor would they find it easy to surmount the scruples of their partisans even if they were able to get over their own. Up till now no one in the United States has dared to profess the maxim that everything is allowed in the interests of society, an impious maxim apparently invented...to legitimatize every future tyrant.[47]

Thus, while in a free society "the law allows the American people to do everything, there are things which religion prevents them from imagining and forbids them to dare"[48] – such as breaking the law. When consciences are active, policemen need be few; citizens are law-abiding willingly. Colonial Americans had already experienced periods of declines in religion, accompanied by a steady rise in moral carelessness. They had also seen religious awakenings lead to tangible improvements in social peace. This is why they all believed that religion "is necessary for the maintenance of republican institutions. That is not the view of one class or party among the citizens, but of the whole nation; it is found in all ranks."[49]

Fourth, Tocqueville again: "Fixed ideas about God and human nature are indispensable to men for the conduct of daily life, and it is daily life that prevents them from acquiring them." But these "fixed ideas" are difficult for most men to reach. Even great philosophers stumble in trying to come to them. But biblical faith provides to reason something that only a very few philosophers, and they only uncertainly, can reach for themselves. Thus, sound religion, tested in long experience, gives a culture an immense advantage. For men cannot act without living out general ideas. Clarity of soul prevents enervation and the dissipation of energies. Some ideas, Tocqueville writes, are a particular boon to free men: Ideas rooted in the unity of humankind, duties to neighbor, truth, honesty, and love for the law of reason. Regarding these essential ideas, the answers biblical religion gives are "clear, precise, intelligible to the crowd, and very durable."[50]

Fifth, religion adds to reason indispensable support for the view that every human being is not simply a bundle of pleasures and pains, a higher kind of cow or kitten or other contented domestic animal.

"Democracy favors the taste for physical pleasures," Tocqueville writes. "This taste, if it becomes excessive, soon disposes men to believe that nothing but matter exists. Materialism, in its turn, spurs them on to such delights with mad impetuosity. Such is the vicious circle into which democratic nations are driven. It is good that they see the danger and draw back."[51] The principle of equality that animates democracies, pulling men downwards, will slowly destroy what is most human in them – their souls. It is religion that checks and reverses this process and, more than that, spurs greatness, Tocqueville thinks. Faith sows its good effects in art and manners, as well as in the arena of practical action. Belief in immortality prods humans to aspire upwards, and in this way grounds their awareness of their own special dignity and natural rights.

Sixth, faith adds to a morality of mere reason an acute sense of *acting in the presence of a personal and undeceivable Judge,* Who sees and knows even actions performed in secret, even willful acts committed solely in one's heart. Thus, faith adds motives for maintaining high standards, and for seeking to do things perfectly *even when no one is looking.* Faith gives us reasons to paint the bottom of the chair, and clean the unseen corners of a room: godliness entails attention to details that no one but God sees. Whereas morality construed within the bounds of reason alone is, at best, a matter of utilitarian calculation or deontological rules, faith sees moral behavior in terms of relations between two persons, ourselves and the God to Whom we owe much. In this vein, Ben Franklin chastised his colleagues at the Constitutional Convention for their ingratitude to their beneficent Friend Who had assisted them when they were in need.

> In this situation of this Assembly, groping as it were in the dark to find political truth, and scarce able to distinguish it when presented to us, how has it happened, Sir, that we have not hitherto once thought of humbly applying to the Father of lights to illuminate our understandings? In the beginning of the contest with G. Britain, when we were sensible of danger we had daily prayer in this room for the divine protection. – Our prayers, Sir, were heard, and they were graciously answered. All of us who were engaged in the struggle must have observed frequent instances of superintending providence in our favor. To that kind providence we owe this happy opportunity of consulting in peace on the means of establishing our future national felicity. And have we now forgotten that powerful friend? Or do we imagine that we no longer need his assistance? I have lived, Sir, a long time, and the longer I live, the more convincing proofs I see of this truth – *that God governs in the affairs of men.* [emphasis in the original] [52]

Seventh, faith in America has had a dramatic effect on mores, especially in the home. In America, Tocqueville writes, religion "reigns supreme in the souls of women, and it is women who shape mores. Certainly, of all the countries in the world, America is the one in which the marriage tie is most respected and where the highest and truest conception of conjugal happiness has been conceived." Tocqueville has no doubt that the "great severity of mores which one notices in the United States has its primary origin in beliefs." The comparative laxity of morals in Europe breeds mistrust even in the home, and even broader ripples of mistrust in the public sphere beyond the home.

> In Europe almost all the disorders of society are born around the domestic hearth and not far from the nuptial bed. It is there that men come to feel scorn for natural ties and legitimate pleasures and develop a taste for disorder, restlessness of spirit, and instability of desires. Shaken by the tumultuous passions which have often troubled his own house, the European finds it hard to submit to the authority of the state's legislators.[53]

When there is no trust in the home, trust in public life is highly improbable. Where there is a lack of self-government at home, self-government in the public sphere has little probability of success. If one cannot say "that in the United States religion influences the laws or political opinions in detail," Tocqueville continues, "it does direct mores, and by regulating domestic life it helps to regulate the state."

In sum, to say nothing of otherworldly benefits, faith adds to reason seven worldly strengths: (1) a *cosmic stage* for the drama of liberty; (2) a *watchful conscience*; (3) *restraint of vice* and gains in social peace; (4) fixed, stable, and *general ideas* about the dynamics of life; (5) *a check on the downward bias* of the principle of equality and the materialism toward which it gravitates; (6) a new conception of *morality as a personal relation* with our Creator, and thus *a motive for acting well even when no one is looking*; and (7) through *the high honor paid to the marriage bond*, the *quiet regulation of mores* in marriage and in the home.

Political Corollaries

This list could be extended to greater length. But, clearly, at least three *political corollaries* follow. The stress of Holy Scripture on the frailty and weakness of the most devoted heroes of the faith – lustful King

David; pusillanimous Peter denying Jesus three times on the night He died – led the founders *to note carefully their own recurring weaknesses and those of republican institutions.* Madison, for instance, wrote a short treatise on *The Vices of the Political System of the United States,*[54] concentrating "his studies upon the vices – the faults and defects and dangerous tendencies – of the kind of government he was supporting."[55] Such systemic self-criticism, rare in the annals of political history, was at least in part the result of the habit encouraged among Christians and Jews of examining all things for their virtues and vices.

Faith not only teaches examination of all things in the light of conscience. It also teaches love for the larger *community*, regard for the public good, and the identification of personal good with the good of all. Donald Lutz quotes a patriot from South Carolina: "The SOCIAL spirit is the true SELFISH spirit, and men always promote their own interest most, in proportion as they promote that of their neighbors and their country."[56] As images of solidarity, the founders turned often to architecture. One of their favorite philosophers was the Roman from Spain, Seneca, who wrote: "We are born to live in society. Our society is very similar to a vault; it would fall if the stones did not support each other, thus holding the whole vault in place."[57] Lutz adds example after example to show the ways in which the founding generation gave priority to the community over the individual.[58]

Nevertheless, faith also taught the founders that every single man and woman, alone, has an *inalienable duty* to choose for or against God. Consider these passages from two separate sermons, the first by Israel Evans:

> Religious liberty is a divine right, immediately derived from the Supreme Being, without the intervention of any created authority. It is the natural privilege of worshipping [sic] God in that manner which, according to the judgment of men, is most agreeable and pleasing to the divine character. As the conscience of man is the image and representative of God in the human soul; so to him alone is it responsible.[59]

The second comes from a sermon entitled "The Rights of Conscience Inalienable" by John Leland of Rhode Island:

> Every man must give an account of himself to God, and therefore every man ought to be at liberty to serve God, and therefore every man ought to be at liberty to serve God in that way that he can best reconcile to his conscience.... It would be sinful for a man to surrender that to man which is to be kept sacred for God.[60]

Add to these this passage from a letter to Benedict Arnold:

> While we are contending for our own liberty, we should be very cautious not
> to violate the conscience of others, ever considering that God alone is the
> judge of the hearts of men, and to Him only in this case are they answer-
> able.[61]

The community plays a crucial role in preparing its individual members, especially its young, to make sound moral choices. But, in the end,
it would be sinful for the community to coerce conscience. Personal
responsibility in conscience is the foundation of rights.

The most religious Americans of the founding generation of 1770-
1800 had every reason, therefore, to rejoice in the American
experiment. They saw both faith and common sense working in unison.
Thus, as William Lee Miller writes:

> For believing Americans in their religious capacity, liberty, republicanism,
> the new nation under the Constitution were not perceived to be inimical to
> the Christian church of Christian beliefs. Rather the opposite. For Madison's
> Baptist supporters in Virginia and elsewhere, the making of America was a
> Second Reformation – another religious triumph.[62]

Indeed, six years after the writing of the Constitution, seventeen
years after the Declaration of Independence, Christian America was still
exulting in the lift given by faith to this nation's great experiment in
liberty:

> May we not consider these as the dawn of brighter days, of a brighter sun
> than ever blessed the world before; as a commencement of the golden age,
> that introduces a better system of religion that enforces moral obligations,
> not a religion that relaxes and evades them; a religion of peace and charity,
> not of strife and party rage?[63]

There is a final passage in Tocqueville, so classic in form and so
important that I must now briefly quote it. This French aristocrat, this
profound (if not always externally devout) Catholic genius, saw in the
two wings of the American experiment a way to unite his two most fundamental passions – for liberty and religion. He sees Anglo-American
civilization as "the product of two perfectly distinct elements which
elsewhere have often been at war with one another but which in America it was somehow possible to incorporate into each other, forming
a marvelous combination. I mean the *spirit of religion* and the *spirit
of freedom*." Far from harming each other, in America "these two

apparently opposed tendencies work in harmony and seem to lend mutual support." In America, Christians and Jews believe that God created men to be free, and that the world of politics is a sphere intended by the Creator for the free play of intelligence.

> Religion, being free and powerful within its own sphere and content with the position reserved for it, realized that its sway is all the better established because it relies only on its own powers and rules men's hearts without external support.
>
> Freedom sees religion as the companion of its struggles and triumphs, the cradle of its infancy, and the divine source of its rights. Religion is considered as the guardian of mores, and mores are regarded as the guarantee of the laws and pledge for the maintenance of freedom itself.[64]

The Most Precarious Regime

Judaism and Christianity provided a great deal more than meets the eye, then, to the American founding. They reinforced in men's minds the role of reason in human affairs, as well as the idea of a cosmos open to liberty, conceived, created, and understood (even in its tiniest details) by a benevolent Deity: Lawgiver, Governor, Judge, and gracious Providence. This Deity would one day ask of each human an accounting for his thoughts and deeds. In His eyes, how humans use their liberty matters infinitely; liberty is the purpose for which the sun and the stars are made. Who denies that America's experiment in liberty is especially dear to Providence? Looking down on it, God smiles. Borrowing from Virgil, the founders inscribed this very image on the Seal of the United States:

ANNUIT COEPTIS.

The other inscription they placed on the Seal in its seventh and final draft called attention to the originality of their new design:

NOVUS ORDO SECLORUM.

In its place, for the first six drafts they had originally had a single word:

VIRTUE.

Given their understanding of liberty, calling attention to *virtue* must have seemed to them too obvious. What they needed to emphasize was the newness and daring of their "new order of the ages." For sometimes experiments go wrong. It is all too easy to see how this one might do so.

For liberty is the most precarious regime. Even a single generation may give it away. One thing our generation must not do is take our republic's longevity for granted.

THREE

The moral government of God, and his viceregent, Conscience, ought to be sufficient to restrain men to obedience, to justice, and benevolence at all times and in all places; we must therefore descend from the dignity of our nature when we think of civil government at all. But the nature of mankind is one thing, and the reason of mankind another; and the first has the same relation to the last as the whole to a part. The passions and appetites are parts of human nature as well as reason and the moral sense. In the institution of government it must be remembered that, although reason ought always to govern individuals, it certainly never did since the Fall, and never will till the Millennium; and human nature must be taken as it is, as it has been, and will be.

– John Adams

Let the pulpit resound with the doctrine and sentiments of religious liberty. Let us hear of the dignity of man's nature, and the noble rank he holds among the works of God…. Let it be known that British liberties are not the grants of princes and parliaments.

– John Adams

THIRD CHAPTER

Immoral Man, Moral Society, Religious Liberty

I n pursuit of their own happiness, human beings have a propensity to trample on the rights of others. This tendency has made religious liberty fragile and very rare.

In overcoming this propensity, the Americans accomplished a revolution which at that time had "no model on the face of the earth."[1] This daring experiment brought together three separate strands of human experience: the loneliness of individual conscience before the Face of God; a new form of community; and a new political architecture – not a *national establishment* of any one religion, but solid public support for a *pluralism of pillars* in many religions.

To weave these three strands together, we need to remember James Madison's reaction against the cruelty shown by Virginia's established church (the Church of England) against the Baptists; the realism in Massachusetts about the fickleness of conscience; and how the Constitutional Convention of 1787 carefully refrained both from establishing a national church and from disestablishing the existing state churches. All three stories spotlight the role of *community* in the founding generation's way of life.

Whereas people of our time are cynical about communities but trust the individual, our founders saw the weaknesses of individuals and trusted union. Without attachment to the Union, independence could not have been achieved. Unless they had taken pride in belonging to a moral community with demanding standards, the American people would not have overcome many internal dissensions and sectional ambitions.

A Whip in the Mouth

In the summer of 1771 in Caroline County in Virginia, an unlicensed Baptist preacher was preaching outdoors when from across the fields a priest of the Church of England galloped up at the head of the Sheriff and other men, thrust a horsewhip in the preacher's mouth, dismounted, and then subjected the preacher to a thorough flogging in an open field, in plain sight of the assembled crowd.

This bloody flogging was not an isolated incident. The Church of England was the established Church of Virginia, and preachers of other denominations were obliged to request a licence from the state. On principle the Baptists refused to apply, holding that their right to preach came not from any state, but from the Word of God. For this "crime" against the state religion, more than forty-five Baptist ministers in Virginia were thrown in jail between 1765 and 1778.[2]

A few weeks after that awful flogging in Caroline County, another assembly of Baptists met in Blue Run Church in Orange County, within four miles of the Madison home. Five thousand turned out, the largest crowd ever assembled in the Commonwealth of Virginia. The leading Baptist preacher in Orange County was bringing some three hundred souls to Christ per year – nearly one per day.

Although not quite twenty years of age at the time, James Madison's heart went out to the Baptists. As a member of the Church of England, he was morally offended when members of his church indulged like "imps of Satan" in the persecution of other believers. During the next twenty years, he often defended the Baptists (the ancestors of Jerry Falwell in Southern Virginia) when they desperately needed help against the establishment of that time.

After his graduation from Princeton three years later, in 1774, Madison stayed on an extra year to study Hebrew and reflect upon the Scriptures. Religious liberty was much in his thoughts. He had fallen under the influence of President Witherspoon, a recent immigrant from Scotland, possibly the most learned man in America, a great devotee of the "natural liberty" of conscience, and a calm but steady foe of "persecution on religion's account." Witherspoon preached liberty both civil and religious: "The magistrate ought to defend the rights of conscience," he wrote, "and tolerate all their religious sentiments that are not injurious to their neighbors."[3] This teaching merged in Madison's mind and heart with the raw trauma of the flogging in Caroline County in 1771. In 1776, just before the Declaration of Independence, though he was only 24, Madison helped to formulate the language of the Virginia Declaration of Rights, all but ending the days of Anglican Establishment in Virginia. He did so gladly, because he believed that a state establishment of religion injured consciences, both among its victims and among its enforcers.

Nine years later, in 1785, Patrick Henry introduced a new tax in Virginia to pay the salaries of all the Christian clergy. Expecting to gain their support, Henry exempted from the tax Quakers and Mennonites, who had no clergy. Now fully allergic to any entanglement of the State with churches, Madison circulated his famous "Remonstrance," announcing firmly that Christian churches – for their own good – should not be dependent on the State at all. While the total number of voters in Virginia numbered only 40,000, similar petitions against the Henry bill were soon signed by 10,929 protesters (especially Baptists), and the bill failed utterly. The older George Mason and the young Madison then got Henry moved out of the legislature and into the Governor's office. Hot for vengeance, Governor Henry, hoping to drive him out of public life, saw to it that on the eve of the next congressional election that young whippersnapper Madison was redistricted.

In Madison's newly drawn district, there were 2,200 voters, most of whom were unknown to him. But he did know the Baptists, including the pastor of Blue Run Church. The quite considerable electoral force of the Baptists enabled him to eke out a narrow win, and thus to participate in the first United States Congress.

> At a critical juncture of his campaign he wrote the Reverend George Eve, the pastor of Blue Run Church where the great protest meeting of Baptists had been held before the Revolution. The Baptists were now even more numerous and active.... In an election in which about 2,200 persons voted, the Baptists had to be a major force. Mr. Madison assured Pastor Eve that he was now committed to amendments to achieve "the most satisfactory provisions for all essential rights, particularly the rights of Conscience in the fullest latitude".... On February 2, 1789, Mr. James Madison was elected over Mr. James Monroe by a margin of 336 votes. The Reverend John Leland wrote at once to congratulate him and to remind him of the Baptists' interest in religious liberty. With the aid of these dedicated evangelicals, by the active intervention of the preachers in politics, Mr. Madison became the spokesman for religious freedom in the Congress that was to begin the government of the United States.[4]

Madison could scarcely forget this critical vote when he led the fight in the first Congress for the Bill of Rights. During the Convention and Ratification debates, he had been opposed to a bill of rights, believing that the Constitution already protected religious liberty and all other rights. He insisted that writing specific rights down would only weaken the protection of rights left unexpressed.[5] The implication might then take root that the government reserved all powers except those expressly written down, whereas the Constitution as a whole had made exactly the opposite assumption. The Baptists, however, did not trust the Anglican Church. They told Madison they wanted their religious rights written down. Madison had no choice but to change his mind.

> Despite his misgivings about the intrinsic merits of bills of rights, Madison saw the necessity to act to gain the support of "the whole community" for the Constitution. He saw a bill of rights, *his* carefully constructed bill of rights, as the most effective solution. If he wrote the amendments, he could win the support of those who were still uneasy, without making any change at all in the constitutional structure. His primary objective was to keep the Constitution intact.[6]

In that first heavily burdened Congress, faced with immense practical problems and little patience for abstract arguments, Madison proposed the Bill of Rights himself.[7]

By Madison's single-handed persistence and legislative skill, the Bill of Rights got through the two houses of Congress, and in only two years sailed through the required state legislatures. That outcome was not greeted with celebrations, parades, fireworks; there was silence. Since about 1948, American elites have emphasized the Bill of Rights, and especially the first amendment, as the single most important part of the Constitution. That is not the way it seemed at the time. Indeed, when Secretary of State Thomas Jefferson dispatched the Bill of Rights to the States for their ratification, he did so in a language drier and more devoid of eloquence than any other passage he ever wrote. He buried the Bill of Rights in news of fisheries and post offices:

> Sir,   March 1, 1792
> I have the honor to send to you herein enclosed, two copies duly authenti-
> cated, of an Act concerning certain fisheries of the United States, and for
> the regulation and government of the fishermen employed therein; also of an
> Act to establish the post office and post roads with the United States; also the
> ratifications by three fourths of the Legislatures of the Several States, of

certain articles in addition and amendment of the Constitution of the United States, proposed by Congress to the said Legislatures, and of being with sentiments of the most perfect respect, your Excellency's

Th. Jefferson[8]

The majorities in Congress who voted for the Bill of Rights did so because the new amendments added nothing to the Constitution and did not weaken it. The Anti-Federalists voted against it for exactly the same reason – they wanted still narrower limits imposed upon the federal state, and a longer list of rights withheld. Yet the Bill of Rights did, in effect, add a new article to the Constitution. The first three articles defined the three separate institutions of limited government: the legislature, the presidency, and the court. Now the Bill of Rights added a "people's article," painting a portrait of the American people and which rights they love. Many voters liked this portrait of themselves. Whereas the first three articles *granted* powers from the people to the three institutions of republican government, the newly added "article" merely described powers *withheld*. Despite bitter arguments in some states, especially Virginia, where Anti-Federalists were many and ably led by the eloquent voices of Patrick Henry, the great George Mason and John Randolph, ratification was swift.[9]

My colleague Robert Goldwin has unveiled the portrait of the people painted by the Bill of Rights, starting with their religious imperatives:

> This is a people who takes religion very seriously, seriously enough to insist that all Americans be free to choose how they will worship, if they choose to worship at all; who cannot be required to follow governmental or any other sort of dictate in matters of religion or be denied the right to follow ancient religious practice, if that is their choice; who will not seek to impose their religious beliefs or practices on others, or allow others to impose their beliefs on them.

But religion is not the only sphere of the human spirit that is important to them. The Bill of Rights goes on:

> This is a people who will insist that their voices be heard, in speech and print; who will not hesitate to broadcast their own opinions, however unpopular, or to hear them from others, no matter how unwelcome they may be; who expect to have much to say about the governing of their nation; and who will gather together, if and when they so choose, to let the government know, peaceably but unmistakably, when they have grievances.

Their portrait is not finished:

> The opening words of the First Amendment, "Congress shall make no law," tell us that this is a people who, though fully committed to the principle of the rule of the majority, understands full well that the majority is not authorized to do whatever it may want; that there are certain things that the majority, as represented in Congress, is forbidden to legislate, by the authority of "the whole community," as expressed in the Constitution by "the People of the United States."[10]

Goldwin also has an excellent discussion of just how the religious freedom clause of the First Amendment got its precise language. The House had debated the establishment clause at great length, and tried out many versions of it. Madison, for instance, had proposed "*nor shall any national religion be established.*" But when it came out of the Committee of Eleven the draft read, "*No religion shall be established by law.*" The objection was immediately raised that that wording "might be thought to have a tendency to abolish religion altogether." Madison, in response, said he thought it meant that "Congress should not establish *a* religion," but for some reason he never proposed that simple and unambiguous wording, using the indefinite article to clarify what it is that Congress must not do. At that moment, Livermore proposed new wording: "*The Congress shall make no laws touching religion.*" The Committee of the Whole House, preferring that form, modified it with wording moved by Fisher Ames (but reportedly written by Madison): "*Congress shall make no law establishing religion.*" The House of Representatives then submitted that version to the Senate.[11]

Then the wording was again changed from "no law *establishing* religion" to "no law *respecting* religion." Delegates from states that already had established churches wanted no tampering at all by the new federal government. They wanted Congress to be declared "blind" to religion – not to make laws about it in one way or the other. Goldwin continues:

> Madison and most other members of the House, it seems safe to conclude..., would have agreed that the purpose of the clause was to keep Congress from favoring one religion in preference to others, but not to indicate hostility or opposition to religion, or anything but approval of it, as consistent with, and even essential to, the well-being of a secular society.[12]

This judgment is reinforced by a review of the six different versions of the First Amendment actually put forward in the congressional debate lined up together by Wilfred Parsons.[13] This sequence, from first to last, displays quite clearly the unfolding will of Congress. The first version came from Madison, and stated clearly three distinct ideas:

1. *The civil rights of none shall be abridged on account of religious belief, nor shall any national religion be established, nor shall the full and equal rights of conscience in any manner or on any pretext be infringed.*

But the Amendment had to be worded in such a way as not to threaten the religious establishments in the separate states. The drafting committee tried one way, then another, to eliminate potential misunderstandings, and to make clear that *Congress* was the body feared:

2. *No religion shall be established by law, nor shall the equal rights of conscience be infringed.*

3. *Congress shall make no laws touching religion, or infringing the rights of conscience.*

4. *Congress shall make no law establishing religion, or to prevent the free exercise thereof, or to infringe the rights of conscience.*

5. *Congress shall make no laws establishing articles of faith or a mode of worship or prohibiting the free exercise of religion; etc.*

6. *Congress shall make no law respecting an establishment of religion or prohibiting the free exercise of religion; etc.*

Left to his own convictions, Madison would have abolished all the state establishments of religion, but many serious partisans of liberty in other states saw in that path sure destruction. Madison wanted the church to pass through society invisibly, never being touched by any notice from the state – no official chaplains (not even in the Navy, at sea), no national days of prayer or thanksgiving, or the like. He (like Jefferson) became so extreme on these issues that he could not hope to carry his contemporaries with him, outside Virginia. His motive was not secularism. On the contrary, he thought the churches would be stronger the freer they were from government assistance (with its inevitable collusion and interference, and even whips in the mouth and jailings). Indeed, Madison boasted in later years that the American model of separation – even if not as pure as he had wanted it – had led to an unprecedented vitality in the churches, especially when compared with Christianity in Europe. "We are teaching the world a great truth," he wrote to Edward Livingston in 1822:

that governments do better without kings and nobles than with them. The merit will be doubled by the other lesson: that Religion flourishes in greater purity without, than with the aid of government.[14]

When he began his term as president, Madison opposed Washington's practice of national days of prayer, but then Madison too was obliged to ask for them – when the raging fires of the War of 1812 made him seek national unity and cry out for help.[15]

Very early, the young Madison had come to the idea that the establishment of a religion, or even the almost universal prevalence of only one religion, rendered the minds and souls of its adherents lazy and torpid, and induced a kind of mental "slavery" unworthy of free men.[16] He made an educated assessment: competition and open debate will prove good for the Christian soul. He predicted that through competition each church group would serve as a sentinel protecting others from state favor and pressure.[17]

On the other hand, Madison's "Remonstrance" asserts that religion must be exercised according to one's conscience and conviction, since each individual stands before his Creator alone, confronted with an interior choice. This view of his is thoroughly impregnated with Christian conceptions. For pagan religions of antiquity, bodily observance was sufficient; "piety" was a matter more of outward observance than of inner meditation and conviction. In the Christian drama of salvation, by contrast, an inward decision is axial. For Christians, religion is a duty owed to a Creator and personal Savior, and this duty hinges on an inward personal commitment that springs from reflection and deliberate persevering choice. That is why acts of conscience are inalienable: a man's destiny hinges on his own act of will, not the will of anybody else. This is the ground on which Madison opens the argument of his "Remonstrance:"

> The religion then of every man must be left to the conviction and conscience of every man; and it is the right of every man to exercise it as these may dictate. This right is in its nature an unalienable right. It is unalienable, because the opinions of men, depending on the evidence contemplated by their own minds cannot follow the dictates of other men: It is unalienable also, because what is here a right towards men, is a duty towards the Creator. It is the duty of every man to render to the Creator such homage and such only as he believes to be acceptable to him. This duty is precedent, both in order of time and in degree of obligation, to the claims of Civil Society.

Madison then goes on to explain that "Before any man can be considered as a member of Civil Society, he must be considered as a subject of the Governour of the Universe." He then adds that a member of civil society, who enters into any local association, must always do so mindful of his duty to the civil authority. Therefore, "much more must every man who becomes a member of any particular Civil Society, do it with a saving of his allegiance to the Universal Sovereign."[18]

This text is vital for two reasons. In its insight into duties, it underlines the precedence of God over Civil Society. And in finding rational ground for religious liberty, it begins with faith, not reason – the duties of the creature who stands alone in the presence of the Creator. In this way, Madison's right to religious liberty is grounded in faith, not reason. It is prior to the formation of civil society. It is beyond the reach of government. Because of this right, government must be limited in power. Because of this right, civil society is also stopped short before the conscience of persons. The genius of the republican form of government, in other words, springs from the inner energies of faith. Only after that propulsion does reason take wing.

Judge John Noonan does a remarkably skillful job in singling out the theological strands that Madison wove together in his famous "Remonstrance:"

1. Religion is "the duty which we owe to our Creator."
2. This duty is to render the homage that each person determines in conscience "to be acceptable to him [the Creator]."
3. The right to determine this duty in conscience belongs to each person and is "unalienable" for two reasons. First, the exercise of that right must depend on evidence, and each person must determine what evidence is sufficient for conviction. Second, this duty is owed to the Creator, and so can never be relaxed by any human being.
4. This duty "is precedent, both in order of time and in degree of obligation," to the claims of "Civil Society," whether those claims are made by society at large or by a legislature. Religion is therefore "wholly exempt" from the "cognizance" of civil society or civil government. That "the Civil Magistrate is a competent Judge of Religious Truth" is a falsehood. That the Civil Magistrate "may employ Religion as an engine of Civil Policy" is wickedness.
5. If freedom of religion is abused, it is "an offense against God, not against man."
6. To rely on governmental support is "a contradiction to the Christian

Religion itself for every page of it disavows a dependence on the powers of the world."

7. To use governmental coercion to support the Christian clergy is to discourage conversion and to surround Christianity "with a wall of defense" characterized by "an ignoble and un-christian timidity."[19]

These seven principles show that Madison's faith in the Christian Church was marvelously pure, possibly even too pure for reality. If men were angels, not even churches would be necessary. As president, he was himself obliged to be more practical.

As Madison worked on the religious freedom clause of the Virginia Declaration of Rights in 1776, later his "Remonstrance" in 1785, then the Constitutional Convention of 1787, and on the Bill of Rights from 1790–1792, he wanted to protect the Baptists, Mennonites, Quakers, and others from beatings, jail, and even death for their religious convictions. He was protecting not just individuals alone but whole religious communities. On the other hand, preachers approached even the vast crowds they addressed (George Whitefield once spoke to an estimated 30,000 persons from one rolling hillside) as if they were speaking to one person at a time, addressing their arguments to the individual conscience of each to lay hold of and "take to heart." Regarding religious liberty, both individuals and community count, both innermost conscience and free public exercise.

Nonetheless, in the admirable principles by which Madison reacted against the abuses he had witnessed, there were two grave dangers he did not see. The first danger was that the nonestablishment of any one religion might turn into antagonism against all religions. The second was that the State would take no care about religion at all, not even about education in the truths of religion. But what, then, about the great religious principles on which the natural right to religious liberty is based: namely, that there is a God, and that each creature owes him worship and gratitude? If these principles are never taught, the foundation of religious liberty crumbles.

So students could not fail to learn those principles, Jefferson himself asked Madison to recommend theological books for the library at the University of Virginia. Madison's list included some Fathers of the Church, St. Augustine, St. Thomas Aquinas, and many others.[20]

Yet Madison seemed otherwise insouciant about religious education in Virginia and the nation. Has the magistrate no responsibility at all to think about such things, and to find some ways, however indirect, to secure knowledge about religious principles in the future? Must religious liberty lose its only footing in young minds, clear knowledge of the duty to worship the Almighty, and the individual right that flows from it? Establishment of the sort Patrick Henry kept angling for may be Charybdis, but is not the pure disestablishment of Madison sailing straight for Scylla? Madison's extreme position, for instance, insisted that the federal government could separate young men from religious services by sending them to sea, but incur no obligation to supply them with chaplains. Is this not one of those attempts to govern as "if men were angels" that Madison himself scorned at other places?[21]

The Virginia solution to the problem of religious liberty purports to be rooted deeply in profound religious principles. Yet, as they grew older, Jefferson and (to a lesser degree) Madison picked the flowers of faith but did not nourish their roots. If they had followed that policy in the beginning, neither the Declaration nor the Constitution would have been acceptable to a religious people. Fortunately, there was much resistance in Virginia at the founding, and even more elsewhere. Fortunately, too, at the founding both Jefferson and Madison had been men of practicality, opposed to "utopic theorists" *(Federalist No. 10)*; their ideal was prudence in the classical sense, not abstract ideology. Madison in particular favored the flourishing of religion in America. In fact, his principle that government should take no notice of religion rested on the "great truth...that religion flourishes in greater purity without, rather than with the aid of government."[22] Still, the phrase "the aid of government" bears more than one meaning.

Jefferson and Madison in their later years led Virginia down one path. Massachusetts under John Adams pursued another. In those days Massachusetts was closer to the national temper.

The Massachusetts Way – Virtue in Community

In Massachusetts, people observed that religious liberty is threatened by human sloth and sinfulness. Left to themselves, people are inclined to take the easiest and most self-indulgent path, to be less than honest with themselves, and to make excuses for their own weaknesses. In addition, they are inclined to have a highly exaggerated self-esteem and to recognize only weakly, if at all, the just claims of the consciences of others. As faith that God sees into the heart grows dim, humans give themselves licence to do as they please. These moral tendencies are universal and persistent; no society "progresses" beyond them. And they bode ill for republican government.

In a letter to James Warren, Sam Adams described the ill effects of certain personal vices in common political life. He linked the treason of a prominent doctor in Boston, thought to be a patriot even as he was selling his services to the British, to his notoriety as an adulterer. There is often a link between private morality and public safety, Adams argued.

> There are Virtues & Vices which are properly called *political*. "Corruption, Dishonesty to one's Country Luxury and Extravagance tend to the Ruin of States."
>
> …He who is void of virtuous Attachments in private Life, is, or very soon will be void of all Regard for his Country. There is seldom an Instance of a Man guilty of betraying his Country, who had not before lost the Feeling of moral Obligations in his private Connections. Before [Dr. Benjamin Church, Jr.] was detected of holding a criminal Correspondence with the Enemies of his Country, his Infidelity to his Wife had been notorious. Since private and publick Vices, are in Reality, though not always apparently, so nearly connected, of how much Importance, how necessary is it, that the utmost Pains, be taken by the Publick, to have the Principles of Virtues early inculcated on the Minds even of Children, and the moral Sense kept alive, and that the wise Institutions of our Ancestors for these great Purposes encouragd [sic] by the Government.[23]

Adams's letter implies a four-step argument: (1) A Republic lives by *liberty*, not licence; (2) Liberty cannot be exercised without an honor guard of *virtues*, such as temperance, self-control, fair-mindedness, courage, and sound practical judgment; (3) That panoply of virtues is highly unlikely to remain vigorous from one generation to another without *religious awakening*; and (4) Religious alertness depends on an experimental, self-critical, and lively religious *education*. Put otherwise, without the good moral habits inculcated by a sound religious education, no free republic will long survive. Government, too, must encourage religious education.

Why is religious education important to political life? Because faith adds many necessary strengths to moral reason. This is, essentially, the argument that John Adams, the father of American independence, took to the people of Massachusetts as they struggled to write a new constitution from 1776-1781. Thus Article III of the Massachusetts Constitution begins:

> As the happiness of a people and the good order and preservation of civil government essentially depend upon piety, religion, and morality, and as these cannot be generally diffused through a community but by...public instructions in piety, religion, and morality....

From which the Constitution drew a stunning conclusion:

> Therefore, To promote their happiness and to secure the good order and preservation of their government, the people of this commonwealth have a *right* to invest their legislature with power to authorize and require, and the legislature shall, from time to time, authorize and require, the several towns, parishes, precincts, and other bodies-politic *or religious societies* to make suitable provision, at their own expense, for the institution of the public worship of God and for the support and maintenance of public Protestant teachers of piety, religion, and morality in all cases where such provision shall not be made voluntarily. [emphasis added][24]

In the public debates that followed, many objected – there were at least six objections – that Article III was an infringement of religious liberty.[25] Jefferson and Madison would surely have said so. People close to Adams replied, No, this article compels no one's belief. But if any citizen wants to benefit from the sound civil order and good habits of liberty essential for the survival of a free Republic, observation will teach him that such habits are the result of a sound religious education, and are not obtainable by most people and in the long run in any other way. Therefore, such a citizen must be willing to contribute to religious education. In this, there is no danger to religious liberty. On the contrary, Article III's many supporters saw it as a necessary condition for religious liberty.[26]

The Massachusetts way, in short, was realism about the weaknesses of individuals such as slackness of will and laziness of intellect, unstable passions, and a fixation on private interests. The Massachusetts way reminds one of Reinhold Niebuhr's putative title *The Not So Moral Man and His Less Moral Societies*.[27] Professor Barry Shain even quotes a host of writers in the founding generation who believed, in large measure from their own experience, that when sin abounds natural liberty ends. It was "when dark and stormy Passions obscured the Light of *Reason*," that "the fair Realm of LIBERTY [was] laid waste, and LICENTIOUSNESS usurped both her Title and Dominion."[28] The loss of innocence meant to early Americans the loss of natural liberty. "LICENTIOUSNESS accompanied the Depravity of Man and immediately succeeded to the Loss of Natural Liberty." Shain points out:

> [A]lmost "no one had much to say of an approving character about natural liberty. It was invariably and pejoratively associated with the lifestyle of 'savages,'" that is, fallen individuals who were bereft of the benefits of God's grace and the restraint of society. For most Americans, then, people could be allowed some measure of natural liberty, but only as mediated by local intermediate social and political institutions, rather than as comprehended by the untrustworthy individual.[29]

Put otherwise, authentic liberty must be restrained, ordered, and taught to take pleasure in the channels of virtue and law. "Liberty *against* Virtue and Laws, is only a Privilege to be unhappy" (emphasis added).[30]

A letter published in a Boston paper in 1763 reads:

> Political liberty does not consist in unrestrained freedom. In governments, that is in societies directed by laws, liberty can consist only in the power of doing what we ought to will, and in not being constrained to do what we ought not to will.[31]

This letter reads uncannily like Lord Acton a century later, who wrote that liberty is not "the power of doing what we like, but the right of being able to do what we ought."[32] The founding generation knew how hard this freedom is to maintain over time. Many deplored the low moral condition of their time. Many in America recognized a lost fervor of purpose and a new licentiousness that had replaced it.

Since most Americans were painfully aware of their own religious dissents from the beliefs of others, the community they looked to for the protection of good moral habits was most definitely not the distant federal government. They cherished their right to dwell in their own associations, as little infringed upon by the state as possible. A few matters such as education and the protection of public morals in public places, however, are too important to neglect in the laws. *Leges sine moribus vanae*, runs the motto of the University of Pennsylvania: "Without sound moral habits laws are empty." Individual states must not undermine the practice of virtue in its local habitats, but encourage the ethos of personal responsibility.

Establishment, No – Pillars, Yes

For this reason, the federal Congress took special pains to inculcate republican principles by teaching religion and morals in the new territories just opening up for future statehood. President Jefferson himself intended (some say only as a feint) to have thousands of copies of his own version of the New Testament printed at government expense, and distributed to the Indians of the Louisiana Purchase.[33] Reasoning that there is no better book of instruction than the principles of republican government, Jefferson did not plan to send a volume of Locke; he planned to send the moral teachings of the New Testament, stripped of all reference to Christ's divinity – his own "Jefferson's New Testament," prepared by his own hands at his own desk. This plan was never carried out, but it does reveal his confidence that the moral teachings of the New Testament are the best foundation of republican government.[34] They are higher and purer than the teachings of the philosophers, Jefferson observes, yet not contrary to reason. They zero in on liberty and accountability.

In one sense, individual liberty is prior to community – an individual's duty to the Creator is in conscience inalienable. In another sense, community is prior to the individual, as a nurturing mother of the families, neighborhoods, and schools that teach the fundamental habits of liberty to individuals. Indeed, the American nation is a community of communities, and guardian of a larger horizon of moral claims.

Without the Union, there could not have been Independence. And only in this larger Union were individual rights safe. For instance, had the thirteen colonies fractured into four or five separate independent nations, some slave and some free, the French, Spanish, and the English would have been glad to pick out likely allies among them, offering bribes and seductions, and furnishing arms to their favorites. In such a world, the slave states might have survived well into the twentieth century. Local tyrants, strengthened by foreign alliances, might have oppressed large minorities. More clearly than most, Lincoln saw that liberty depends on Union. To his eyes, liberty was the golden "apple" of liberty mentioned in the Psalms, Union the "silver frame."[35] Perish the Union, perish liberty.

Union, therefore, became an almost religious term. And so was the

other term that Lincoln favored, *covenant*. The Union born in the blood
of patriots in 1776, and forged in the communal process of ratification
in every participating state after 1787, was not formed by a mere legal
contract but by a sacred covenant, which could not be sundered. To
defend it was a sacred duty. The very term *Union* inspired men to give
their lives for it.

The preservation of the Union is important to a theology that flows
from the social constitution of the human being, *"communio* theology"
as it is nowadays called. Individual liberty is achieved only within a
historical social structure and only by a brotherhood of common effort.
Only Union saved liberty in 1776 and again in 1863.

In brief, one of the central ironies of American history is that
many today boast of our being a nation of individuals, whereas a crucial
reality for which our ancestors fought and died was the large community, the Union. Further, a widespread belief among our founders was
that individuals by themselves are morally untrustworthy; in order to
live in liberty, individuals depend on strong moral communities.

On this basis, the Americans developed an original conception of
the "pillars" of republican virtue. In Europe, to have religion as a moral
foundation meant to establish one religion – *cujus regio, ejus religio* –
with prescribed doctrines and rituals to ensure a unified public ethos.
Uneasily at first, for want of knowledge of any better way, these European traditions of church and state had been carried over to America.
Here it became clear by trial and error that that traditional method had
destructive consequences both for the church and for the state. For
instance, Catholic Maryland, having learned a salutary lesson from the
sad experience of Catholic states in Europe, had launched an early and
tentative experiment in religious liberty; seven-hundred armed Protestants, inspired by Britain's "Glorious Revolution" of 1688, imposed
English penal laws in Maryland, depriving Catholics of the right to vote
and to hold office, prohibiting their public worship, and disallowing
Catholic schools. "Until the American Revolution, Catholics in Maryland were dissenters in their own country, living at times under a state
of siege, but keeping loyal to their convictions, a faithful remnant await-
ing better times."[36] European habits persisted and, as in Europe, they
repressed religious liberty.

Under the Quakers, by contrast, Pennsylvania did experiment
with religious liberty, and made it work. Six other colonies (including

Massachusetts) maintained modified established churches, most of these continuing to thrive until at least two generations after independence.[37] In these colonies before 1776, heretics were lashed, imprisoned, tormented, even hanged. From 1776 onward, however, these establishments were "mild," limited to the education of the citizenry in the virtues necessary for freedom, not aimed at doctrinal uniformity. They no longer coerced consciences, but they did give official and public favor to Protestants.

The European alliance of throne and altar had saddled the *state* with tasks for which it had little or no competence, and for its efforts bred hostility and resentment among religious dissenters and nonbelievers. That traditional arrangement had also saddled the *church* with practices that, however common they had been in the past, had come to seem from painful experiences inimical to Christian ideals and aspirations – the use of the state to punish or to banish heretics, for instance, as had happened in Massachusetts in the case of Roger Williams.[38]

Therefore, in order to strengthen both the church and the republican state, the founding generation decided not to establish a *national* church. Virtually every America leader of the time was Protestant, and rejected the idea of one national church. So did Charles Carroll, one of the few Catholics among them (and one of the richest men in America):

> To obtain religious, as well as civil liberty, I entered zealously into the Revolution, and observing the Christian religion divided into many sects, I founded the hope that no one would be so predominant as to become the religion of the State.[39]

These leaders elected, instead, to build the foundation of the republic on the exercise of everyday religious life in every locality and state. Through the open, visible, and often publicly encouraged practice of a vigorous religious life, following the sage advice of President Washington's "Farewell Address," the American people would publicly exhibit those religious habits of the heart necessary for the proper working of republican institutions.[40] And these religious habits of the heart, demonstrated daily in private and in public behavior, would be the moral foundation of the republic.

Thus, when Madison wrote that our rights are not protected by "parchment barriers," but by the habits and institutions of the American people,[41] the strong foundation he was taking for granted was made up of sound moral habits and local institutions. Adams and other Northerners believed that the disestablishment of the Anglican church in Virginia was overdue; that its long continuance had bred the lassitude that allowed slavery to thrive in the South. They noted, too, that the fires of Independence were lit by dissenting preachers, seldom by Anglican priests. Some Southerners disliked Northern religious intensity and its starchy whiff of moral superiority. Sectionalism and local diversity seemed a natural expression of liberty.

It is important to savor the originality of this American solution. Most scholars and lawyers note exclusively its effect on the *state*. But its most striking originality lies in its advantages for religion in general and Christianity in particular. Before the founding of America, the injunction of the Lord – "Give unto Caesar that which is Caesar's, and unto God that which is God's" (Matthew 22:21) – had ended in a contradiction. When a church was established by the state, Caesar became (as the King of England did) the head of the church. Experience showed that both church and state were harmed, but especially the church. After Independence, no American church wanted a single national church established; all wanted freedom from the national state. The American version of "establishment," even when it continued in individual states, was neither national nor doctrinal. It was practical, aimed at cultivating the moral habits necessary to the practice of liberty.[42] Its most obvious flaw was the persistence in some states of religious tests for holders of public office; only Protestants could serve.

The first part of the American solution, therefore, was a self-denying ordinance on the part of the *federal government*; the people expressly declared the *federal* government incompetent in theological matters beyond those essential for the common good. "*Congress shall make no law* respecting an establishment of religion" (emphasis added).[43] Thus, the people cleared the way as never before for the citizenry to give to God His full due in divers and plural ways. They limited the power of the national Caesar.

Nonetheless, the founding generation grasped this principle within a communal horizon. Individual conscience is inalienably personal in the responsibility it faces,[44] but it is not isolated in solitariness. Most American Protestants of 1776 understood themselves as participants in a historic community of belief, for whom conscience in its depths is *always social*, not atomic. For them, religion was not for private exercise alone. When believers engaged in the "free exercise" of their religion, they often did so in the public square, as in open meetings in public parks, and parades down public streets. Congress itself often issued decrees for public fasting, petition, and thanksgiving to God. For many years, the largest religious service in the nation took place in the U.S. Capitol Building and later in the Supreme Court Building itself. Thomas Jefferson not only took part in them with regularity, but also provided music for them at public expense.[45]

Two things are strictly forbidden, Madison explained to Congress: the establishment of *a* religion by the national Congress,[46] and also the *dis*establishment of the already established religions of the several states. In Madison's own "Remonstrance," the basis for this decision was a fundamental Christian conception, viz., the dignity of the human person, rooted in the act of freedom by which each responds to the call of his Creator. That conception had never before been given such a highly developed political articulation as in the Virginia Bill for Establishing Religious Freedom and the Bill of Rights.

Under a regime in which government is limited, respectful of individual rights, and under the rule of law, the national government is no longer the only or even the chief actor in the public square. In a free society, there is plenty of room in the vast open spaces of civil society for the public exercise of religion by individuals, associations, churches and other religious assemblies. ("Public" is an equivocal term; it does not apply solely to the activities of the state. Many other institutions, including the churches, are public actors.) Moreover, in the federal republic, the generation of Madison, Jefferson, and Adams permitted ample room for "mild" establishments of religion by individual states.

A crucial ambiguity in this arrangement remains. Has not the federal Caesar, as well, a responsibility to pay public homage to God? While the U.S. Constitution makes no public provision, traditional practices do, from the very first motion of the very First Continental Congress. The Constitution expressly avoids the explicit confession of Christian faith found in the Constitutions of several of the states. On the other hand, the U.S. Congress works under the prayers and counseling of a salaried pastor. Presidents issue proclamations of Days of National Thanksgiving, and both Congress and presidents have declared national days of prayer and fasting in moments of urgent national crisis. The U.S.

government pays for the installation of Stars of David and crosses on the graves of U.S. servicemen buried overseas. From the beginning, the American tradition has not been separation *simpliciter*. From 1776 to 1948 the dominant metaphor for church-state relations was that public officials must act as "nursing fathers" to the religious and moral habits of the people (the phrase in quotes comes from Isaiah).[47] Jefferson's phrase "wall of separation" from a letter of 1802 lay totally unnoticed until it was cited by the Supreme Court in 1879 in *Reynolds v. United States* in a mistaken transcription of Jefferson's original letter; the focus in 1879 was not on "separation" but on the term "*legislative* powers" (which the transcriber had written instead of Jefferson's original clearly formed handwriting "*legitimate* power"). The metaphor otherwise lay unused and virtually unknown until Justice Black drew it from obscurity in 1947 (still using the erroneous translation).[48]

Still, federal homage to the Creator and Source of all our rights – the Lawgiver, Governor, Providence and Judge mentioned in the Declaration of Independence – has been quite limited, more limited than the public homage openly paid by states and localities. Nonetheless, in maintaining a sphere of reverential silence in which its citizens give to the transcendent God the particular names that they have learned in their traditional communities and personal investigations, the American federal state may be paying a form of homage proper to a pluralistic people. It is not an achievement without ambiguity, but it is a great achievement.

Thus, what Madison wrote in *Federalist No. 14* about the body of the Constitution might with even greater force be said of the originality of the founders with respect to religious liberty:

> They accomplished a revolution which has no parallel in the annals of human society: They reared the fabrics of governments which have no model on the face of the globe.[49]

That the American model is original does not mean, of course, that it will endure forever. And that possibility, indeed probability, of impermanence led to another step in the logic of the framers.

The Corruptibility of Liberty

What is original about America is that it places its foundation in the

minds and habits of its own people, in local communities. This is a fragile foundation. If its principles are forgotten or its virtues go
unexercised, this foundation disintegrates. A single generation can turn
out the lights and walk away from commitments earlier made. Free
regimes live or die by free decisions.

No one can argue that the founders did not foresee these dangers.
Thomas Jefferson made George Washington's Farewell Address
required reading at the University of Virginia, since in it Washington
sets forth the "pillars" of the free society, and highlights the perils it
must weather. Washington does not call religion "optional." The word
he uses is "indispensable."

> Of all the dispositions and habits which lead to political prosperity, *Religion
> and morality are indispensable supports*. In vain would that man claim the
> tribute of Patriotism, who should labour to subvert these great *Pillars* of
> human happiness, these firmest props of the duties of Men and citizens.
> The mere Politician, equally with the pious man ought to respect and cher-
> ish them. A volume could not trace all their connections with public and
> private felicity. Let it simply be asked where is the security for property, for
> reputation, for life, if the sense of religious obligation desert the oaths, which
> are the instruments of investigation in Courts of Justice? *And let us with cau-
> tion indulge the supposition, that morality can be maintained without
> religion*. Whatever may be conceded to the influence of refined education
> on minds of peculiar structure, *reason and experience both forbid us to
> expect* that National morality can prevail in exclusion of religious princi-
> ple.
>   'Tis substantially true, that *virtue or morality is a necessary spring of
> popular government*. The rule indeed extends with more or less force to
> every species of free Government. Who that is a sincere friend to it, can
> look with indifference upon attempts to shake the foundation of the fabric?
> [emphasis added][50]

John Adams was even clearer in his warning in 1798:

> We have no government armed with power of contending with human pas-
> sions unbridled by morality and religion. Avarice, ambition, revenge, or
> gallantry, would break the strongest cords of our Constitution as a whale
> goes through a net. *Our Constitution is made only for a moral and reli-
> gious people. It is wholly inadequate to the government of any other*.[51]

So strongly did John Adams believe this that when he wrote to his cousin
Zabdiel, a minister of the Christian gospel, two weeks before the adop-
tion of the Declaration of Independence, he described his fears for the

future, and urged upon Zabdiel the importance of his work in religious ministry:

> Statesmen my dear Sir, may plan and speculate for Liberty, but it is Religion and Morality alone, which can establish the Principles, upon which Freedom can securely stand.

For Adams, the alternative to virtue in the people is tyranny:

> *The only foundation of a free Constitution is pure Virtue*, and if this cannot be inspired into our People, in a greater Measure, than they have it now, They may change their Rulers, and the forms of Government, but they will not obtain a lasting Liberty. – They will only exchange Tyrants and Tyrannies. [emphasis added][52]

No one ever promised our founders that their experiment in liberty would last forever. Nearly all the founders voiced their fears about that. George Washington had three particular worries:

> *Since* there is no truth more thoroughly established, than that there exists in the economy and course of nature, an indissoluble union between virtue and happiness; between duty and advantage; between the genuine maxims of an honest and magnanimous policy, and the solid rewards of public prosperity and felicity:
>
> *Since* we ought to be no less persuaded that the propitious smiles of Heaven can never be expected on a nation that disregards the external rules of order and right, which Heaven itself has ordained: and
>
> *Since* the preservation of the sacred fire of liberty, and the destiny of the republican model of government, are justly considered as *deeply*, perhaps as *finally*, staked on the experiment entrusted to the hands of the American People.... [emphasis on *since* added][53]

For all these reasons, a way must be found to inspire virtue in our people, or independence is in vain. The pillars of the American republic are not found in an established church; they are sunk into the religious and moral habits of its people. This is a foundation deeper and stronger – and truer to Christianity – than the establishment of a national religion. It is, however, a foundation that is subject to moral entropy. We are not doomed to self-destruction, but the risk is real.

If You Can Keep It

As they were leaving the Convention Hall with the Constitution completed, some of the delegates were struck by the design of a bursting sun painted on the chair back on which General Washington had been seated. They were pensive about how their Constitution – their words on paper – would actually work, once put into practice. Looking at that sun, Ben Franklin wondered whether it was a rising sun, or a setting sun.[54]

Then, at the banquet soon after to celebrate the conclusion of the Constitutional Convention, a Philadelphia matron rushed toward its most senior delegate: "O! Mister Franklin," she gushed. "What have you gentlemen wrought, after so many weeks of secrecy behind those thick doors?"

Franklin is said to have adjusted his glasses before offering his famous retort: "A republic, madam. If you can keep it."[55]

FOUR

*Our liberties do not come from charters; for these
are only the declarations of preexisting rights.
They do not depend on parchment or seals; but come
from the King of Kings and the Lord of all the earth.*
—John Dickinson, 1776

FOURTH CHAPTER

A Religious Theory
of Rights

merica is the most democratic country in the world, and at the same time, according to reliable reports, it is the country in which the Roman Catholic religion is making the most progress.... If Catholicism could ultimately escape from the political animosities to which it has given rise, I am almost certain that that same spirit of the age which now seems so contrary to it would turn into a powerful ally.... —Alexis de Tocqueville[1]

We consider the establishment of our nation's independence, the shaping of its liberties and laws as a work of special Providence, its framers "building better than they knew, the Almighty's hand guiding them." And if ever the glorious fabric is subverted or impaired, it will be by men forgetful of the sacrifices of the heroes that reared it, the virtues that cemented it, and the principles on which it rests.
— The Catholic Bishops of the United States,
The Third Plenary Council of Baltimore (1893)[2]

The Concept of Dignity

The great American majority, as Robert Goldwin has pointed out,[3] was a religious people, who believed they owed their liberty to the Creator, Lawgiver, Judge, and Providence Who had by His "signal interventions" at critical moments seen to their victory over seemingly impossible odds. They believed that Providence had contrived all of history as a dramatic struggle to build free institutions worthy of human dignity. This great majority believed that Judaism and Christianity, whether taken straight or taken broadmindedly, were the best religions that history had ever uncovered for two earthly tasks: for inspiring and guiding republican government, and for fitting a people's habits to the tasks of republican government. They wanted their right to exercise this religion publicly, protected against the federal government. They insisted, therefore, on the First Amendment. Their most powerful motive for the Bill of Rights was not just suspicion of central authority, but above all piety toward those religions for which the ultimate liberty of each individual is the indispensable precondition, Judaism and Christianity.

The moral reasoning behind natural rights that arises from Jewish and Christian theology – compatibly with the great line of the *philosophia perennis*, which includes deference to Aristotle, Cicero, Seneca and other philosophers of public right[4] – is based upon a special concept of human dignity: the dignity of having been created by God, called to be a friend of God, and being inalienably responsible to God for one's use of liberty.

This concept of dignity has both a theological and a philosophical foundation. The theological ground was stated by John Adams when he wrote before the Revolution,

> Let the pulpit resound with the doctrines and sentiments of religious liberty. Let us hear the danger of thraldom to our consciences from ignorance, extreme poverty, and dependence, in short, from civil and political slavery. *Let us see delineated before us the true map of man. Let us hear the dignity of his nature, and the noble rank he holds among the works of God, – and that God Almighty has promulgated from heaven*, liberty, peace, and goodwill to man! [emphasis added][5]

The philosophical ground is also set forth by John Adams:

> Let it be known, that British liberties are not the grants of princes of parliaments, but original rights, conditions of original contracts.... *Let them search for the foundations* of British laws and government *in the frame of human nature, in the constitution of the intellectual and moral world.* [emphasis added] [6]

The philosophical ground is set forth in another version by Walter Berns, who has written that the American founding derives directly from the philosophy of John Locke, and that this philosophy in fact undermines, and is intended to undermine, the classical and Christian understandings of human nature:

> The origin of free government in the modern sense coincides and can only coincide with the solution of the religious problem, and the solution of the religious problem consists in the subordination of religion.[7]

A third version is set forth by Michael Zuckert in a recent study of the philosophical and religious wings of the American founding, entitled *The Natural Rights Republic*,[8] a wondrous mine of historical analysis. In a related essay, Zuckert presents an especially clear exposition of the argument in its philosophical form.[9] Although we earlier alluded both to the debt of the American founders to Locke and their distinctive originality, these matters must now be explored more closely, in order to grasp the full rounded sense of human *dignity* in which the founders actually grounded their concept of human rights.

Zuckert's Exposition of Jefferson

Zuckert begins by setting forth the six "truths" enunciated by Jefferson in the early part of the Declaration. He groups these truths in three historical "phases," a narrative that begins with the *pre-political phase*; moves to the *political*; and ends with the *post-political*. Each phase represents a truth about history and evokes a corresponding principle.

The *pre-political phase* is "All men are created equal." It yields this truth: "endowed with certain inalienable rights."

The *political phase* is "Governments are instituted to secure these rights." It yields this truth: "deriving their just powers from the consent of the governed."

The *post-political* or declining phase is "If government becomes destructive of those ends, there is a right to alter or abolish it." In this phase, the corresponding truth is: "and institute new government."

In this metaphoric frame, Zuckert says, we see the historical context in which Jefferson meant us to understand "All men are created equal."

> By nature, or in nature, human beings are equal, in the sense of not being subject to the authority of any other. Neither God nor nature has established rule among human beings; they do this for themselves. By stating that men are created equal in this sense, the Declaration is saying what some political philosophers said when they posited the original condition as a "state of nature," a state in which no rightful authority exists by nature.[10]

This is a helpful exposition of Jefferson as Enlightenment philosophers understood him. However, you will recall from our first chapter that, before signing the Declaration of Independence, Congress added two further references to God, using names dear to the biblical tradition, "Supreme Judge" of our consciences and "divine Providence." These additions substantially enlarged the metaphysical framework suggested by Jefferson. Other actions of the founders – chronicled in earlier chapters – gave further expression to a biblical sense of reality. Moreover, as we saw earlier, Madison's ground for the natural right to religious liberty is not the state of nature, but rather the inalienable duty of each rational creature to pay his Creator due adoration and thanksgiving; that is, Madison begins with faith in God. No creature has any right to interfere in that surpassing duty, and that duty is peculiarly inalienable, since it must flow from deliberate personal choice.

In other words, the actual ground on which the founders turned to natural rights was the ground of faith. That is where they grasped the dignity of every individual and hence the inalienable right of every individual. What they saw by reason alone was rather different. Reason sees that each man can be a threat to the life of every other, and that self-preservation is the first of all duties. But this is not a lesson in equality. On the contrary, it reveals life-or-death inequalities in the brains and physical strength of individuals; it is a lesson in the survival of the fittest. When the islanders of Melos pleaded for reason before the advancing Athenian navy, the Athenians replied with scorn:

> You know as well as we do that right, as the world goes, is only in question between equals in power, while the strong do what they can and the weak suffer what they must.[11]

Throughout nature, everywhere we look we see inequality, slavery, oppression. Even in personal relations, individuals find it hard to deny themselves the last word in argument, the put-down, the show of superiority even in trivial matters. It is not equality that characterizes the pre-political state of human beings, but inequality.

Indeed, the ancients systematized this insight by teaching that while a few men may be "made" of gold, and a larger minority may be of silver, the large majority of humans have the passions and the souls of slaves, and so they deserve to be. Until modern times, and still today in large sectors of the globe, broad-scale slavery has been so frequent a condition of human beings as to have often been mistaken as natural.

The struggle for freedom and equality has been relatively rare; suffering passivity is common. One enterprising journalist pointed out in 1776 that of the 750 million persons alive on earth at that time, barely 39 million were living as free men.[12]

Whence, then, came the "truth" that "all men are created equal"? Its roots lie in Judaism, carried around the world by Christians. Jefferson himself believed that, if shorn of its miracles, there was no better ethic than that of the New Testament for instruction in republican self-government. Yet, although Jefferson and his companions were deeply anti-Catholic, the ideal of equality was taught by the Catholic Church long before there was an America. As Tocqueville rightly sees,

> Among the various Christian doctrines Catholicism seems one of those most favorable to equality of conditions. For Catholics religious society is composed of two elements: priest and people. The priest is raised above the faithful; all below him are equal.
>
> In matters of dogma the Catholic faith places all intellects on the same level; the learned man and the ignorant, the genius and the common herd, must all subscribe to the same details of beliefs; rich and poor must follow the same observances, and it imposes the same austerities upon the strong and the weak; it makes no compromise with any mortal, but applying the same standard to every human being, it mingles all classes of society at the foot of the same altar, just as they are mingled in the sight of God.
>
> Catholicism may dispose the faithful to obedience, but it does not prepare them for inequality. However, I would say that Protestantism in general orients men much less toward equality than toward independence.[13]

To the extent that the Enlightenment depends upon the principle of "created equal," it depends upon Jewish metaphysics and Christian faith.

Locke's contention that by nature no man is intended to be ruled by another comes not from observation, not from history, and not exactly from philosophical argument, but from an appeal to a biblical metaphysic. Indeed, it never entered into the consciousness of philosophers in any part of the world, unless they had first had contact with Christianity. The one overwhelming reality that reduces all humans to equality is the Face of their Creator, Who is not impressed by men's power, wealth, or earthly might. This Judge, however, has no interest in making them feel small; His aim is to awaken them to their potential greatness. Their equality arises from their relation to Him. Witness this argument from faith even in Locke's *Second Treatise*:

The state of nature has a law of nature to govern it, which obliges every one; and reason, which is that law, teaches all mankind who will but consult it that, being all equal and independent, no one ought to harm another in his life, health, liberty, or possessions. For men being all the workmanship of one omnipotent and infinitely wise Maker – all the servants of one sovereign Master, sent into the world by His order, and about His business – they are His property....[S]haring all in one community of nature, there cannot be supposed any such subordination among us that may authorize us to destroy one another, as if we were made for one another's uses, as the inferior ranks of creatures are for ours. Every one, as he is bound to preserve himself... so by the like reason, when his own preservation comes not in competition, ought he, as much as he can, to preserve the rest of mankind, and may not, unless it be to do justice on an offender, take away or impair the life, or what tends to the preservation of the life, the liberty, health, limb, or goods of another.[14]

In those days, faith permeated philosophy and lifted it above its own limitations.

Thus, we come to the need to explain in crisper detail the moral and religious theory that actually moved our founders. Some philosophers hold that "natural rights" are incompatible with Christian faith. The American founding, they say, is through and through anti-Christian, and its aim is to subordinate religion to politics in such fashion that religion will be driven impotently into the private realm and wither as a public social presence. The evidence presented in these chapters forces us to a much less extreme conclusion. The vast majority of the American founders and the whole ratifying people thought and acted in the conviction that the American theory of rights is religious as well as reasonable. Have they been deceived?

The reason there is a lively debate on this central question lies in a peculiar historical vulnerability in classical Protestant thought. Philosophers and historians have trouble explaining the continuity – and discontinuity – between the two great covenantal "foundings" of the United States, the first in 1620, the latter in 1776. The first consisted in the two covenants, not quite simultaneous, of the Mayflower Compact of 1620 and of the covenant set forth in John Winthrop's famous sermon on the *Arbella* not long afterwards. It is clear that some themes of the Declaration of Independence were already foreshadowed in these early comments – for example, that humans properly form political societies on the basis of covenants, and that good societies are founded on "the consent of the governed."[15]

Zuckert notes as well important discontinuities, of which he emphasizes three: the early covenants do not begin from the equality of all men, but recognize many ranks and degrees, even including the authority of the king; they mention the historical rights of Englishmen, but do not mention natural rights that inhere in all individuals by nature; and they are expressly Christian in their form, purpose, and sacred language. By contrast, the Declaration of 1776 relies on natural equality and natural rights, and is mostly "secular" in form, purpose, and expression.[16]

The question, then, is why American political philosophy changed so much between 1620 and 1776. Zuckert offers a truly delicate and complex analysis of three interwoven traditions: the Protestant Whig traditions imported from Britain into America; the early Christ-centered Pilgrim tradition of Massachusetts Bay; and the closely reasoned Puritan tradition that later developed. Regarding the last, he draws upon the work of others to show how New England preachers welcomed the appeals to reason made by Algernon Sidney and John Locke.[17] These preachers accustomed churchgoers throughout the colonies to hearing simultaneous arguments both from Scripture *and* from reason.[18]

Still, for Protestant interpreters of the founding the problem of the high role for reason remains acute. Classic Reformation figures such as Martin Luther and John Calvin tended to reject with great force the earlier Scholastic ways of relating faith and reason by declaring that the Catholics laid too little emphasis upon Scripture and too much on reason. Against this, classic Protestant writings emphasized the severe inadequacies of reason and put their trust in *Sola Scriptura*. Thus, it is not easy to show that the fairly chaste appeal to arguments of reason in the Declaration – and the relative delicacy and restraint of its appeals to Scripture (as in the names it uses for God: Creator, Judge, Providence) – is continuous with American Pilgrim traditions. In form, substance, and language, the Declaration seems to break from the Protestant past.

This question of the development between 1620 and 1776 appears in a quite different light to Catholic thought. Indeed, Zuckert makes this very point: Where, on the one hand, classical Protestantism looked to *Sola Scriptura*, "Locke's official formula, on the other hand, echoes the understanding put forward by the mainline Catholic thinkers from

Thomas Aquinas to Francisco Suárez and Robert Bellarmine, and part of the initial Reformation impulse was to reject such accommodation."[19] Catholic thinkers after 1260 stressed the ability of reason to discern the basic laws of human flourishing. In that year, the long-lost Greek text of Aristotle's *Nichomachean Ethics* was translated into Latin, so the evidence of Aristotle's admirable use of reason in ethics exploded in Christian consciousness. As the later paintings of the Sistine Chapel recall, the medievals saw analogies in the laws discovered by the wise Greek and Roman lawmakers, the law of Moses, and the New Law of the Gospels. They rooted all of these in the living mind ("Light," "Law") of the Creator – the Eternal Law, now and always effective in concrete things.

In this traditional scheme, the legitimacy of government flows both from the consensual reasonings of the governed, able to recognize the light of God's intelligence in human affairs, but also from the measuring rods God has established for justice, which even rulers must heed. In other words, just because rulers have the consent of the governed, they may not violate justice as they please. It is not only the consent of the governed that legitimates them, but also their adherence to canons of justice. That is why even legitimately established kings, once they become tyrants (offenders against justice), invite disobedience. "Disobedience to tyrants is obedience to God," as Franklin worded it.

It is true that no Catholic thinker of that time had developed a theory of natural rights, based on arguments taken both from reason and from Scripture, equal to Locke's achievement. The best that Suárez and Bellarmine achieved falls short of a modern theory of rights; but it is not insignificant. First, Catholic thinkers had held for centuries that kings do *not* rule by divine right, but *under* divine law and its worldly expression, natural law.[20] Not only in this respect was the principle of limited government, as Lord Acton points out, known from at least the thirteenth century.[21] Second, Catholic thought had established the principle that political power flows from the consent of the governed; and thus, that a tyrant who abuses the dignity of his subjects may lawfully be deposed.[22] Finally, Catholic thought, in its emphasis upon the reflection and deliberation required for acts of genuinely free will – *i.e.*, human liberty, properly so called – had already established a high concept of the dignity of the human person.[23] Catholic thought extolled the human being as the most noble among God's creatures, fallen and needy, but noble in creation and calling. This teaching fell short of enumerating a declaration of the rights of the human person in a modern idiom. But it was already sufficient for making *ad hoc* defenses of particular rights; *e.g.*, the right to private property;[24] the right of association (defended by Aquinas in his defense of the rights of Dominicans and Franciscans to form independent associations[25]); and the right (also the duty) to follow conscience, even in cases in which conscience is erroneous.[26]

These tentative beginnings of a full-dress theory of rights were never articulated in a complete theory before the time of John Locke. There is little doubt, however, that Locke knew of these beginnings, particularly the work of Suárez.[27] The honor of putting such beginnings together in a comprehensive way fell to him and to no Catholic thinker. These beginnings, however, led the historian of liberty Lord Acton to call Thomas Aquinas "The First Whig."[28]

To help explain this – to others perhaps surprising – affinity between America and the Catholic tradition, it would be interesting to see what a Catholic interpretation of the Declaration, even articulated *ex post facto*, would look like. By reputation, the United States is a Protestant country and Catholics were asserted to be unsuited for it. Yet virtually every Catholic writer or thinker who has visited America since 1607 has been excited by the country's extraordinary consonance with Catholic faith. This is true of a host of prominent persons from Hector St. Jean Crèvecoeur to Philip Mazzei, from Thaddeus Kosciuszko and Casimir Pulaski to the Marquis de Lafayette and Alexis de Tocqueville, from the Jesuit chroniclers of North America to the U.S. Catholic Bishops at the Third Plenary Congress of Baltimore in 1893, and on to Jacques Maritain, Raymond Bruckberger, John Courtney Murray, and others.[29] On this point the many enthusiastically pro-American papers given at Catholic University in the autumn of 1889 at the first national Catholic Lay Congress are quite stunning.[30]

The Logic of Liberty

The logic of the founding has its own originality, which is not that of any earlier group of Christian people. It is an amalgam of certain practical strains in the ethic of Aristotle, Cicero, Seneca, and other writers about natural and civic virtue, mixed with biblical insights and reflections, and fed by many profoundly new reflections on human experience, both ancient and contemporary. The sermons of Witherspoon and Cooper, discussed in chapter two, illustrate this blending beautifully.[31]

Put in its starkest form, this logic moves through seven steps. First, the founders saw in the two uniquely human activities *reflection* and *choice* the engines of liberty. Second, these activities suggest a highly *moral* concept of the natural right to liberty. This understanding of liberty draws upon both revelation and reason with the result that, third, in matters of liberty, revelation and reason seem to be allies, not foes.

Fourth, as experience teaches, without virtue (that is, habits of certain kinds) liberty cannot be sustained; unless you "confirm your soul in self-control," you cannot exemplify self-government.

Fifth, given the changeability of human morals over time and the persistent tendency of morals to decline, the free society is inherently precarious. Sixth, only a source stronger than moral reflection but inwardly linked to it can arrest this remorseless entropy, and that source is religion of a certain kind. Seventh, trial and error teach that the advantages of liberty and the virtues it inculcates are better secured when religion is *not* established.

Why did the American founders believe that religion is a sound foundation for a republic, when Europeans of the Enlightenment held liberty and religion to be foes? The Americans followed two different paths in arriving at their own distinctive concept of natural rights, and both paths reached to the same point. As the founders understood them, both reason and revelation locate the evidence for this natural right in man's moral nature – "in the frame of human nature," as John Adams put it, "in the constitution of the intellectual and moral world."[32]

This distinctive American understanding of natural rights is implicit in the opening lines of *Federalist No. 1*, which characterize the entire process of ratifying the Constitution, as the people were then doing. Here are the crucial words:

> It seems to have been reserved to the people of this country, to decide the important question, whether societies of men are really capable or not, of establishing good government from *reflection* and *choice*, or whether they are forever destined to depend, for their political constitutions, on accident and force. (emphasis added)[33]

The question is not whether humans merely *have* these two capacities, "reflection" and "choice." If they didn't, there would be no point in proceeding with public debates, arguments in journals and pamphlets, and long deliberations. The question is whether these observed capacities are *strong* enough for the great social task of forming governments.

Since no other earthly creature except human beings acts from these two capacities, reflection and choice are nature's testimony to human destiny. To live according to reflection and choice is, therefore, the law of nature. It is also the law of God. Since both nature and God command humans to exercise their liberty, it follows that humans must have a natural right to liberty. Without such a right, they could not obey either the law of their own nature or the law of God. Further, since to be free is to incur responsibility for one's own deliberate choices, no one can hand off his liberty to others; liberty is not alienable.

To violate a person's natural liberty is, therefore, to deface, deform, and frustrate the laws of nature and nature's God. It is both a sin against justice that cries out to heaven and a crime indictable before the tribunal of humankind. In religious terms generic enough not to be limited to Christians solely, Jefferson wrote: "The God who gave us life gave us liberty at the same time."[34] It is a self-evident step from this conviction to the phrase of the Declaration, "endowed by their Creator with certain inalienable rights."

Skills in constitution-writing, however, are not the same as skills in metaphysics. The founders were not primarily metaphysicians; they were nation-builders. They were less concerned to publish precise disquisitions on liberty than to contrive practical institutions of liberty, institutions that would work – and work among people as they were, not some imagined species. This point was emphasized on the eve of the constitutional convention by John Adams in *A Defence of the Constitutions of Governments of the United States*, with a sharp elbow in John Locke's eye:

> A philosopher may be a perfect master of Descartes and Leibniz, may pursue his own metaphysical inquiries to any length, may enter into the innermost recesses of the human mind, and make the noblest discoveries for the benefit of his species; nay, he may defend the principles of liberty and the rights of mankind with great abilities and success; and, after all, when called upon to produce a plan of legislation, he may astonish the world with a signal absurdity. Mr. Locke, in 1663, was employed to trace out a

plan of legislation for Carolina; and he gave the whole authority, executive and legislative, to the eight proprietors, the Lords Berkley, Clarendon, Albemarle, Craven, and Ashley; and Messieurs Carteret, Berkley, and Colleton, and their heirs. This new oligarchical sovereignty created at least three orders of nobility.... Who did this legislator think would live under his government? He should have first created a new species of beings to govern, before he instituted such a government.[35]

The American founders, evidently, were quite clear about who would live under their new government. They wanted an independent republic and a constitution that would work in America – would both endure among Americans and be worthy of American hopes. Through and through, such a project had to exhibit reflection and choice at work, in order to meet the standards of the natural right to liberty for which it was designed. Such a requirement, in turn, would endow the building of the republic with substantive moral purpose. An entire citizenry had to be taught how to pursue the public business – and to conduct their private lives – in ways compatible with sober reflection and reasoned choice.[36]

For it is soon a matter of immediate experience, if not of self-evidence, that not every human all the time is in the frame of mind required for reflection and deliberate choice. Passion, ignorance, bias, interest, fear – all these are common motives and conventional means for cutting reflection short and acting in ways contrary to dispassionate choice. The free citizen must be able to summon up at will a capacity for sober reflection and duly measured choice, such as the authors of *The Federalist* properly demanded of them. Thus, citizens who depend upon reflection and choice will necessarily depend upon an array of inclinations, dispositions and habits that, when duty calls, clear their souls of passion, ignorance, bias, interest, and fear.

George Washington, in particular, grasped the inner dependence of the republican experiment upon the sound habits of its citizens. For this reason alone, at full risk to his own reputation (with everything to lose, nothing to gain), he could not refuse to come out of retirement to guide the first generation of citizens of the new republic through its first foundational years. His principle was this: A nation, like a child, forms its character around its earliest transactions. Therefore, Washington determined to lead the nation at large through the ways in which a citizenry called to self-government must comport itself. The people themselves must become an example to the world of reflection and deliberate choice, and the enabling and supportive virtues on which these capacities depend.[37]

This distinctive concept of natural rights embodied a national moral project that can be expressed through the two-sided meaning of "self-government." A republican experiment is an experiment in public self-government through public institutions on the part of the whole people. At the same time, such public self-government can only succeed if its citizens also practice self-government in their personal lives. The citizens of a republic must comport themselves with capacities for sober reflection and deliberate choice at the ready. It is not necessary for all or even most to be saints. Nonetheless, to suppose that a republican government could succeed without at least a modicum of virtue in its citizens would be a pipe dream.[38] Actions taken without reflection and choice may be licentious; they cannot be examples of liberty.[39]

Further, it is the great merit of the Protestant Christian religion (which in this is remarkably close to Orthodox Judaism) that it emphasizes both religious and personal responsibility and self-mastery. It emphasizes these virtues for reasons that are both prudent in the ways of the world and religious. These virtues are commanded equally by the laws of nature and nature's God. That is to say, actions flowing from virtues of this sort are necessary for the fulfillment of the distinctively human potential, and in that sense in accord with natural law. But actions flowing from virtues of this sort are also necessary for making the commitments required by religious faith, hope, and charity – commitments of conscious choice, made after due reflection, and apt to be persevering and *semper fidelis* – and thus in accord with the New Law of God. For grace, too, uses and perfects nature, lifting it up to new possibilities that do not contradict its instinctive longings but fulfill them in a surprising and undeserved way.

In this respect, the American founding was also established in a carefully modulated language, which could be understood by freethinking atheists in one way, by 'broadminded' Unitarians such as Jefferson in another, and by devout Presbyterians such as Witherspoon and partially secularized Puritans such as John Adams in yet others. The key to this code is the analogy between faith and reason (and its parallels, grace and nature). While the American eagle rises on both wings, some individuals use both wings comfortably, but others feel at home only on the propulsion of one or the other. For the majority of the founders it was not rationalism but "piety" that lifted their courage.

Consider only the eighty-nine founders who signed either the Declaration of Independence or the Constitution or both (see Appendix). Most lived in states whose Constitutions required of them, even for holding office, that they be Protestant Christians. Most so lived, wrote, and argued. Men of a purely rationalist temper, most of them thought, are not likely to be morally reliable in times of stress and danger and ambiguity. Men of a purely rationalist temper were certainly not representative of the majority on whose broad shoulders the fate of the republican experiment rests. For most people, and in the long run, the moral entropy that levels the high achievements of an age of moral heroism, and lowers the moral practice of a people, can be countered only with an awakening brought about by God's "amazing grace." From the beginning, the battle hymns of the American people have reflected this dual reality of the moral entropy of nature and a new "rebirth of freedom." Condensed in a single phrase, this insight is still expressed even by our most secular presidents in the last line of many a presidential address: *God bless America!*

A Religious Interpretation of the Founding

The passing years have exposed serious moral and intellectual deficiencies in Lockean regimes. Self-preservation, for instance, prompted the white population of the South to cling to slavery: to overcome slavery, a more vigorous, moral definition of natural right had to be brought to bear.[40] This moral definition arose in precisely those parts of the country where the original theory of natural rights was a moral and religious theory, rooted in human dignity. In a more general framework, after those periods of laxity which must be foreseen in the long cycles of all societies, the very flatness and insipidity of Locke's ethical vision – its frequent reduction of the higher to the lower – leave it unlikely of itself to inspire nobility of spirit.[41] To meet such inescapable necessities, the doctrine of natural right must be given auxiliary supports.

Tocqueville himself predicted that at some time in the future, prudent in the ways of the world, Catholics might come to the defense of the American Republic.[42] In at least four ways the American Republic more closely matches the Catholic vision of the good City than any prior civilization in history. It is by no means the City of God. It is flawed and full of faults. Nonetheless...

• In its very founding, this Republic rested upon the classical activities of reflection and choice – the very guts of the Thomistic vision of liberty – as manifested in the ratification debates. In a Fourth of July speech given during the summer following the Constitutional Convention, James Wilson of Pennsylvania described the thrill of that great debate:

> A people, free and enlightened, ESTABLISHING and RATIFYING a system of government, which they have previously CONSIDERED, EXAMINED and APPROVED! This is the spectacle, which we are assembled to celebrate; and it is the most dignified one that has yet appeared on our globe.
>
> You have heard of SPARTA, of ATHENS and of ROME. You have heard of their admired constitutions, and of their prized freedom. In fancied right of these, they conceived themselves to be elevated above the rest of the human race, whom they marked with the degrading title of *Barbarians*. But did they, in all their pomp and pride of liberty, ever furnish to the astonished world an exhibition similar to that which we now contemplate? Were their constitutions framed by those, who were appointed for that purpose, by the people? After they were framed, were they submitted to the consideration of the people?.... Were they to *stand* or *fall* by the people's approving or rejecting vote? To all these questions attentive and impartial history obliges us to answer in the negative.[43]

• This Republic took flight upon a relation between faith and reason that is quite congenial to Catholics, less so to many Protestants (who underplay the duality). In one of G. K. Chesterton's mystery stories, Father Brown unmasks a villain who is masquerading as a priest when the latter uses derogatory comments about reason in order to magnify faith; no Catholic priest would ever do that.[44] A brief summary of the historical Catholic tradition of relying on both wings is found in John Paul II's *Fides et Ratio*:

> Faith and reason are like two wings on which the human spirit rises to the contemplation of truth; and God has placed in the human heart a desire to know the truth – in a word, to know himself – so that, by knowing and loving God, men and women may also come to the fullness of truth about themselves.[45]

• Third, this Republic is open to the transcendent God, both in its characteristic symbol system and in its legal forms – in the all-seeing

Eye above the deliberately unfinished pyramid on the Seal of the United
States; in its public acts of supplication and thanksgiving; and in the
language of the First Amendment, "Congress shall make no law respecting an establishment of religion or prohibiting the free exercise thereof."
The power of Congress is limited. It cannot either enter into the sphere
of the Almighty or seal it off. Cardinal Gibbons of Baltimore explained
this in Rome in 1887 on his installation as a Cardinal:

> For myself, as a citizen of the United States, and without closing my eyes to
> our shortcomings as a nation, I say with a deep sense of pride and grati-
> tude, that I *belong to a country where the civil government holds over us the
> aegis of its protection, without interfering with us in the legitimate exercise
> of our sublime mission as ministers of the Gospel of Christ. Our country has
> liberty without licence, and authority without despotism.*[46]

• Fourth, in honoring the civic virtues of the natural man, without
ceasing to honor prayerfulness and piety, American political culture
respects something like a Catholic vision of the proper relation between
the natural virtues and grace. *Gratia non tollit sed perficit naturam*,
runs the Thomistic proverb: Grace does not take away but makes natural virtue perfect. Grace carries nature beyond itself, to become itself
more fully. We have already seen many other ways in which grace "perfects" nature (chapter 2) . In battle, for instance, it inspires a hope and
courage and perseverance that increase the frequency of heroic actions
and the probability of victory.

Before the age of Aquinas (1225-1274 A.D.), the standard textbook answer to the question: "Can a man without grace be good?" was:
he cannot. By contrast, the answer of the young Aquinas was that there
is a distinction between "saving" acts and "good" acts.[47] If "good"
means performing up to the best possibilities of one's nature in the
earthly city, as when one speaks of a good citizen, then the answer is yes.
If "good" means worthy of salvation, then the answer is no, for it is
only through the grace of Christ that men are saved. This different
answer was facilitated by the fact that Aquinas was the first philosopher in the West to have in his hands a fresh translation of Aristotle's
Nicomachean Ethics, which had been lost for upwards of a thousand
years, and had been available only in Arabic. Thus he had empirical
evidence, so to speak, that a distinction between good and evil can be
drawn in terms of natural virtues and vices, because Aristotle had done
it very well indeed.

ENCOUNTER BOOKS
900 Broadway
New York, New York 10003-1239

www.encounterbooks.com

Please add me to your mailing list.

Name

Company

Address

City, State, Zip

E-mail

Book Title

For Aquinas, nature as we actually find it in history is fallen, disordered, thrown off center, weakened, dulled. But it has not been destroyed. It has admirable powers still. For Aquinas, a man in approaching God need not go down on all fours; God desires the worship and the friendship of men who are free, not slaves. He gives His grace to heal human weaknesses and to elevate human capacities beyond their natural range. He does not take nature away, destroy it, raze it to the ground. Quite the contrary.

For God, there are no afterthoughts. All of history is present to Him not as it is to us in the long sequence of consecutive hours, days, and eras, but in a single immediate glance. In God there is no "foreknowledge." All of God's knowledge is simultaneous; the term "foreknowledge" is an adaptation to a human way of speaking. Thus, in creating us, God knew in the same instant our creation, fall, and redemption. For Him, these matters interpenetrate one another: creation is simultaneously (in His eye) pristine, fallen, and disordered, and redeemed. Before time was, and after time will be completed, God is. "I AM WHO AM," the great Hebraic text (Exodus 3:14) teaches. On this text, Aquinas founded his fundamental insight into the priority of existence to essence.[48] In daily experience, Aquinas had a very sharp sense of the brevity of life: of what it is to exist with exquisite consciousness for a time, and then to be no more. This insight lies behind his reflections on how we are led by daily experience through reason itself, even apart from faith, to some sense of God.

In the philosophy of Aquinas, the human person is the one creature in the universe created as an end, not solely as a means, because capable of self-governing behavior through reflection and choice – although, of course, often enslaved to passion, self-interest narrowly conceived, and self-gratifying weaknesses of will. Aquinas further believed that the source of all political power rests in the consent of the people, and that the ideal regime is an admixture of monarchical, aristocratic, and democratic principles.[49] He held that monarchs are subject both to the moral law, which is superior to their own power, and to the consent of the people, such that a monarch who abuses either one of these is a tyrant, whose power is illegitimate; and that tyrants may be deposed. For all such reasons, Aquinas has been singled out as "the first Whig," that is, the first philosopher in the party of liberty, whose first writings on this subject are virtually contemporaneous with the Magna Carta, and wholly in keeping with it.[50]

The secular partisan of John Locke is likely here to ask with a certain asperity: But if Aquinas is such a Whig, why did the world have to wait until Locke's *Letter on Toleration* and even the First Amendment in order to get a doctrine and a practice of religious liberty? In social systems such practical discoveries are made by trial and error; the mind is not led to them by logic alone. Before the question of "natural rights" could arise in the form in which Locke addressed it in 1680, for instance, a number of other practices and doctrines had to be tested by experience.[51] As Lord Acton says, the requisite development of conscience and a fuller understanding of liberty did not arise until the seventeenth and eighteenth centuries.[52]

In *Centesimus Annus*, in summary form, John Paul II lists three natural rights of great antiquity: the right to private property; the right to association; and the right to religious liberty. Both the social practice and the intellectual justification of two of these rights – private property and association – long antedate Locke. The argument establishing the first is at least as old as Aristotle, and the *locus classicus* of the second lies in the defense of the Dominicans and Franciscans against those who wished to banish such associations from the University of Paris circa 1250 A.D.[53] The *theological* principle of religious liberty – namely, that the decision whether or not to accept the word of God is of its nature wholly personal and inalienable – is not new. "Whoever loves father or mother, son or daughter, more than me is not worthy of me. He who will not take up his cross and come after me is not worthy of me" (Matthew 10:37). No one, not even members of our own family, can perform that task for any of us. Thus, the family of Thomas Aquinas could not in the end prevent him, even by kidnapping him and holding him prisoner, from answering his personal call.[54]

Nonetheless, under Providence it remained for the United States to erect before the world "a new model" of liberty never seen before, and thus to work out in institutional form the *political* and *institutional* principle that the power of the state is severely limited in the sphere of conscience. The *theological* principle had been known ever since St. Ambrose (339-397 A.D.) forbade Roman soldiers from entering the Cathedral in Milan.[55] This matching of the *politics* of liberty to the *theology* of liberty had never before been achieved.

This achievement in the United States may be flawed, but it

remains one of the most noble achievements of the human race; as Pope John Paul II recounted to the new American Ambassador to the Vatican in 1998,

> The Founding Fathers of the United States asserted their claim to freedom and independence on the basis of certain "self-evident" truths about the human person: truths which could be discerned in human nature, built into it by "nature's God." Thus they meant to bring into being, not just an independent territory, but a great experiment in what George Washington called "ordered liberty."...
>
> The American democratic experiment has been successful in many ways; millions of people around the world look to the United States as a model in their search for freedom, dignity, and prosperity. But the continuing success of American democracy depends on the degree to which each new generation, native-born and immigrant, makes its own the moral truths on which the Founding Fathers staked the future of your Republic....
>
> I am happy to take note of your words confirming the importance that your government attaches, in its relations with countries around the world, to the promotion of human rights and particularly to the fundamental human right of religious freedom, which is the guarantee for every other human right. Respect for religious convictions played no small part in the birth and early development of the United States. Thus John Dickinson, chairman of the Committee for the Declaration of Independence, said in 1776: "*Our liberties do not come from charters; for these are only the declarations of preexisting rights. They do not depend on parchment or seals; but come from the King of Kings and the Lord of all the earth.*" Indeed it may be asked whether the American democratic experiment would have been possible, or how well it will succeed in the future, without a deeply rooted vision of divine Providence over the individual and over the fate of nations.[56]

It is obvious that our reflections so far stimulate many further questions.

FIVE

The only foundation for a useful education in a republic is to be laid in religion. Without this there can be no virtue, and without virtue there can be no liberty, and liberty is the object and life of all republican governments.

—Benjamin Rush, 1798

FIFTH CHAPTER

Ten Questions
About the Founding

"American historical scholarship," Wilfred M. McClay wrote recently, "has largely neglected the study of religion. Precious little in the story of American history that survives in our standard textbooks even hints at the abiding religiosity of the American people."[1] As a result, even the most elementary questions go publicly unmentioned, even those that need to be mastered anew by each generation. Principles are kept intelligently alive only by inquisitive generations. The following are questions frequently asked in this generation.

1. You wouldn't pray to "nature's God," would you? (What for?) In other words, in the Declaration of Independence, isn't "nature's God" a term of art, or an engine in the Newtonian machinery?

Let's stipulate – but just for a moment – that "nature's God" is a part of the Newtonian machinery. The same Declaration speaks of Creator, Judge, and Providence. And under such names one does pray to the God of Abraham, Isaac, Jacob and of Jesus and his apostles. The founders also prayed to that God, Father of all, Almighty Governor of the universe.[2]

But now let me go back and retrieve "nature's God." Whatever Newton (or Locke) may have meant by it, the signers of the Declaration brought that phrase into the Jewish and Christian orbit, and by a traditional method, too. When St. Paul addressed the Athenians, he pointed to the statue of the unknown god in their own city square, and

spoke there (and elsewhere) of the God all men know from the observation of nature around them (Acts 17:22-28). Through reason alone
not much can be learned about God, but a few things can.

That such a God exists can be inferred, and some sense of that
God's infinite might, the intricacy and delicacy of God's wisdom, and
the disproportion between God and our own minds. We can gain some
sense, too, of God's overall benevolence, even though the evils and
sufferings that we endure temper our judgments, and incline us to
waver as to how good God really is. From reason alone, though,
philosophers did not come to the idea of creation in time (Aristotle's
unmoved mover could have maintained eternal cycles in this material
world); nor Final Judgment; nor Redemption. About the character and
"personality" of God (if any), reason alone leaves us in darkness. From
the observation of nature around us and within us, philosophers have
learned a few things about "the God of nature," but not much.

But neither St. Paul nor other thinkers thought it impermissible
to unite what they learned about God from the revelations made
through the Hebrew prophets and through the Son of God – that is,
what they learned from the way of knowing called faith – with what
they learned from reason. They understood these two ways of knowing,
reason and faith, as complementary. For what they could not learn
from reason alone, God in his mercy supplied them in the light of revelation, if they were willing to accept the credibility of his witnesses,
and through them come to some obscure direct sense of his presence.

The benefits of having two sources of knowledge are four. First,
what is accepted through faith confirms what is known from reason.
Second, faith offers us propositions to test through daily living; for
instance, that to take up the cause of liberty may be to involve oneself
in travail and suffering ("to take up the cross daily"), but it is certainly to enjoy the favor of Providence. Third, faith is rich with
motivations just where reason is poor. For instance, faith counsels us
that even our hidden acts of courage, unnoticed by others, will not
escape the eye of our Judge. To act always in confidence that one's
deeds are fully observed and accurately weighed is to act far beyond
the bounds of reason alone, while trusting in the ultimate reach of reason. Fourth, when we turn to action, the God of Jews and Christians,
being the Source of reason, the ultimate reason for our trust in reason, extends the range of our confidence and our firm reliance on His

assistance. He emboldens us to act beyond what may seem reasonable in the light of reason alone, and thus to dare great things boldly "with a firm reliance on Divine Providence."

So He did for the founders of our nation.[3]

Thus, if what we mean by "nature's God" is only that which can be known through reason, we might not pray to such a God – although it seems that pagans have in fact supplicated such a God not infrequently. We would certainly not know to pray to Him as "Our Father which art in heaven." Yet if we mean by "nature's God" the same who is Creator, Judge, Providence, and Father of all, as He is known through the Hebrew prophets and lastly though Jesus, then, yes, we might well pray to Him: "Love who moves the sun and other stars," Morning Star, Lord of the firmament, Maker of the mighty mountains, Source of all running waters and streams, "Our Father which art in heaven, hallowed be thy name."

Reciting such praises from the Psalms of David in their Psalters and hymnbooks, the founders of our nation prayed to the God of nature and history, not only in their churches, but also on official and public days of thanksgiving, fasting, and supplication during the celebration of governmental events, and in the sermons that invariably accompanied them.

2. **Many of your examples show that the founders held that their religion was *useful* to them. Doesn't that turn religion into a mere means? Isn't their religion, then, purely utilitarian? Even Tocqueville observed that American preachers spoke little of doctrine, preferring to emphasize the relevance of religion for this world.**

Yes, Tocqueville did write that "Priests in the Middle Ages spoke of nothing but the other life; they hardly took any trouble to prove that a sincere Christian might be happy here below." Then he went on:

> But American preachers constantly come back to earth and only with great trouble can they take their eyes off it. To touch their listeners better, they make them see daily how religious beliefs favor freedom and public order, and it is often difficult to know when listening to them if the principal object of religion is to procure eternal felicity in the other world or well-being in this one.[4]

But in this same passage Tocqueville defended the American emphasis on self-interest rightly understood – and commended it. After all, Jesus in the Gospels preached in just this way, picturing the alternatives as eternal punishment and eternal bliss, and urging humans to choose which is in their true self-interest. Where should they lay up their treasure? Which course is truly useful to them? To present religion in utilitarian terms does not falsify the presentation. True religion is, in fact, useful.

It may be that humans ought to choose the love of God for its own sake. And some will. But we humans are very weak, and nearly all of us at some moments need every ounce of motivation we can summon, however crassly utilitarian some of it may be, in order to get us to do the right thing. Tocqueville quotes Montaigne: "When I do not follow the right path for the sake of righteousness, I follow it for having found by experience that all things considered, it is commonly the happiest and most useful."[5]

Tocqueville goes on to make a deeper point. Americans, more than any aristocratic culture ever did, value what is useful, not merely what is "beautiful."[6] Americans turn away from the pretensions of the nobility, who have been taught to prefer the "noble" and the "beautiful," and to disdain the useful and the lowly. Americans, even wealthy Americans, do not fear getting their hands dirty, and do not shirk manual work, even if they own plantations or are of high military rank. They consider it manly to share common hardships and to put their shoulders to the wheel. Indeed, so completely have Americans turned against aristocratic pretensions, that even when they do something because it is good for its own sake, they disguise this good deed by pointing out that it is actually useful for them in the long run.

> Americans, on the contrary, are pleased to explain almost all the actions of their life with the aid of self-interest well understood; they complacently show how the enlightened love of themselves constantly brings them to aid each other and disposes them willingly to sacrifice a part of their time and their wealth to the good of the state.[7]

Americans prefer the conceit of practicality and utility, even when describing the noble.

Permit me a contemporary example. Once when teaching for a semester at the University of Notre Dame, I noted posters advertising for student volunteers to give up their summers to help poor villagers put up housing in Central America. Designed by the university chaplain's office, the largest lettering on some signs announced that such volunteering would be: THE BEST INVESTMENT YOU EVER MADE. Across the bottom (I cite from memory), the banner read: YOU'LL GIVE MORE TO YOURSELF THAN YOU WILL TO THEM. Thus do chaplains even today present the act of generosity, solidarity, and pursuing the common good as an act of self-aggrandizement.

Facing a rugged, unsettled wilderness, the first Americans had much to accomplish, and little time to waste. If they wanted a roof over their heads, they had to put it up. If they wanted a bridge over a stream, they had to build it. If they wanted a church, there wasn't one from the eleventh century that they could just use; they had to construct one. Moreover, they didn't have at hand all the manufactured goods and tools that Europeans had; they had to import them from great distances, or learn how to make substitutes for them. No wonder the *useful* gained value in their eyes, and seemed very near to the *true* and the *good*. When you learn to "make do," you try to make the substitute as good as the original. Inventive artisans can even improve upon the original. Invention became an American passion. Americans started producing new models of the *true* and the *good*, which had never been seen before, and many of these were also demonstrably *useful*.

Metaphysically speaking, Americans were expanding the linguistic universe of the aristocratic cultures of the past, within which the terms "the noble" and "the useful" had their assigned places. "Useful" had been associated with *servile* and was beneath the notice of aristocrats, but in America the landed gentry could not afford to ignore the useful, and took pride in their useful inventions and utilitarian skills. They considered the expenditure of brain power on useful things an important service to the common good as well as to themselves. When Benjamin Franklin demonstrated some of the properties of electricity with his ingenious experiments, the *truths* he was uncovering about the *good* for humankind inherent in electricity led him to *useful* instruments such as lightning rods. He did not consider such concern with utility an ignoble use of talent.

In such a milieu, to describe a religion as useful is not to demean it, or to place it below things good in themselves or true for their own sake. To describe religion as useful is not unlike saying that man was not made for the Sabbath, but the Sabbath for man. In an age quite intent on what is practical and useful, to emphasize that certain things in themselves true and in themselves good are also quite useful is high praise.

It would be very odd of God, indeed, if obeying His commandments and following His word were always dysfunctional, useless, in vain. The Hebrew and Christian religions are, in fact, useful guides to living a good personal life. They are also good maps for how to make a republic work, not in some utopian future, but in this present world of sinful and fallen human beings. Judaism and Christianity offer not only a vision of a free and self-governing society – a "shining city on the hill" – but also a realistic ethic, including the means of repenting and starting over after moments of weakness and fall. This vision suggests the need for a system of checks and balances, and an elaborate diffusion of the division of powers.[8]

Such advantages accrue for one reason only: this religion is *true*. It is verifiable against the facts of human experience. If Christianity and Judaism were not in themselves true, they would not likely be solid reeds on which to depend, when the going gets tough. Anyone proposing Christianity as a religion only because it is useful, while knowing full well that it is neither true nor good in itself, is a fool. For what purpose would it be "useful"? The savor in the salt of religion lies in its being true:

> I therefore do not believe that the sole motive of religious men is interest; but I think that interest is the principal means religions themselves make use of to guide men, and I do not doubt that it is only from this side that they take hold of the crowd and become popular.
>
> I therefore do not see clearly why the doctrine of self-interest well understood would turn men away from religious beliefs, and it seems to me, on the contrary, that I am sorting out how it brings them near to them.[9]

For men and women who know that their religion is true, the commendation that it is also of unparalleled usefulness is not a denial of its truth or goodness. It is an additional reason for giving thanks. In an age that prides itself on using practical intelligence, it is the latest seal of approval.

Such seals, of course, change with the fashions. Nowadays, in our own time, mere practicality is out of fashion. But this change in fashion does not falsify the claim made by our forebears, *viz.*, that in training up citizens committed to self-government, the Hebrew and Christian religions are uniquely useful. Nothing so demonstrates the utility of certain traditional moral disciplines as today's lack thereof. "Confirm thy soul," the old hymn says, "in self-control/Thy liberty in law."

For the Puritan and Anglican divines, the Source of *being* and *true* and *good* is one and the same God. The notion that following His law is not useful for personal and national life would have seemed to them an insult to God. That they praised this usefulness more than other generations in other cultures is to their credit, but only up to a point. For sometimes the founders so emphasized the practice of religion, the usefulness of religion, that they neglected the doctrine and the exact understanding of what they had inherited. "It is in our lives and not our words that our religion must be read," Jefferson wrote.[10] He, like other founders, constantly praised practice and often spoke disdainfully of doctrines, formalities, and exact definitions of things religious. During his term in the White House, Jefferson composed a "Philosophy of Jesus Christ," and he later enlarged it into *The Jefferson Bible*, a compendium (in four languages) of the moral teachings of Jesus. In his version of the New Testament, Jefferson deleted all references to miracles, divinity, and doctrine; all that survived was the practical moral teaching of Jesus. In the words of the Virginia Declaration of Rights,

> That Religion, or the duty which we owe to our Creator, and the manner of discharging it, can be directed only by reason and conviction, not by force or violence; and, therefore, all men are equally entitled to the free exercise of religion, according to the dictates of conscience; and that it is the mutual duty of all to practise Christian forbearance, love, and charity, towards each other.[11]

It is better to practice love of fellows, Jefferson and others liked to say, than to quibble over divisive issues of doctrine. Their impulse is understandable, but it also violates Pascal's law, that the first moral obligation is to think clearly. A faith careless about its intellectual content is reduced merely to a sensibility; after a time, it sinks to sentimentality. In two generations, it will leave its followers inarticulate: "Yes, faith is important to me, but it's not something I can put in words."

In summary, religion *is* useful, but it cannot be reduced to the useful.

The religious sense is close to a sense of beauty, but it cannot be reduced to an aesthetic sense. Religion makes arduous ethical demands, but it cannot be reduced to ethics. The utilitarian, the beautiful, the ethical and the religious – these four – are each specifically different from the others. The religion of the founders was stronger in the domains of the useful and the ethical than in the domains of the beautiful and the holy. They felt more at home speaking of religion as a useful public good and an important moral guide. Facing the huge practical difficulties of getting a new experiment in republican self-government underway, this concentration of energies may have been wise, but it was limited. The price later generations have paid for that concentration is the gradual retreat of religious faith from the field of intellect. Fervent practice has not made up the ground lost through intellectual weakness.

After the tremendous gains achieved by the founding generation, it would have been better if later generations had added to the American religious patrimony a religious sense of awe before the holy, accompanied by intellectual inquiries of great depth and clarity. Even if the conditions of frontier life hardly accommodated themselves to such tasks, their absence is today sorely felt. Our national sense of the holy and the beautiful is thin.

When all is said and done, however, it is unfair to accuse the founding generation of reducing religion to the useful. Their sense of their own weakness before the might of the British fleet, their trust in Providence, their oft-expressed and fervent thanksgiving for the "signal interventions" of that Providence in their behalf during the course of a long and difficult war, and their acts of fasting and humiliation go far beyond the bounds of the secular and the utilitarian. Yet it is fair to say that in their approach to religion they proceeded too narrowly. They left their religious inheritance unnecessarily vulnerable to intellectual attack and to cultural decline.

3. **The American eagle rises on two wings: reason and faith. Some of the founders, we are told, were comfortable with one or the other of these two wings and some with both. But it is not clear exactly what these two wings are. For instance, is the wing of reason to be identified exclusively with common sense? But common**

sense means many different things to different thinkers. For Thomas Jefferson, for example, common sense meant Enlightenment rationalism. And what is meant by faith? Does it mean personal religious conviction in general, or is it faith as expressed in creedal statements and institutional religion?

To speak in a general way appropriate for the full range of the beliefs of the founders, it is necessary to use definitions broad enough to apply to all. The "common sense" philosophy of the Scottish philosophical tradition, for instance, so beloved of many of the founders, belongs in part to the Aristotelian tradition of practical wisdom and partly to the practical school of Cicero and Seneca. But it reflects also that distinctive love for concrete things that English and Scots collegians at the University of Paris (Duns Scotus was one) were already known for in the middle ages, and that love for inductive methods and individual cases that distinguished British common law from the more abstract, deductive traditions of the Continent. The Anglo-Saxons demonstrate a love for reason all right, but theirs is not quite the "Reason" of the Continental Rationalists.

Jefferson *was* more Continental in his preferences, as he demonstrated in his praise for the French Revolution of 1789. That preference made him a good choice as author of the American Declaration of 1776, since one of the aims of the Declaration was to appeal to the French mind, and to provide France with a way of coming to the aid of an independent nation, rather than to the aid of seditious subjects rebelling against the British king. Jefferson's most famous philosophical passage – "We hold these truths to be self-evident," etc., is abstract, timeless, and dramatic. By contrast, most of the rest of the Declaration consists of a long list of concrete violations of the traditional rights of Englishmen – case by case – modeled on earlier lists of such grievances in British history, such as that of the British Declaration of Rights of 1689. These parallels are drawn out in Pauline Maier's great study of the Declaration.[12]

In the title of this book, I used the term "common sense" rather than "reason," in order to emphasize that the founders were not Enlightenment philosophers but men of affairs, political leaders, statesmen. They were following the ways of practical philosophy, not theoretical philosophy. For this, "common sense" seems the better name, not least because so many of them (Witherspoon, for one) were partial to the "common sense philosophy" that some of them inherited from Scotland.

Allow me an aside. One of my early favorite books was Bernard Lonergan's *Insight: A Study of Human Understanding*.[13] Lonergan has two penetrating chapters on how insight works in common sense, and on the weaknesses inherent in common sense. More than any academic philosophers today, Lonergan both praised and measured the exact strengths and creative possibilities inherent in knowledge by common sense; it is the kind of knowledge most often employed by ordinary people and persons of practical affairs. In politics and in the law, as well, common sense is indispensable. Of course, as Lonergan points out, common sense does not rise to the level of theory. Its reliance on one case in one situation, another in another, opens it to seeming contradiction. Thus, on one occasion, a shrewd man may cite the proverb, "An empty barrel makes the most noise." In a contrasting situation, he may say, "The wheel that squeaks the loudest gets the grease." People who are quick, glib, and articulate can always raise difficulties about such statements. Each proverb has its truth, but only within certain contexts. People of common sense have a good instinct for which bit of wisdom fits which context. But you might tie them up in knots if you ask them for a theory that irons out all the edges and wrinkles in what they say. They don't think theoretically. They try to take the facts in context, case by case, and reach back in memory for the appropriate wisdom. They do not look for a theory, but for a ray of practical wisdom helpful just now.

Nowadays, television commentators and other intellectuals who sound off on op-ed pages in national publications often poke fun at political leaders who are not articulate in the abstractions of public policy analysis. They thought Adlai Stevenson smart and Eisenhower dumb; Carter smart and Reagan "an amiable dunce;" Gore articulate and Bush slow. The rationalistic prejudices of the modern outlook block many today from having the sort of common sense found almost everywhere in the founding generation. Wise men often fly beneath the radar of the quick and glib. A wise man and a wise guy operate on different frequencies.

Faith, like reason, was also a term of many meanings in 1776, as it also is today. Those founders who were graduates of Columbia, Princeton, Harvard, or Yale knew the traditional medieval distinctions between natural theology and faith. Standard exams at such universities included questions from natural philosophy (a discipline developed by reason alone), as distinguished from faith (questions approached through using both reason and Holy Scripture, such as questions about God as Creator, Providence, Redeemer, Judge). Many of the founders were as knowledgeable as intelligent laymen would be about the major differences among Protestant understandings of "faith;" not with theological precision, perhaps, but with enough knowledge to place themselves in this tendency or that.

The great gap, in their eyes, was that between atheism and belief in God. Benjamin Rush of Philadelphia, whom many thought was the most learned of the founders, preferred "Mahometans" to atheists; his was a common view. The founders tended to classify all beliefs about God as "faith," even if they derived what they thought about God mainly from reason (as Tom Paine expressly did). Thus, when they spoke of the Governor of the universe, the Creator, Judge, or Providence, they called such beliefs "faith," but they did so in an almost philosophical tone of voice, not a confessional voice. "Faith" meant for them those things humans know about God, even apart from attendance in any church. They surmised that almost all reasonable people come to similar understanding about the Divine, through observation of nature and human experience. They thought atheism willfully irrational.

The Unitarian tendency in American thought at the end of the eighteenth century, the tendency that Jefferson most clearly represented, approached God without any reliance on "faith" as a supernatural gift of God, but solely in the light of reason alone. But such persons were also, even in their own eyes, persons of faith, not atheists. Even though they did not think of Jesus Christ as the Son of God, or believe in the miraculous events recorded in the Bible, they did believe that reason alone leads humans to recognize the hand of God in nature and human affairs. They believed in a Divine Governor of the universe, Whom they even deigned at times to refer to as Providence (as Jefferson did in his First Inaugural Address[14]). They spoke sometimes of God as the Judge Whom all meet at death. These latter tendencies showed that they were deeply influenced by the Christian, or at least Hebrew, convictions in whose atmosphere they had been raised. They were more influenced than the term "Deist" suggests.

None of the signers of the Declaration or Constitution, so far as I can see, ever went so far into "Transcendentalism" – transcending Hebrew notions such as Creator, Providence, and Judge – as Ralph Waldo Emerson and, later, Walt Whitman were to do. Some were not orthodox Christians. But as distinguished from atheists, they were men of faith.

I believe that a usage similar to this is appropriate for today, because a typical contemporary outlook (philosophical, scientific, taken-for-granted) embodies premises and methods that screen God out of nature or human experience. On those premises, and by those methods, God simply doesn't appear. To have an idea that God exists, or any idea that God is a Lawgiver or Governor of the universe, the modern outlook holds, is a matter of faith. Reason itself knows nothing of God.

Those who confine themselves to the modern outlook find it hard to believe that the founders could have been serious in using faith to lift their project off the ground. Many today imagine that the founders, being men of the Enlightenment, could not really have taken faith seriously. And if they did, well, that part of their inheritance is no longer valid or credible, but belongs in the attic with knee britches and powdered wigs. What remains valid from the founding is only what meets the test of reason: a few principles from Locke, the secular philosophy of natural rights detached from Judaism and Christianity. That is the way most historians and political philosophers seem to present the founding. That interpretation does not fit the historical record.

4. **The majority of the founders were men of religious belief. They were able to avoid divisions of religious sentiment and find common ground by appealing to the God of the Hebrews and the religious heritage of the Torah, a "Biblical metaphysics." Today, however, no such religious consensus exists. Not only does no religious consensus exist, but the Supreme Court has become "an agency of aggression," as a recent dissenting opinion of Chief Justice Rehnquist puts it, exhibiting "bristling hostility toward religion." What has transpired in American society today, such**

that religious consensus has vanished? Is there now broad judicial antagonism to religion? Is this the outcome of a fundamental flaw in the constitution of our republic? Or something recent? When did things go wrong?

Great question: When?

When did things go wrong? Right in the beginning? If not then,…when?

Far from having a hostility toward religion, the founders counted on religion for the underlying philosophy of the republic, its supporting ethic, and its sole reliable source of rejuvenation. The historical record does not allow the fault to be fairly laid at the feet of the founders.

We may grant that the founding was not perfect. The continuation of slavery – out of necessity, but clearly contrary to the founding principles – shows just how steeped in fault the founding was. We have also conceded that an excessive emphasis on the utility of religion, and insufficient intellectual clarity about the nature of religion, Judaism and Christianity in particular, weakened the young nation, much as a bad knee thrown out in youth is liable to buckle at unexpected times during a man's maturity.

An inability to be articulate about what Judaism and Christianity require of a free people raises the probability that these requirements will not be met. Without articulate defense, the intellectual basis of republican government will begin to deteriorate, and the sound habits of the people will turn squishy. Thus, serious weaknesses were present at the founding. Still, there is no perfect work of man. In the ways of the world, in the long course of human history, the founding of our nation was as perfect as it gets. As the American bishops said at the Third Plenary Council of Baltimore, the founders, guided by Providence, built "better than they knew."[15]

When did the nation go wrong? Not knowing the answer with certainty, I have three suggestions for further research. First, beginning in the late nineteenth century, American academics began to look to Germany and other European centers to emulate, considering America backward and the ideological ferment of Europe more advanced.[16] This new pattern reversed the earlier conviction (shared by Tocqueville) that America was the leader and model, and the "Old World" the latecoming pupil. By 1900, the ideologies of Europe had begun to be used as the lens through which to interpret the American founding. This process was greatly advanced by Beard and Parrington.[17] The distinctive contributions of American Judaism and Christianity, their emphasis on the fall of man and their anti-utopian modesty, were overlooked. The Europeanization of American intellectual life betrayed American originality and led to forgetfulness of the true first principles of the American republic.

Second, the traditional alliance of religion and liberty in the United States came under assault after World War II from the rejection of Judaism and Christianity by many secular liberals in the academy, the law, and journalism. A concerted effort, led by Leo Pfeffer, attempted systematically to secularize American public life, by filing law suits against every perceived "entanglement" of the American state with Christianity.[18] Protestants and Other Americans United for the Separation of Church and State enthusiastically joined in this effort, as did the American Civil Liberties Union. Such groups symbolized the public presence of religion in public life as an infectious disease that ought to be quarantined. A determined effort was made to banish religion from American public life. Beginning about 1948, one Supreme Court case after another turned the judiciary (and the law schools) into aggressive enemies of religion in public life.

Finally, although Hollywood got its start much earlier, by the post-war era of the 1950s intellectual and artistic elites acquired even more formidable powers over the public ethos through the appearance of two new technologies of communicating, slick national news magazines and television. For the first time in history, the media gave national elites decisive dominance over local elites, such as pastors, preachers and editorialists, school principals and other local authority figures in law and medicine. These national elites now set the agenda for what is to be considered "in" or "out," signalled thumbs up or thumbs down to decide what is acceptable. Even parents could scarcely withstand the onslaught.[19]

Further, these new elites were decidedly secular, indeed vigorously adversarial – anti-Jewish, anti-Christian.[20] For the first time in American history on so grand a scale, religious figures began to be systematically ridiculed and satirized. A new "nonjudgmental" secular morality was rigorously imposed, and the traditional morality was relentlessly mocked and marginalized. The unmistakable subtext of the morality plays produced by the new artistic class was that a new morality is "blowing in the wind," and that the dying of the old ways should be celebrated as liberation. In the wake of this cultural cyclone, roaring in behind it, radical feminism, the celebration of homosexual life, and the relentless logic of "non-judgmentalism" raced forward unchecked.[21]

Perhaps I am not correct in identifying all the forces that have turned the American spirit in a new direction. But I am fairly confident in placing its inception after World War II. For if one reads the letters and memoirs of those who fought in World War II, and revisits the films made during that time, their continuity with the earliest mores of America is quite stunning by comparison with the culture of sixty years later. American institutions, not least in the law and among the guardians of the public ethos, underwent a huge shift just after World War II. I do not agree with those who attribute the shift mostly to the "counterculture" of the 1960s, although no doubt that shift played its own mischievous role in the entire process. The factors I have pointed to seem much deeper, and they began to unfold well before the 1960s.

One reason the drive to secularize public life through the Courts succeeded so quickly after 1945 may have been that for some decades the historians and political philosophers had already been dismissive of the powerful religious forces that had propelled the founding; they preferred a strictly agnostic view of the philosophy of natural rights. Lending emotional and imaginative support to that drily skeptical tone was the literature of disillusionment which arose like whiffs of poisonous gas from the trench warfare of World War I and wafted like the smoke of cigarettes over the tinkling pianos of the Jazz Age.

5. Maybe the "establishment clause" in the Bill of Rights has allowed for the flourishing of religion in America, as Madison predicted. But has the Bill of Rights also led inadvertently to an increase in "indifferentism"? Is it not implicit in Madison's thought, and embodied in the "establishment clause," that no religion is more true than any other? Finally, did not the "establishment clause" inevitably lead to the constitutional protection of the very atheism that the founders generally abhorred?

It is a mistake to make two clauses where the Constitution so closely knits together one. The authors of the Constitution, as the constitutional debate and the sequence of drafts demonstrate, wished to protect the free exercise of religion in the states, *including* the establishment of religion in some states. To that purpose, they insisted that the *federal* government could neither establish one religion nor abolish the establishments existing in some states. The purpose of most of the founders was far removed from wishing to ban religion from public life altogether; it was almost directly the opposite. Most could not accept the antiseptic Virginia model favored by Jefferson and Madison.[22] As Presidents, neither Jefferson nor Madison could practice their own preferred principles; they, too, found it better to yield to already well-established traditions of public prayer and thanksgiving to God. Thus, the Constitution did not stifle the existing, strong, and public religious practice of the land.

Independently of the U.S. Constitution, Christian faith requires that individuals be free to reject God's proffered friendship, to turn away from God, and to declare themselves atheists. It also allows for the possibility that some of those who call themselves atheists actually walk in darkness with God and are dear to Him, notably, those who pursue the truth in total fidelity to their own consciences, with courage and fidelity. Only God reads the souls of humans. Although Christians have often failed in this duty, their own faith requires them to respect the consciences of all. This, too, the Constitution tries to institutionalize.

Nothing in the U.S. Constitution nor anything I have discovered in Madison's thought requires the proposition that one religion is as true as another, or the proposition that freedom of conscience entails indifference to questions of truth.[23] On the contrary, awareness that there is a God Who commands an inalienable response in the conscience of each individual is the reason why a sound polity must respect freedom of religion, even when some who enjoy that liberty fail to use it to render thanks to God.

No one of us possesses the truth.[24] We are bound in conscience to be faithful to it, as best we can see how to be. To do this, we must have some room for trial and error. Besides, we can learn from others. The doctrine of original sin (verified in personal observation) teaches us that there is bound to be some self-interest and lack of courage in our own fidelity to truth, and thus some error in our truth. Our awareness of our own finitude and dependence on many other persons instructs us that there is bound to be some truth even in those who otherwise offend us or seem to be our enemies. Respecting freedom of conscience is in our own interest, so that we may come to see both our own errors and also the truth in the positions taken by others, where we do not at first see it.

To be tolerant is by no means the same thing as to believe that any proposition is as true as any other. In our continuing desire to press onward toward a greater insight into the truth, all propositions must be assessed in the light of evidence. We need to discard the false, and to press onward toward the true. Sometimes we tolerate what seems to us untrue, in the hope that we will come to see at least some truth in it. Most of the time, we tolerate – that is, we put up with, show respect for, suffer the burden of, make the extra effort for – the person we think to be in error, not because of the error but because we know them to possess part of the truth, hidden from us. Experience shows that in this effort we often learn a great deal that we did not expect to learn. Besides, respecting the dignity of others *qua* others is a good thing in itself. From a Jewish and Christian point of view, there is something of God in each of us. Respecting this something, listening for it, is seldom in vain. (Sometimes, though, it can be costly. Some people are at times a pain.)

The respect our Constitution implies we ought to show for the diverse consciences of each of us does not violate orthodox Christianity. On the contrary, the imperative for that respect *comes from* Jewish and Christian teaching. Our Constitution does not reduce tolerance to some form of moral equivalence, to disregard for the truth of things, to moral indifferentism, relativism, or nihilism. Quite the opposite. On the basis of moral equivalence (or moral indifferentism, relativism or nihilism), why would liberty of conscience be morally better than servility of conscience? On such grounds, what value can liberty of conscience possibly have? Precisely because conscience is ordered to truth, and only to truth, conscience is sacred. Here are Madison's words:

> It is the duty of every man to render to the Creator such homage and such only as he believes to be acceptable to him. This duty is precedent, both in

order of time and in degree of obligation, to the claims of Civil Society. Before any man can be considered as a member of Civil Society, he must be considered as a subject of the Governour of the Universe.[25]

Truth is not solely a property of propositions but the name of a person – a divine Person who made all things, who understands them from inside-out, loves them, wills them to be, and so causes them to come into existence, like sparks in the night. Truth is a relation between persons. No human being has the right to interfere with the relation between a human being and his Maker, or even the right to treat another human being with less than the respect due to a person whose liberty is held in respect even by its Maker.

This is the argument that Madison makes in his Remonstrance, all its implications drawn out. This is, I believe, the assumption behind the moral authority that suffuses our Constitution and the Declaration.

6. **You said earlier that Madison's "Remonstrance" is considered a vital text because "in finding rational ground for religious liberty, it begins with faith, not reason – the duties of the creature who stands alone in the presence of the Creator." You say on this ground that Madison's right to religious liberty is grounded in faith, not reason. What is the exact sense of "faith" that you are using here? If one regards the obligation of a creature to give due worship to his Creator as one of the fundamental precepts of the natural law, this would seem to be a matter of reason, not faith.**

The distinction between faith and reason implied in this question is the classical one. It parallels the classical distinction between natural philosophy (based on reason) and theology (based on propositions at least one of whose premises is from God's revelation).

But that sense is not the sense in which I am using the words. Because of the looser usage of the founders, and also because of the contemporary inability of philosophy as it is currently construed to reach as far as God, I am using "faith" for all propositions about God, even those that in earlier times would have been reached by pre-Christian "pagan" philosophers who wrote of God. In earlier times, as you suggest, these propositions would have been considered the work of reason and proper to philosophy.

I am using "reason" or "common sense" for the practical form of sustained thinking exercised by the founders, the practical reasoning of thoughtful men of affairs, statesmen, well-read in the ancients, in history, and often enough in the common law. The founders did not find "reason" in this sense antithetical to Jewish or Christian faith, but complementary. Not the same, but companionable, and mutually reinforcing.

7. **Historically, Catholics have been favorable to the American experiment and even predisposed to it by the Catholic tradition of natural virtue and nature perfected by grace. But it is also part of the Catholic tradition that the civic order is under obligation to foster the spiritual interests of the Church. It is the duty of the civil order to promote in the natural order that which is conducive to the full moral development of its citizens and their peaceful coexistence in the community. Given the sinful condition of mankind, it is incumbent on the civil order to cooperate with the Church for the spiritual means necessary for the full moral development of its citizens. Thus the Church has the right to demand that the civil order cooperate with her and recognize her legitimate authority for the spiritual good of the citizens. In the American system, however, neither the Catholic Church nor any other church can impose obligations on the civil order. Does this not de facto subordinate the authority of the Church to the civil order and create a system to which no Catholic can ever be fully amenable?**

Such language makes it look as though "the civic order" is a human person with a conscience. Just which human beings speak for "the civic order"? I would think the civic order is made up of far more than the organs of the state. For instance, in Poland circa 1987-1989, Lech Walesa spoke for "the civic order" for *Polonia* (as the Poles call it when they mean that mystical reality that is rather more than any state). The power of his voice overturned the then-existing Polish State.

Similarly, in the United States, not the President or the Congress or the Supreme Court or any other state body is empowered to establish a Church, or even to identify only one Church "to turn to," so that it might impose on the citizenry those moral obligations necessary for the well-being of the Republic. The Catholic Church does not require that sort of recognition, or even desire it, even though in the past such a relation between church and state was understood to be normal. The evils that flowed from such a close relation are well-documented in history. Much that is fruitful for Christian living has been learned by hard experience.

Much, in particular, has been learned about the possibilities of differentiating responsibilities into countervailing institutions, to minimize the probabilities of corruption in any one institution by an inappropriate mixture of political and ecclesiastical power. Thus, for instance, political power has been differentiated from economic power, and both have been differentiated from cultural, spiritual, and moral power. The state has limited roles; so does the church. These roles are not the same. The state need not tell the church what to do, nor the church the state. In principle, neither one is "subordinate" to the other. Each guards a realm in which it passes judgment on and limits the other.

In contemporary Iran and Iraq, by contrast, it has happened that one institution gains control over all three fundamental forms of power – political, economic, and moral. One institution – one person even – decides when to wage war and declare peace, how much oil to pump, at what level prices should be set, what punishment should be meted out for adultery, which sorts of writings should be censored or proscribed as seditious, etc. Such concentration of power raises high probabilities of abuse.

One should not confuse a medieval arrangement of powers with the ideal set forth by orthodox Christian faith today. Catholic social teaching, in particular, has advanced steadily through each generation by learning from worldwide social experience. It has changed much, through learning from practical experience, while remaining faithful to certain basic principles. It has also come to new insight into the meaning of its own first principles, such as individual liberty. For instance, there is no doubt that it understands the theology of personal liberty in the light of the inalienable individual responsibility for the act of faith much more fully at the end of the twentieth century than in earlier times, through advances in psychological knowledge, in the phenomenology of freedom, and in the political, economic, and social dimensions opened up by new institutions. To confirm this, one can turn to the testimony of *Gaudium et Spes*, the Instruction of Vatican II on the "Church in the Modern World,"[26] and also Pope John Paul II's *Centesimus Annus*[27] and *Tertio Millennio Adveniente*,[28] among others.

Should the radically secular interpretation of the U.S. Constitution favored by the ACLU and other aggressive secularizing forces take exclusive control over American institutions, however, American Christians might well have to move into nonviolent opposition to the new regime, for it would make loyalty to the Constitution repulsive to them. Indeed, it would make loyalty to the Constitution tantamount to a suicide pact.[29]

A fatal flaw in the secularizing impulse, universally ignored by its partisans, is its authoritarian ambition. What Tocqueville wrote about princes describes them perfectly:

> It is clear that most of our princes are not content simply to govern the nation as a whole. They seem to hold themselves responsible for the behavior and fate of their subjects as individuals, and have undertaken to guide and instruct each of them in all they do, and will, if necessary, make then happy against their will.[30]

When people in Oklahoma read about people in New York who clamor for rent controls and a cherished long list of left-wing illusions, they shrug and think that New Yorkers are illogical and silly, but they consider that New York's business, not theirs. By contrast, when Manhattanites read at breakfast that Oklahomans pray publicly at high school football games, some spit out their coffee and pledge to put a stop to that.

The Manhattanite retorts: But *they* want to keep us from having abortions.

The reality is actually the reverse. In *Roe v. Wade*, American elites convinced the Supreme Court to throw out the law under which Americans had consented to live for many generations. Thus, the Court arrogated to itself, without the consent of the people, and on no ascertainable constitutional principle, the power of reversing laws that had governed the land for many generations. Moreover, it did so regarding a fundamental moral and legal principle, which entails decisive implications for the law regarding life not only in its beginning but also at its end. Laws of such sweep and magnitude must be established only through the consent of the people, and not least when they implicate the most fundamental of the natural rights, the right to life. This right is necessarily antecedent to the right to liberty and the right to pursue happiness.

8. For a hundred years, the second wing of the eagle – faith, religion – was comparatively neglected by historians and theorists. The Enlightenment received preponderant attention. Why?

It is not as though historians and theorists totally ignored the religion of the founders; they made mention of it. But the overriding intellectual assumption of the era preceding ours was the thesis that religion is a steadily receding force, and secularization is the dominant trend. In this light, it seemed reasonable to stress the "ascendant" and "living" elements — those of secularization. Only today, with the collapse of the secularization thesis,[31] and the growing recognition that faith is not only a permanent characteristic of human behavior but one of rising importance in world affairs, has it become necessary to give the religion of the founders its due attention. The founders did not think that the constitutional government they were erecting could survive without Hebrew-Christian faith. This premise must be given due weight.

9. If Thomas Aquinas was the first Whig, why did it take so long for the right to religious liberty to become an operative part of political constitutions?

Aquinas is called the first Whig[32] because of the centrality he gave to human liberty in nature and history. The human person, he thought, is the most beautiful creature in all creation,[33] the only one created as an end in himself.[34] In his or her liberty the person is made in the image of the Creator. Aquinas further saw that political power arises from the consent of the governed. (In the Dominican order, all positions of authority are assigned by regular elections, constitutionally ordered, in which all the brothers have equal votes.) He also taught the traditional vision of limited government, limited both by moral law and by constitutional devices such as the mixed regime, and that justice sometimes demands that a tyrant be deposed.[35]

But there are many further social advances beyond this set of ideas before one can come to a political regime of religious liberty. One must learn to differentiate the sphere of the state from that of society, noting that the relevant authorities in the two spheres are not one and the same. Second, one must differentiate the sphere of culture from that of politics, in such a way that loyalty to the state does not require unity of thought and belief. Third, one must develop a theory of rights that sees justice (*jus*, right) inhering not only in things but in persons; not only, for example, in three acres of land in which John has ownership (the right of property), but in John as the owner of the right to deploy his own liberty of conscience. That is, one must grasp that rights inhere in *subjects*, not things.

As Brian Tierney points out with great subtlety and care in his admirable historical essays on the origin and development of *The Idea of Natural Right*, it is not likely that Aquinas had reached the subjective idea of natural right, although there is some controversy on the point.[36] What Aquinas did do is develop the idea of personal liberty in exquisite analytic detail, with precisions beyond the ken of earlier writers concerning such concepts as the will, practical wisdom, *liberum arbitrium*, conscience, synderesis, and other aspects of liberty. He passed along to the practical-minded canonists who worked in his wake ample materials and abundant distinctions, so that they might apply his thought to practical problems in ever new contexts. These new practical conundrums led them to adapt the Thomistic language they inherited to new uses, beyond those employed by Aquinas himself but – so some canonists argued – entirely consistent with his approach.[37] Give the credit to the canonists; they saw that individuals have property in certain natural rights, just as they have dominion over their own liberty.

Tierney cites multiple uses of the concept of a natural right inhering in individual persons in the work of the canonists during the thirteenth and fourteenth centuries, and in newer contexts right up until the seventeenth century – in other words, well before Locke (1632-1704), Hobbes (1588-1679), and even Ockham (1285-1349). Tierney finds that the theory developed by Leo Strauss and many of his students, that there is an unbridgeable chasm between the medieval era and modern natural right theory (after Hobbes, say), is untenable in the light of the historical evidence. When Tierney finds Walter Berns writing that "natural rights and traditional natural law are, to put it simply yet altogether accurately, incompatible," his rejoinder is terse:

"Such views seem based on the mistaken idea that modern rights theories are derived entirely from Hobbes." Such views ignore "the history of the concept of *jus naturale* before the seventeenth century."[38]

Tierney's chapter on the work of Francisco de Vitoria, Francisco Suárez, and Bartolemeo de las Casas, and the struggle of the Salamanca School of Spain to vindicate the natural rights of the Indians of America, well before the work of Hobbes and Locke, is especially illuminating. Tierney's work fills out with crisp and full detail what earlier writers had touched on.[39] I wish I had known years ago about the massive evidence Tierney adduces.

Tierney's work shows that many generations were required before ideas reached abstractly in philosophy could be fully deployed in practical contexts and then in successively newer contexts. Out of this long process, fresh generalizations arose and new concepts became necessary. In this fashion, practical work inspired philosophical inquiry, just as earlier philosophical work had inspired new practical experiments. A rich and pluralistic intellectual tradition assimilated all this forward movement, at some points registering the need for invention, at other times suggesting from its own past experience the redirection of attention, in order to test for earlier but forgotten patterns. (Intellectual traditions keep alive by changing often, while maintaining historical perspective.) By being placed in a radically secular context, at times even explicitly anti-religious, some forms of medieval natural rights theory were made to seem radically new. In this case, much of the novelty came from the context, not from the concept of a subjective natural right in itself, whose lineage is far older.[40]

Tierney's broad historical canvas presents an analog to the argument I have been working on here. Tierney sees in the actual history of the concept of a subjective natural right both the impulse of Jewish-Christian faith and the impulse of philosophy.

> The idea of natural rights grew up – perhaps could only have grown up in the first place – in a religious culture that supplemented rational argumentation about human nature with a faith in which humans were seen as children of a caring God. But the idea was not necessarily dependent on divine revelation, and later it proved capable of surviving into a more secular epoch. The disinclination of some Enlightenment skeptics to regard God's law as a sufficient ground for moral behavior, and the widespread tendency, after Hume, to doubt whether reflecting on human inclinations could yield moral insights, raised new problems about the justification of rights

that are still matters of dispute. But the appeal to natural rights became more prominent than ever in the political discourse of the eighteenth century. The doctrine of rights shaped by the experience of previous centuries turned out to be still of value in addressing the problems of a new era. The proponents of the secularized rights theories of the Enlightenment had often forgotten the remoter origins of the doctrines they embraced; but their rhetoric about the rights of man becomes fully intelligible only when it is seen as the end product of a long process of historical evolution.[41]

It has been said that a conservative is one who thinks his ancestors were at least as intelligent as he, and possibly wiser. But a conservative is also one who delights in seeing progress through trial and error, progress through invention and discovery. A conservative who delights most of all in the progress of the idea of liberty (Friedrich Hayek suggests) is perhaps better described as a "whig."[42] It is a name that the founders embraced, as when Jefferson wrote to a friend, "But with respect to our rights...there was but one opinion on this side of the Water. All American whigs thought alike on these subjects."[43]

10. In your reading over the years, have you encountered one story about the founders that you particularly treasure?

My favorite story is that of Joseph Warren of Massachusetts, the best known physician in Boston, Massachusetts, in the early 1770s. He had delivered the Adams babies, and was a favorite of Abigail Adams. For some years, he was active in the local Sons of Liberty, one of the organizations of patriots who resisted the encroachments of arbitrary power and taxation.

Joseph Warren stood with the other amateurs among Minutemen at Lexington, and took a bullet through his hair above the ear. Two months later, just commissioned a Major General in the Massachusetts militia, he learned that 1500 patriots had crept up Bunker Hill at night and silently erected earthen walls. Shocked at daylight to discover this, battalions of Redcoats were assembling for an afternoon attack. Some of them put all of Charlestown to the torch, and tongues of flame from five hundred houses, businesses, and churches leapt into the sky. Breathless, Abigail Adams watched from a distant hillside and heard the cannons of the warships bombarding Bunker Hill for five long hours. As they did so, Joseph Warren rode to Boston and took a position in the ranks on Bunker Hill.

The American irregulars proved their discipline that day – and the accuracy of huntsmen firing in concentrated bursts. Twice they broke the forward march of 3500 British troops with fire so withering they blew away as many as 70 to 90 percent of the foremost companies of Redcoats, who lost more than a thousand dead that day. Then the ammunition of the Americans ran out.

While the bulk of the Massachusetts militia retreated, the last units stayed in their trenches to hold off the British in hand-to-hand combat. That is where Major General Joseph Warren was last seen fighting, as a close-range bullet felled him. The British officers had him decapitated and bore his head to General Gage.

Freedom is always the most precarious regime. Even a single generation can throw it all away. Every generation must decide.

Joseph Warren had told the men of Massachusetts:

> Our country is in danger now, but not to be despaired of. On you depend the fortunes of America. You are to decide the important questions upon which rest the happiness and the liberty of millions not yet born. Act worthy of yourselves.[44]

EPILOGUE

How Did the Virginians
Ground Religious Rights?

Walter Berns' Thesis

A colleague of mine at the American Enterprise Institute, Walter Berns, has written that the philosophy of John Locke was decisive in the American founding. According to Berns, Locke's disguised but unmistakable aim was, first, to break with the traditional Christian understanding of nature and, second, to drive religion out of politics decisively by confining it in the private sphere.[1] Professor Berns invokes Jean-Jacques Rousseau to set the horizon and framework of this interpretation, and thus makes the European Enlightenment a hermeneutical key to the American founding.[2] Further, he neglects the testimony of John Adams, Benjamin Rush, Alexander Hamilton, John Dickinson and others of the founders whose views on the source of natural rights are far more religious than those of Locke (narrowly interpreted). Finally, Berns largely ignores the practice of the founding generation, which accommodated a far more public role for the free exercise of religion than the American Civil Liberties Union now tolerates.[3]

Nonetheless, the Berns thesis does throw some doubt upon the generous and affectionate view of the American founding propounded by the genial Catholic philosopher Jacques Maritain, one of the thinkers who prepared the way for the Universal Declaration of Rights. If Berns is right, Maritain cannot be. And vice versa.

Jacques Maritain's Thesis

In a series of three books, Maritain set forth his argument that modern democracy of the American type cannot be understood apart from the inspiration of the gospels of Jesus Christ, which works in secular history as yeast in dough. In *Man and the State*, Maritain introduced his thesis in these terms:

> Far beyond the influences received either from Locke or the XVIIIth Century Enlightenment, the Constitution of this country is deep-rooted in the age-old heritage of Christian thought and civilization.... Peerless is the significance, for political philosophy, of the establishment of the American Constitution at the end of the XVIIIth Century. This Constitution can be described as an outstanding lay Christian document tinged with the philosophy of the day. The spirit and inspiration of this great political Christian document is basically repugnant to the idea of making human society stand aloof from God and from any religious faith. Thanksgiving and public prayer, the invocation of the name of God at the occasion of any major official gathering, are, in the practical behavior of the nation, a token of this very same spirit and inspiration.[4]

Later, in *Reflections on America*, Maritain quoted at length these words by Peter Drucker:

> The unique relationship between religion, the state, and society is perhaps the most fundamental – certainly it is the most distinctive – feature of American religious as well as American political life. It is not only central to any understanding of American institutions. It also constitutes the sharpest difference between American and European institutions, concepts, and traditions. This country has developed the most thoroughgoing, if not the only truly secular state.... The United States is, however, also the only country of the West in which society is conceived as being basically a religious society.
>
> By its very nature the sphere of the state has to be an autonomous sphere, a sphere entirely of the "natural reason." But also, by definition, a free society is only possible if based solidly on the religious individual.... This leads to the basic American concept: the state must neither support nor favor any one religious denomination.... But at the same time the state must always sponsor, protect, and favor religious life in general. The United States is indeed a "secular" state as far as any one denomination is concerned. But it is at the same time a "religious" commonwealth as concerns the general belief in the necessity of a truly religious basis of citizenship.[5]

Maritain's own comments on this passage are as follows:

This description of the American situation is clear and plain enough. I shall only add, with respect to my own personal experience, that the first time I heard the President of the United States (it was Franklin Roosevelt) speaking on the radio, address a prayer to God – I realized all of a sudden that the expression "separation between Church and State" does not have, to be sure, the same meaning in French and in American.[6]

A little later, he added:

The Founding Fathers were neither metaphysicians nor theologians, but their philosophy of life, and their political philosophy, their notion of natural law and of human rights, were permeated with concepts worked out by Christian reason and backed up by an unshakeable religious feeling.[7]

Meanwhile, in the first chapter of his little book *Christianity and Democracy*, Maritain traced out in considerable detail a long series of presuppositions and assumptions (seven in all), which over the centuries the secular conscience has absorbed from Judaism and Christianity. "The secular conscience has understood," he repeated,

that progress does not lead to the recovery of paradise by Revolution tomorrow; it *tends to the carrying over of the structures of conscience* and the structures of human life to better states, and this *all through history* up to the advent of the kingdom of God....

... Under the often misunderstood but active inspiration of the Gospel, the secular conscience has understood the *dignity of the human person* and has understood that the person, while being a part of the State, yet *transcends the State....*

... Under the inspiration of the Gospel at work in history, the secular conscience has understood the *dignity of the people and of the common man.* Faithful people, God's little people, kingly people, called to share in the work of Christ; people in the sense of the community of the citizens of a country, united under just laws; people in the sense of the community of manual labor and of the stock and resource of humanity in those who toil close to nature – the notion of the people which the secular conscience has gradually formed stems from the meeting and mingling of all these elements, and it is from the heritage of Christendom that this notion proceeds. ... By virtue of the hidden work of evangelical inspiration, the secular conscience has understood that the *authority of rulers,* by the very fact that it emanates from the author of human nature, *is addressed to free men* who do not belong to a master and is exercised by virtue of *the consent of the governed.*

... The secular conscience has understood that the political realm and the flesh and blood paraphernalia of the things that are Caesar's must nevertheless be subject to God and to justice.... What has been gained for the secular conscience, if it does not veer to barbarism, is the *condemnation of the politics of domination*... and the conviction that the cause of the welfare and freedom of the people and the cause of political justice are substantially linked.

... Under the often misunderstood or disfigured but active inspiration of the Gospel, *the secular conscience has awakened* not only to the dignity of the human person, but *also to the aspirations and the élan which are at work* in his depths.... What has been gained for the secular conscience, if it does not veer to barbarism, is the sense of freedom and *the conviction that the forward march of human societies is a march toward the conquest of a freedom consonant with the vocation of our nature.*

... The secular conscience has understood that in the misfortunes and suffering of our existence, crushed by the iron laws of biological necessity and by the weight of the pride, injustice and wickedness of men, *a single principle of liberation, a single principle of hope, a single principle of peace can stir up the mass of servitude and iniquity and triumph over it,* because this principle comes down to us from the creative source of the world, stronger than the world.... What has been gained for the secular conscience, if it does not veer into barbarism, is *faith in the brotherhood of man,* a sense of *the social duty of compassion* for mankind in the person of the weak and the suffering, the conviction that the political work par excellence is that of *rendering common life better and more brotherly* and of working so as to make of the structure of laws, institutions and customs of this common life a house for brothers to live in.[8]

Coming from radically secular France, where the Revolution of 1789 also began with an invocation of "natural rights," but in a quite different sense and on a quite different foundation, and where the revolutionaries seized, profaned, and closed Christian institutions throughout the republic, Maritain fears that Americans will not hold fast to their own originality:

Let me say, as the testimony of one who loves this country, that a European who comes to America is struck by the fact that the expression "separation between Church and State," which is in itself a misleading expression, does not have the same meaning here and in Europe. In Europe it means, or it meant, that complete isolation which derives from century-old misunderstandings and struggles, and which has produced most unfortunate results. Here it means, as a matter of fact, together with a refusal to grant any privilege to one religious denomination in preference to others and to have a State established religion, a distinction between the State and the Churches which is compatible with good feeling and mutual cooperation. *Sharp distinction and mutual cooperation, that's an historical treasure,* the value of which a European is perhaps more prepared to appreciate, because of his own bitter experiences. Please to God that you keep it carefully, and *do not let your concept of separation veer round to the European one.*[9]

This difference between France and America stimulated Maritain's philosophical reflections. Yet Maritain seldom cites a particular text of the founding period, such as the Declaration, the Constitution, *The Federalist* or other classics. It is not apparent that he read much of Madison, Jefferson, Hamilton, Adams or other founders.

Therefore, one wonders, lovely as Maritain's thesis is, does it stand up to a close reading of the essential documents? Professor Berns, like other students of Leo Strauss, points out that apparently religious documents such as the Declaration of Independence require a special kind of care, since the surface meaning of the words may often be belied by the more hidden subtext. For instance, one must grasp the particular philosophical problem that John Locke faced, namely: How *not* to seem like a heretic, while actually proposing a heretical solution to the political-religious problem. While seeming to cite religious arguments and to pay obeisance to traditional terms, Locke was actually reducing religion to subordinate status. He *intended to* eliminate the centuries of competition between religious authority and political authority by subordinating religion to secular law. [10]

In making this argument, Professor Berns leans heavily upon James Madison's *Remonstrance* of 1785, a pamphlet which Madison circulated throughout Virginia in resistance to an initiative by Governor Patrick Henry. Henry had proposed a bill to raise taxes for salaries of clergymen in all those churches that would accept such aid. [11] In other words, Henry hoped to engineer a way around the recent disestablishment of the Anglican Church of Virginia by including all churches within the ambit of state aid. Madison feared that this ploy was reintroducing the entanglement of church and state. So in a fuller way than anyone yet had, although building upon earlier classics largely written by George Mason and Thomas Jefferson, Madison spelled out the ground of his argument for the natural right of religious liberty. As a major test of the argument between Maritain and Berns, it seems useful to examine the reasoning of these three Virginians in some detail.

Virginia's Conception of Religious Liberty

The way in which Virginia approached the question of religious liberty was very different from the path chosen by Massachusetts and other states,[12] but the Virginia way has become the standard by which American liberals today measure the relations of church and state – and even of religion and society. "Church" and "state" refer to institutions, of course, whereas "religion" and "society" refer more broadly to the habits and practices of individuals, sometimes acting singly, sometimes acting along with others. Citizens often work together through diverse associations and civic relationships, in various contexts and activities, in order to achieve their social ends and purposes independently of the state. The sphere of "society," therefore, is much larger than that of the "state."[13]

Massachusetts and others among the founding thirteen states, while protecting the full religious liberty of citizens under their new constitutions after Independence, maintained an established church, and entrusted important moral and educational tasks to church communities with state support, direct or indirect. Virginia, too, agreed that the protection of morals and education in republican habits was indispensable to the survival and well-being of republican government.[14] However, abuses of religious freedom led three leading Virginians to draw an exceedingly bright yellow line between the state and not only the church but even religion more generally. This line was defined by four major documents: George Mason's *Virginia Declaration of Rights* of 1776, Thomas Jefferson's *Virginia Bill for Establishing Religious Liberty* in 1779, James Madison's *Memorial and Remonstrance against Religious Assessments* in 1785, and again his *Act for Establishing Religious Freedom* of 1785.[15]

Three features of this decade-long struggle deserve note. First, Virginia trod this path almost alone among the founding states.[16] Second, the puritanical passion of Jefferson and Madison on this point was bitterly resisted by many in Virginia, as well as in the other states, and in practice proved nearly impossible to observe to the letter. The dependence of the Republic upon the concepts and habits inculcated by Jewish and Christian religions proved to be too conspicuous to ignore. As presidents, for example, both Jefferson and Madison expended many efforts to show their personal support for religious worship; by many official acts, they nurtured religious activities.[17] The actual practice of the early Republic exhibited many and various friendly accommodations between the state and religious citizens that sharply distinguished the American way from the rigorous hostility Maritain had known in France. While the American Republic had no established church, the American state took a positive and benign attitude toward the full, free and quite visibly *public* exercise of religion, not least at major state functions and national celebrations. Moreover, the religion shown in such public exercises was not just "religion in general," but quite distinctively Protestant Christianity, albeit, typically, in a fairly nondenominational form. And this public choice was not a matter of mere reflex without argument on its behalf. Public figures and public documents widely asserted that *this* particular stream of religion was of decisive importance in the history of liberty and indispensable to its survival.

But the third feature of these founding documents is even more striking and profound. For it is quite stunning that the four documents in question depend for their *intelligibility* and their *credibility* upon a distinctively Jewish and Christian view of man's relation to God. The hinge of the argument in each document is a fact of Jewish and Christian faith: that each individual conscience stands in the presence of its Creator. Further, in virtue of having been created from nothing, each individual owes a primordial duty to her or his Creator. This duty is of so intimate a nature that no other person can perform it in that individual's stead. It is an *inalienable* duty, which can be taken up by no other.

This particular religious view is held by only two religions. It is not found in Buddhism nor in Hinduism; not in animism nor in pantheism; not in the religions of the ancient Greeks or Romans; nor in the religions of the Incas or the Mayans; and not even in that one other religion which also recognizes a Creator separate from the created world, Islam.

These other world religions are satisfied by outward obeisance. Do your duty, and no one inquires into what your secret thoughts may be. Since only outward ritual acts were demanded, not even the great Greek or Roman philosophers worried over the assent of conscience to the worship of the gods. By contrast, Jews and Christians trembled if asked to make outward obeisance to idols, for they recognized in that act a terrible sin of idolatry, forbidden by the Second Commandment.

Only Judaism and Christianity among all world religions developed, and still nourish and celebrate, the three central ideas necessary to the American conception of rights. Only they hold to the doctrine that *there is a Creator* (and Governor of the universe); that *each individual owes a personal accounting* to this Creator at the time of Judgment, a Judgment that is prior to all claims of civil society or state; and, third, that *this inalienable relation between each individual and his Creator occurs in the depths of conscience and reason,* and is not reached merely by external bows, bended knee, pilgrimages or other ritual observances.

To summarize: Jews and Christians conceive of the Creator as Spirit and Truth. The arena in which humans meet the Creator is, therefore, the inward conscience. The entire American theory of the foundation of natural rights hinges on this conception. Let us consider a few central passages in some detail.

The paragraph of the *Virginia Declaration of Rights* (1776) dealing with religion, paragraph 16, makes explicit its dependence on a distinctively Christian understanding of religion:

> That religion, or the duty which we owe to our Creator and the manner of discharging it, can be directed by only reason and conviction, not by force or violence; and therefore, all men are equally entitled to the free exercise of religion, according to the dictates of conscience; and that it is the mutual duty of all to practice Christian forbearance, love, and charity towards each other.

Thomas Jefferson's *Bill for Establishing Religious Freedom,* submitted in 1779 but not passed by the legislature until 1785, also picks up an explicitly Christian motif:

> Well aware that...*Almighty God hath created the mind free, and manifested his Supreme will that free it shall remain,* by making it altogether insusceptible of restraint: That all attempts to influence it by temporal punishments or burthens, or by civil incapacitations, tend only to beget habits of hypocrisy and meanness, and are a departure from *the plan of the holy author of our religion, who being Lord both of body and mind, yet chose* not to propagate it by coercions on either, as it was in his Almighty power to do, but to extend it by its influence on reason alone....

Then comes the operative paragraph:

> We the General Assembly of *Virginia* do enact, that no man shall be compelled to frequent or support any religious worship, place, or ministry whatsoever, nor shall be enforced, restrained, molested, or burthened in his body or goods, *nor shall otherwise suffer, on account of his religious opinions or belief;* but that all men shall be *free to profess, and by argument to maintain, their opinions in matters of religion,* and that the same shall in no wise diminish, enlarge, or affect their civil capacities.

Then, since no assembly can pass an irrevocable act that another assembly of equal powers cannot rescind, Jefferson's bill adds a deeper understanding of the ground of this act:

> we are free to declare, and do declare, that the rights hereby asserted are of the natural rights of mankind, and that if any act shall be hereafter passed to repeal the present, or to narrow its operation, such act will be an infringement of *natural right.*[18]

Thus, in the acts put forth by Mason and Jefferson, the concept of natural right is argued for in the language of Jewish and Christian belief about the Creator, who wishes to be worshiped in spirit and truth. For this God, the arena of conscience is sacred, in such wise that the duty and therefore the natural right of the individual who stands in that arena are also sacred. In that sacred space that stands between the individual and the Creator, no state, society, or other human person dares to intervene.

First Penn, Then Madison

William Penn of the Society of Friends first established religious liberty in the colonies and supplied the Christian rationale for it. In Penn's vision, Almighty God conceived of this universe we inhabit and brought it into being so that somewhere in it there would be at least one creature with whom He could establish friendship. And since God wished the friendship of free women and men, not slaves, He constituted human beings free. For Penn, friendship is the purpose of the universe, and friendship's necessary precondition is liberty:

> There can be no Friendship where there is no Freedom. Friendship loves a free Air, and will not be penned up in straight and narrow Enclosures. It will speak freely, and act so too; and take nothing ill where no ill is meant.[19]

Religious liberty was the first natural right that Penn recognized in his new colony – religious liberty for all.[20] One can see this metaphysical scheme behind the words of Mason and Jefferson in the two acts of the Virginia Assembly quoted above: "that all men are equally entitled to the free exercise of religion, according to the dictates of conscience; and that it is the mutual duty of all to practice Christian forbearance, love, and charity, towards each other."

Penn's scheme also lies behind Madison's eloquent *Remonstrance*, but Madison adds a deeper and more profound point, viz., that the relation of the intelligent creature and his Creator is not only inalienable in the sense that no one else may stand in for another, but also in the sense that this is a relation prior to all other relations, even those of civil society. Religious liberty, then, is not a natural right that comes into existence along with civil society. It is prior to civil society. It is rooted in nature itself, in the primordial relation of intelligent creature to Creator. In an astonishing tour de force, the young Madison goes beyond Locke and even deeper than Mason and Jefferson. His argument begins where Article 16 of the *Virginia Declaration of Rights* left off, and so he quotes directly from that text:

> Because we hold it for a fundamental and undeniable truth, "that Religion, or the duty which we owe to our Creator and the manner of discharging it, can be directed only by reason and conviction, not by force or violence." [*Virginia Declaration of Rights*, Art. 16] *The Religion then of every man must be left to the conviction and conscience of every man: and it is the right of every man to exercise* it as these may dictate. *This right is in its nature an unalienable right.* It is unalienable, *because the opinions of men, depending only on the evidence* contemplated by their own minds *cannot follow the dictates of other men: It is unalienable also, because what is here a right towards men, is a duty towards the Creator.* It is the duty of every man to render to the Creator such homage and such only as he believes to be acceptable to him. *This duty is precedent,* both in order of time and in degree of obligation, *to the claims of Civil Society. Before any man can be considered as a member of Civil Society, he must be considered a subject of the Governour of the Universe.*[21]

It is important to pause here and take in Madison's point. The relation of an individual to his Creator is precedent to his entering into civil society; it arises from nature itself. Yet this view of nature is in fact derivative from an expressly Christian understanding of the world expressed in philosophical rather than in exclusively theological or scriptural terms.[22] According to Madison, an individual by nature is "a subject of the Governour of the Universe." On that fact, deep and inviolable, his natural right is grounded as on a rock.

In paragraph 4, Madison next establishes the fundamental equality of all individuals, considered as subjects of the Governour of the Universe.

> If "all men are by nature equally free and independent," [*Virginia Declaration of Rights*, Art. 1] *all men are to be considered as entering into Society on equal conditions;* as relinquishing no more, and therefore retaining no less, one than another, of their natural rights. *Above all,* are they to be considered as retaining an "*equal* title to the free exercise of Religion according to the dictates of Conscience." [*Ibid.*] *Whilst we assert for ourselves a freedom to embrace, to profess and to observe the Religion which we believe to be of divine origin, we cannot deny an equal freedom* to those whose minds have not yet yielded to the evidence which has convinced us. *If this freedom be abused, it is an offence against God,* not against man: To God, therefore, not to man, must an account of it be rendered. [emphasis added]

In the next eleven paragraphs of the *Remonstrance*, Madison gives several expressly Christian arguments for the natural right of religious liberty. He calls Governor Henry's bill, against which he is remonstrating, "*a contradiction of the Christian religion itself*, for every page of it disavows a dependence on the powers of this world" [emphasis added]. Indeed the Christian church survived centuries of direct opposition by the mighty Roman Empire. "Nay, it is a contradiction in terms, *for a Religion not invented by human policy, must have pre-existed and been supported, before* it was established by human policy."[23] Note well Madison's description of Christianity: "a Religion not invented by human policy."

In paragraph 12, Madison declares that "the policy of the Bill is adverse to the diffusion of the light of Christianity. The first wish of those who enjoy this precious gift ought to be that it may be imparted to the whole race of mankind." But attempts to enforce Christian conscience have the reverse effect, dispelling seekers after truth in aversion and fear. In paragraph 15, Madison begins his ringing conclusion:

> Because finally, "the equal right of every citizen to the free exercise of religion according to the dictates of conscience" is held by the same tenure with all our other rights. If we recur to its origin, it is equally the gift of

nature; if we weigh its importance, it cannot be less dear to us; if we consult the "Declaration of those rights which pertain to the good people of Virginia, as the basis and foundation of Government," it is enumerated with equal solemnity, or rather studied emphasis.

Madison's *Remonstrance* denounces Governor Henry's assessments as a dangerous usurpation of a power which, according to natural right, the governor does not possess, and concludes with a prayer to Almighty God:

> earnestly praying, as we are in duty bound, that the Supreme Lawgiver of the Universe, by illuminating those to whom it is addressed, may on the one hand, turn their Councils from every act which would affront his holy prerogative, or violate the trust committed to them; and on the other, guide them into every measure which may be worthy of his blessing, may redound to their own praise, and may establish more firmly the liberties, the prosperity and the happiness of the Commonwealth. [emphasis added]

In brief, Madison visibly argues as a Christian, with the purest ideals of Christianity in mind, and with a view to his faith's flourishing. He does not argue as an atheist, materialist or apostate from Christianity. Quite the contrary.

Can followers of any other faith except the Jewish and the Christian make Madison's argument? It is obvious that no Muslim argument is yet available (although some day one might be), arguing on Islamic grounds the natural right of all persons, of whatever religious beliefs. If there exists a Buddhist or Hindu argument to this effect, let it be adduced. Madison's terms are specifically Christian and derived from Christian traditions.

Only Judaism and Christianity have a doctrine of God as Spirit and Truth, Who created the world in order to invite those creatures endowed with intelligence and conscience to enter into friendship with Him. Only the Jewish and Christian God made human beings free, halts the power of Caesar at the boundaries of the human soul, and has commissioned human beings to build civilizations worthy of the liberty He has bestowed on them. So high is *this* God's valuation of human liberty of conscience that, even though He has launched a divinely commissioned religion in history (in two covenants, Jewish and Christian), he would not have either of these religions imposed on anyone by force. ("The God who gave us life gave us liberty at the same time," Jefferson wrote.)[24] So devoted were the American founders to this understanding of religious liberty that, as Thomas Jefferson wrote in his *Autobiogra-phy* (1821), in the *Virginia Bill for Establishing Religious Freedom* they modestly held back from mentioning the exact name of the "holy author of our religion." Here is how he tells the story:

> Where the preamble declares, that coercion is a departure from the plan of the holy author of our religion, an amendment was proposed, by inserting the word "Jesus Christ," so that it should read, "a departure from the plan of Jesus Christ, the holy author of our religion"; the insertion was rejected by a great majority, in proof that they meant to comprehend, within the mantle of its protection, the Jew and the Gentile, the Christian and the Mahometan, the Hindoo, and Infidel of every denomination.[25]

Madison gives powerful Christian reasons for such forbearance. Alone among the religions of the world, Judaism and Christianity place so high a valuation upon religious liberty, because of their own doctrine that the relation God seeks with humans is friendship.

Summation

The explicitly Christian language of Madison, and the background of God-human relations on which it plainly draws, strongly suggest that as between Maritain and Berns, it is Maritain who is correct. While Madison's use of the Christian tradition employs a restricted, even chaste use of theological language – the name Jesus Christ is never mentioned, only "divine Author of our religion" – there can be no doubt that his worldview is no other than Christian. It is certainly not Kantian nor Hobbesian, not Greek nor Roman, not Voltairean. It is certainly not a full-blooded Thomist vision. On the other hand, it embraces too many theological elements to be merely secular, philosophical, or unbeliev-ing. It is neither rationalist nor relativist, and it is more than merely theist or, as the conventional jargon of historians puts it, "deist." In itself, while it does not affirm everything that orthodox Christian faith affirms, Madison's vision is sufficiently impregnated with Christian faith to be not only unconvincing, but *unintelligible* without it.

Some may assert that Madison's formulations may *appear* to be superficially Christian, while in reality standing as typical Enlighten-ment philosophizing. But one has only to compare them with texts from Rousseau, Voltaire and other secularist figures of the time to see how much Christian sentiment and metaphysics they embody in their simple, elegant statement of a man's duties in spirit and truth to his Creator. Although to my knowledge, he did not consider these classic Virginia texts in detail, neither citing nor quoting from them, nonetheless Maritain's judgment about the American founding seems utterly just, affirming only enough and not a word more than the facts require. Recall Maritain's words: *"The Constitution of this country is deep-rooted in the age-old heritage of Christian thought and civilization."* It is *"tinged with the philosophy of the day."* It is *"a lay – even, to some extent rationalist – fruit of the perennial Christian life-force."* Also:

> The Founding Fathers were neither metaphysicians nor theologians, but their philosophy of life, and their political philosophy, their notion of natural law and of human rights, were permeated with concepts worked out by Christian reason and backed up by an unshakeable religious feeling.[26]

Apart from Christian conceptions of a Creator Who asks to be worshiped in spirit and truth, and a Christian conception of the inner forum of inalienable conscience, George Mason's *Virginia Declaration of Rights*, Jefferson's *Bill for Establishing Religious Freedom*, and Madison's *Remonstrance* would lose all cogency and sense. These documents owe their derivation to a Jewish and Christian worldview, and do not spring naturally from any other.

Some Precisions

Some scholars insist that John Locke lies behind all the American references to natural right, and that Locke's intention with his formulation was to subordinate religion to the state once and for all. Three classic texts from Jefferson and/or Madison are deployed to support this interpretation. One text that my friend, teacher and colleague Walter Berns (not alone) sometimes emphasizes in Jefferson's *Bill for Establishing Religious Freedom* of 12 June 1779 is this one:

> ...that our civil rights have no dependence on our religious opinions, any more than our opinions in physics of geometry... [27]

This text is sometimes used to suggest that the right to religious liberty has no dependence on religious beliefs. However, the words that immediately follow indicate an altogether different meaning, viz., that our religious beliefs should never be the occasion for our losing civil rights. Here is the immediately following passage:

...that therefore the proscribing any citizen as unworthy the public confidence by laying upon him an incapacity of being called to offices of trust and emolument, unless he profess or renounce this or that religious opinion, is depriving him injuriously of those privileges and advantages to which in common with his fellow-citizens he has a natural right...

Jefferson's sole way of reaching the natural right to religious liberty was by way of his Jewish-Christian convictions about the nature of the Creator and the Creator's relation to men and women, whom He created to be free.

The second text that Berns and other scholars bring to bear is this one, in Berns' formulation:

Instead of establishing religion, the Founders established religious freedom, and the principle of religious freedom derives from a non-religious source. Rather than presupposing a Supreme Being, the institutions they established presuppose the rights of man, which were discovered by Hobbes and Locke to exist prior to all government – in the state of nature to be precise. To secure these rights, men must leave the state of nature, which they do by giving their consent to civil government. Nevertheless, the rights presuppose the state of nature, and the idea of the state of nature is incompatible with Christian doctrine. According to Christian doctrine, "the first and great commandment" is to love God, and the second, which is like unto it, is to love one's neighbor as oneself. In the state of nature, however, man is not obliged to love anyone, but merely to preserve himself and, what is more to the point, "to preserve the rest of mankind [only] when his own preservation comes not in competition."[28]

But five hundred years before the Declaration, Thomas Aquinas also pointed out that under natural law, the first moral obligation is self-preservation.[29] He even interpreted the Second Commandment in this light: One is instructed to love one's neighbor *as oneself*.[30] In other words, love for self is the prime analog for love of others, and a necessary condition for it. In addition, Christian writers have for centuries taken careful note of the way humans actually behave. Regularly, humans are proud, avaricious, addicted to "the world, the flesh, and the devil," and in practice every bit as selfish as Hobbes and Locke describe. Christian writers attribute this real state of affairs in the world to the flaws and wounds in human nature – i.e., original sin. On the everyday level, Christian realism is as pessimistic about humans as anything in Hobbes and Locke; yet it also glimpses, as the latter do not, the healthy possibilities in practical reason and the

occasional nobility made possible by God's grace, which they see as abundantly available to those who ask.

The third text that Berns and others cite hinges on their interpretation of "Nature's God." The God invoked by the Declaration, Berns writes,

> is "Nature's God," not, or arguably not, the God of the Bible, not the God whom, today, 43 percent of Americans (a number far exceeding that in any of the other Western democracies) claim regularly to worship on the Sabbath. Nature's God issues no commandments, no one can fall from his grace, and therefore, no one has reason to pray to him asking for his forgiveness; he makes no promises. On the contrary, he endowed us with "certain unalienable Rights," then left us alone, and with the knowledge, or at least the confidence, that he will never interfere in our affairs. Moreover, he is not a jealous god; he allows us – in fact, he endows us with the right – to worship other gods or even no god at all.[31]

But Berns forgets to mention that the Declaration contains three other names for God, and each of these is of specifically Jewish and Christian derivation. For hundreds of years, theologians had pointed out that although Aristotle, Plato, Cicero, Plotinus and other "pagan" philosophers had reached admirable notions of God, it was not open to reason, but only to revelation to grasp that the world had been created by a Creator, that humans were held to a strict accounting in the final judgment in the eyes of their Creator, and that the details of their lives and of all the affairs of men were governed by His Providence. In this way, just as the long theological tradition of several hundred years standing had done, the Declaration brought the God reached by reason alone, "Nature's God," to the family of notions associated solely with the God of revelation, Creator, Judge, and Providence.

APPENDIX

*I have already said enough to put Anglo-American
civilization in its true light. It is the product
(and one should continually bear in mind this point
of departure) of two perfectly distinct elements
which elsewhere have often been at war with
one another but which in America it was somehow
possible to incorporate into each other, forming
a marvelous combination. I mean the* spirit of
religion *and the* spirit of freedom.

—Alexis de Tocqueville

The Forgotten
Founders

What do we know about the lesser known signers of the Declaration and the Constitution, giving particular attention to two factors: their religious views, and the personal price some of them paid for signing the Declaration of Independence? Herewith a few notes to stimulate further researches.

Most Americans know only a few of the founders at all well; they have probably heard most about Washington, Adams, Jefferson, Franklin, and Madison. A handful of other names would come to their minds: Alexander Hamilton, Aaron Burr, Patrick Henry. One day it occurred to me that I knew remarkably little about George Mason, James Wilson, Benjamin Rush, Charles Pinckney, and a great many others whose names are prominent in the early debates about Independence and the Constitution. Consider, for instance, a list of the signers of the Declaration and a list of the signers of the Constitution. (There is surprisingly little overlap on these two lists; see next page.)

If we ask ourselves, What did the top hundred leaders of the founding generation think about reason and faith, not to mention about human nature and the essence of human liberty, we discover our own ignorance. Or at least I did. The investigations that follow are an attempt to understand the term "founders" in a larger universe than I was earlier accustomed to. Indeed, the term "founders" must at least include **all** those Americans who ratified by their actions the Declaration of Independence and the Constitution. What did they think about the basic questions of human nature and destiny, and the project of republican self-government?

Here is a test. How much do you know about each of the following?

Signers of Both the Declaration and the Constitution

George Clymer	Robert Morris	Roger Sherman
Benjamin Franklin	George Read	James Wilson

Signers of the Declaration of Independence

John Adams	William Hooper	John Penn
Samuel Adams	Stephen Hopkins	Caeser Rodney
Josiah Bartlett	Francis Hopkinson	George Ross
Carter Braxton	Samuel Huntington	Benjamin Rush
Charles Carroll	Thomas Jefferson	Edward Rutledge
Samuel Chase	Richard Henry Lee	James Smith
Abraham Clark	Francis Lightfoot Lee	Richard Stockton
William Ellery	Francis Lewis	Thomas Stone
William Floyd	Philip Livingston	George Taylor
Elbridge Gerry	Thomas Lynch, Jr.	Matthew Thornton
Button Gwinnett	Thomas M. McKean	George Walton
Lyman Hall	Arthur Middleton	William Whipple
John Hancock	Lewis Morris	William Williams
Benjamin Harrison	John Morton	John Witherspoon
John Hart	Thomas Nelson, Jr.	Oliver Wolcott
Joseph Hewes	William Paca	George Wythe
Thomas Heyward, Jr.	Robert Treat Paine	

Signers of the Constitution

Abraham Baldwin	Thomas FitzSimons	James McHenry
Richard Bassett	Nicholas Gilman	Thomas Mifflin
Gunning Bedford, Jr.	Nathaniel Gorham	Gouverneur Morris
John Blair	Alexander Hamilton	William Paterson
William Blount	Jared Ingersoll	Charles Pinckney
David Brearley	Daniel St. Thomas	Charles Cotesworth
Jacob Broom	Jenifer	Pinckney
Pierce Butler	William Samuel Johnson	John Rutledge
Daniel Carroll	Rufus King	Richard Dobbs
Jonathan Dayton	John Langdon	Spaight
John Dickinson	William Livingston	George Washington
William Few	James Madison, Jr.	Hugh Williamson

1. *A Secular Hurrah!*

To celebrate James Madison's 250th birthday, the Library of Congress
hosted a symposium attended by the country's most distinguished Madison scholars; the probing of Madison's religious views played a
significant role. Afterward, one noted scholar told me that since he was
himself a secular man, "The more secular Madison's position turns out,
the more I cheer." For him, I suppose, "secular" means good, progressive, forward-looking. So, yes, the fitting response is *hurrah*. "Religion"
may be linked to intolerant, divisive, backward, dying, passé. That suggests at least a quiet *boo*.

In this vein, the concentration of historians and political theorists
on the least religious of the founders makes perfect sense. Why highlight
what is least relevant to the future? The three figures of the founding era
most studied nowadays are the figures regarded as the least religious:
Jefferson, Madison, and Franklin. That there is such a concentration
is not in dispute; it characterizes some Straussians on the right as well as
mainline academics on the left.

By contrast, Madison's two companions in writing *The Federalist*, John Jay and Alexander Hamilton, are relatively little studied. Even
though John Adams was the man most admired of the age as the Father
of Independence, the preeminent parliamentarian, and the leading
jurist of constitutional law and history, he has today been almost forgotten. About John Dickinson, George Mason, Benjamin Rush, James
Wilson, Sam Adams, John Witherspoon and other first-class minds we
have been taught very little. For most of these important leaders, worthy biographies are not available, and their writings go relatively
unstudied.

2. *Sherman, Williams, Williamson, R. T. Paine, Paca, Morris*

Virtually all the signers of the Declaration and Constitution were
churchgoing men. Several were ministers or chaplains, others had
trained to become ministers, and still others were conspicuously learned
in religion. Of the 56 signers of the Declaration, 34 were Anglican, 13
Congregationalist (once known as Puritans), 6 Presbyterian, and one
each Baptist, Catholic and Quaker.[1] The proportions regarding the
Constitution were nearly the same.[2]

A man who had roomed with Alexander Hamilton wrote of having admired the latter's habit of dropping to his knees to pray before
retiring, and the seriousness of his religious reading and his replies to
objections to his faith.[3] The son of Jonathan Edwards, also a distinguished clergyman, wrote of Roger Sherman of Connecticut, who was an
active participant in two congregations, that "he could with reputation
to himself and improvement to others converse on the most important
subjects of theology. I confess myself to have been often entertained,
and in the general course of my long and intimate acquaintance with him
to have been much improved by his observations on the principal subjects of doctrinal and practical divinity."[4]

William Williams of Connecticut entered Harvard at sixteen and
after graduation devoted himself to the study of theology for several
years. Hugh Williamson of North Carolina studied medicine at Edinburgh, London, and Utrecht before becoming a licenced Presbyterian
preacher, but was never ordained. Robert Treat Paine served as a chaplain to the troops of Massachusetts Bay. William Paca of Maryland,
having become Governor after the War, addressed the Maryland Assembly with these words: "The sufferings of the ministers of the gospel of
all denominations, during the war, have been very considerable; and the
perseverance and firmness of those who discharged their sacred functions   under   many   discouraging   circumstances,   claim   our
acknowledgments and thanks."[5] As happened in many states, the legislature made financial provision for the support of the several
denominations in Maryland. The legislators of Maryland, like the governor, were "thoroughly convinced of the powerful influence of religion"
upon "the happiness and welfare of our people."[6]

Throughout the new states, the opinion was universal – save only
in the case of Madison[7] – that religion added to the resources available
to reason powerful new motives for learning good moral habits, and for
this important reason, among others, religion had indispensable civic
utility. This utility did not detract from the transcendent good of religion in and of itself, but it did offer practical reasons why governments
should not be careless in its assistance.

Thus, Gouverneur Morris of Pennsylvania, who spoke more frequently (173 times) than anyone else at the Constitutional Convention,
especially on the subject of the untrustworthiness of human reason and
morals, voiced the most common sentiment of all the founders when he

wrote in his "Notes on the Form of a Constitution for France:" "Religion is the only solid basis of good morals; therefore education should teach the precepts of religion, and the duties of man toward God.... But each one has a right to entire liberty as to religious opinions, for religion is the relation between God and man; therefore, it is not within the reach of human authority."[8] Morris's two almost universally shared principles, that religious liberty is equally a natural right of every man (given the sacredness of the creature's duties to his Creator) and that neither human nature alone nor reason alone is a dependable support for moral life in a republic, are the distinctive marks of the American mind in the founding period. The first principle went beyond Locke in its grounding for natural rights, and the second marked a distinct chasm between American realism and the "idle theories" of human perfectability then sweeping Europe.[9]

3. *Alexander Hamilton*

With a realism equal to that of Morris, Alexander Hamilton once wrote in a letter, "Nothing is more fallacious than to expect to produce any valuable or permanent results in political projects by relying merely on the reason of men. Men are rather reasoning than reasonable animals, for the most part governed by the impulse of passion."[10] He had written in the same vein in *Federalist No. 15:*

> There was a time when we were told that breaches, by the States, of the regulations of the federal authority were not to be expected; that a sense of common interest would preside over the conduct of the respective members, and would beget a full compliance with all the constitutional requisitions of the Union. This language, at the present day, would appear as wild as a great part of what we now hear from the same quarter will be thought, when we shall have received further lessons from that best oracle of wisdom, experience. It at all times betrayed an ignorance of the true springs by which human conduct is actuated, and belied the original inducements to the establishment of civil power. Why has government been instituted at all? Because the passions of men will not conform to the dictates of reason and justice, without constraint. Has it been found that bodies of men act with more rectitude or greater disinterestedness than individuals? The contrary of this has been inferred by all accurate observers of the conduct of mankind; and the inference is founded upon obvious reasons. Regard to reputation has a less active influence, when the infamy of a bad action is to be divided among a number than when it is to fall singly upon one. A spirit of

faction, which is apt to mingle its poison in the deliberations of all bodies of men, will often hurry the persons of whom they are composed into improprieties and excesses, for which they would blush in a private capacity.[11]

On the other side of man's nature, however, Hamilton saw brilliant light: "The sacred rights of mankind are not to be rummaged for among old parchments or musty records. They are written, as with a sunbeam, in the whole volume of human nature, by the hand of Divinity itself, and can never be erased or obscured by mortal power."[12] It is not to be forgotten that Hamilton, who had served with Washington as an artillery commander since the tender age of nineteen, also drafted President Washington's classic and justly famous "Farewell Address," with its eloquent recognitions both of the noble and ignoble sides of human nature.

I recall being stunned when I first read of Alexander Hamilton's tender requests that the Holy Eucharist might be brought to him on his death bed. I had heard much of his hardheadedness; I had not heard of his piety. At an early age, Hamilton lay dying from the festering wound suffered in his one-sided duel with Aaron Burr.[13] Bishop Moore at first refused his request for the sacrament, lest the solemnity of the Eucharist be diminished by the scandal of dueling. On the second day, moved by Hamilton's humble pleading and tender piety, the bishop brought the Eucharist, much to Hamilton's joy.[14] Nothing in the standard portraits of Hamilton had prepared me for this scene. I had not earlier encountered, either, the tenderness of the religious convictions expressed in this last of his letters:

> This letter, my dear Eliza, will not be delivered to you, unless I shall first have terminated my earthly career, to begin, as I humbly hope, from redeeming grace and divine mercy, a happy immortality. If it had been possible for me to have avoided the interview, my love for you and my precious children would have been alone a decisive motive. But it was not possible, without sacrifices which would have rendered me unworthy of your esteem. I need not tell you of the pangs I fell from the idea of quitting you, and exposing you to the anguish I know you would feel. Nor could I dwell on the topic, lest it should unman me. The consolations of religion, my beloved, can alone support you; and these you have a right to enjoy. Fly to the bosom of your God, and be comforted. With my last idea I shall cherish the sweet hope of meeting you in a better world. Adieu, best of wives – best of women. Embrace all my darling children for me.[15]

4. *Princeton's John Witherspoon*

Still another figure loomed larger in my imagination, once I began reading widely about the religious views of the forgotten founders. In 1768,
after much pleading by separate delegations of distinguished Americans,
the Reverend John Witherspoon, a Presbyterian professor of religion in
Glasgow, at last agreed to come to America to accept the presidency
of the newly founded College of New Jersey at Princeton.[16] The
Presbyterians were a dissenting church, opposed to the Anglican Establishment, but there were already some five-hundred Presbyterian
congregations around the country. The young Witherspoon was a first-
class scholar, a learned and eloquent preacher, and a teacher
compelling enough to induce James Madison to stay on for an extra year
to plumb the deep connection between civil and religious liberty and to
study Hebrew (the better to read the Bible). The lesson Witherspoon
wanted graduates of Princeton to grasp was that all other rights spring
from one source: the dignity of the free decisions each individual must
make in the presence of the Creator. These decisions can be made by
no one else but that individual, and in that precise sense are inalienable;
made in God's presence, they are sacred. Because they are linked to all
other decisions, they are also full of implications for civil society. Witherspoon's grasp of both biblical history and church history was so firm
that he could illustrate this connection, age after age, in context after
context until the young Madison could grasp the historical power of the
proposition, as well as the philosophical.

It was a matter of principle to Witherspoon not to speak of politics
in his sermons. He had few beliefs deeper than that church should not
mix in state matters, nor state in church, lest the two liberties – civil
and religious – do harm to one another. His greatest jealousy was on the
side of divinity; he wished to preserve the purity and integrity of the
gospel. When the devout Christian meets his duties to civil society, he
should do so with honor, integrity and jealousy for the purity of religion.

On his arrival in America, Witherspoon scoffed at idle talk about
independence and rebellion. He cherished the British traditions of
rights and liberties. Gradually, however, particularly after the misbe-
gotten interventions of the king in Massachusetts in 1774, Witherspoon

came to judge that the king was too far from America to grasp its reality fairly, and by wrong and destructive misjudgments was undercutting
his legitimacy as a just ruler. Inexorably, Witherspoon was drawn
toward the cause of Independence.

With much trepidation but firm resolve, he was finally moved to
preach publicly on the subject in May of 1776, choosing as his theme
how Providence acts in the affairs of men, often taking away the
strengths of the powerful, and instructing the weak in the necessity of
uncommon virtue and brotherly unity. The powerful are often brought
down by their own actions, and the weak raised up beyond their deserts.
He cited instances from the history of the first Israel (it was common to
think of America as the second).

As we have noted in chapter two above, there has rarely been a
more influential professor in American history. Besides being the
teacher of one President (Madison, B.A. 1771) and one Vice-President
(Burr, B.A. 1772), Witherspoon was a delegate to the Continental Congress, a signer of the Declaration of Independence, a member of three
standing committees during the Revolutionary War and of more than
one-hundred-and-twenty Congressional committees.[17] He was often
chosen by his colleagues to be the draftsman of important congressional
decrees. After the war, Witherspoon later became an active champion of
New Jersey's ratification of the federal Constitution.

Witherspoon's learning, his authority, and his bearing brought the
Congress weightiness, sobriety, wisdom, and courage. He was a tower
of strength to his younger colleagues. In paintings and stained-glass win-
dows of the early founders, his is a distinctive presence. No university
president since, not even Wilson at Princeton or Eisenhower at Columbia, has played so great a role in shaping this nation's character.

5. Livingston, King, and Henry

Some of the signers were troubled in their Anglicanism because of its
persecution of dissidents such as the Baptists of Virginia, or because of
its ties to England in a time of Independence, or because of its establishment or its too Catholic liturgy. On the other side, the stricter forms
of Calvinism created intellectual crises for several of the signers, in some
cases because of too severe a castigation of the powers of reason, in
other cases because of too inflexible and forbidding a notion of predestination, in still others cases because of too severely literal a reading of

Scripture or too constrained an insistence on "Scripture Alone." Serious study and intelligent discussion of religious matters among intelligent laymen was far more common in those days than in ours. Thus, for instance, William Livingston of New Jersey, in whose home Alexander Hamilton lived for some time as a youth, made a name for himself among Calvinists by correcting those among his followers who interpreted predestination to imply dependence on "a superior and irresistible agency," which reduced them to "mere machines, void of intelligence and free volition." He insisted that Calvinists must be governors of their own lives, take hold of their capacities for moral direction, positively choosing against evil and for good.[18] His influence on behalf of robust activism was quite marked. A member of the Continental Congress, a signer of the Declaration, he took command of the New Jersey Militia in 1776, and then was elected Governor of the new state, in which capacity he served until his death in 1790.[19]

Rufus King of New York was one of those who left the Congregational Church for the Anglican, becoming warden at St. Paul's Episcopal Church right in the teeth of the War, in 1782. Like the others, he thought religion the foundation of social stability, essential to strengthening moral conduct throughout the society and a source of personal strength in adversity. His reputation as an active Christian layman was such that he was asked to join the board of the American Bible Society; he strongly approved of its work, but declined at that time.[20]

After nasty public attacks on his character, Patrick Henry once wrote to his daughter as follows:

> Amongst other strange things said of me, I hear it is said by the Deists that I am one of their number; and indeed, that some good people think I am no Christian. This thought gives me much more pain than the appellation of Tory; because I think religion of infinitely higher importance than politics; and I find much cause to reproach myself that I have lived so long, and have given no decided and public proofs of my being a Christian. But, indeed, my dear child, this is a character which I prize far above all this world has, or can boast.[21]

6. Rush, Dickinson, and Wilson

Three overlooked stars from Benjamin Franklin's Pennsylvania are John Dickinson, Benjamin Rush, and James Wilson. John Dickinson was an avid reader in history and law. His commonplace books show a wide-ranging mind, devouring authors from Tacitus to Blackstone. In the midst of eminent colleagues, he dared to write, not without reason, that he had "acquired a greater knowledge in history, and the laws and constitution of my country than is generally attained by men in my class."[22] Worried by encroachments of British arrogance in the colonies, he became an outspoken champion of freedom. He even composed a drinking ballad, whose rousing chorus went as follows:

> In Freedom we're born and in freedom we'll live,
> Our right arms are ready,
> Steady, men, Steady.
> Not as slaves but as freemen, our lives we will give.[23]

The freedoms he loved came not from brute nature: "We claim them from a higher source, from the King of Kings and Lord of all the earth. They are not annexed to us by parchments and seals. They are created in us by a decree of Providence which established the laws of our nature.... They are founded in the immutable maxims of reason and justice."[24] He knew, however, that liberty is a fragile gift, easily lost through lassitude: "Slavery is ever preceded by sleep."[25] In 1776, John Dickinson, faithful both to his instructions and to his Quaker convictions, didn't sign the Declaration of Independence, but then went home and formed a company of militia to lead into battle in support of General Washington.

Like several others of the signers, Rush first wished to study for the ministry before choosing his final profession, medicine. Despite the primitive condition of medical knowledge in his time, which led him into some fearfully mistaken practices (with fateful consequences during Philadelphia's serious epidemics), Rush and his assistants proved themselves heroes in ministering to the stricken multitudes even at great danger to themselves.[26] Dr. Rush was reputed to be the single most learned man in the colonies, working at the frontiers of medical investigations and the systematic researches just then being made in Europe (where he regularly went to study), but he had to compete for that honor with two of his most steady correspondents, John Adams and Thomas Jefferson. Like the other Pennsylvanians, Rush was outshone by the polymath genius, geniality and international fame of Benjamin Franklin. But while Franklin was abroad representing the fledgling nation in London and Paris, Rush and the others were carrying on the governance of the crucial war, whose outcome would determine whether they would all hang as traitors or live as free men.

Rush was a physician, but his mind ranged far into philosophical, religious, and civic matters, and he corresponded with like-minded persons both in Europe and here. In his shrewdly chosen texts from the founders, *Our Sacred Honor*, William Bennett cites a marvelous passage from Rush's tract (1773) condemning the practice of slavery. This passage foretold of an impending tragedy, and artlessly revealed both philosophical and religious grounds for the doctrine of natural rights:

> Ye men of sense and virtue – *Ye advocates for American liberty*, rouse up and *espouse the cause of humanity and general liberty. Bear a testimony* against a vice which degrades human nature, and dissolves that *universal tie* of benevolence which should connect all the children of men together in one great family. – *The plant of liberty is of so tender a nature, that it cannot thrive long in the neighbourhood of slavery.* Remember the eyes of all Europe are fixed upon you, to preserve *an asylum for freedom in this country*, after the last pillars of it are fallen in every other quarter of the globe.
>
> But *chiefly – ye ministers of the gospel*, whose dominion over the principles and actions of men is so universally acknowledged and felt, – Ye who *estimate the worth of your fellow creatures by their immortality*, and *therefore must look upon all mankind as equal*; – let your zeal keep pace with your opportunities to *put a stop to slavery*. While you inforce [*sic*] the duties of "tithe and cummin," neglect not the weightier laws of justice and humanity. Slavery is an Hydra sin, and includes in it every violation of the precepts of the Laws and the Gospels.[27] [emphasis added]

All the founders believed that the impulse to vindicate natural rights is born, like our knowledge of our rights itself, in religious faith. Obviously, the founders had in mind Jewish and Christian faith; yet, they also held, as Benjamin Rush points out, that the opinions even "of Confucius or Mahomed" are to be preferred to atheism. The murderous atheism of the French Revolution confirmed even Tom Paine in this view after 1789, but most had cherished it from the beginning. They may have been shaky about orthodox Protestant doctrines, but they were solid in seeing the ground of rights, morals, and republican principles in the Old Testament and New. As Rush explained:

> [T]he only foundation for a useful education in a republic is to be laid in Religion. Without this there can be no virtue, and without virtue there can be no liberty, and liberty is the object and life of all republican governments.

Such is my veneration for every religion that reveals the attributes of the Deity, or a future state of rewards and punishments, that I had rather see the opinions of Confucius or Mahomed inculcated upon our youth, than see them grow up wholly devoid of a system of religious principles. But the religion I mean to recommend in this place is that of the New Testament.

It is foreign to my purposes to hint at the arguments which establish the truth of the Christian revelation. My only business is to declare, that all its doctrines and precepts are calculated to promote the happiness of society and the safety and well being of civil government. *A Christian cannot fail of being a republican. The history of the creation of man, and of the relation of our species to each other by birth, which is recorded in the Old Testament, is the best of refutation that can be given to the divine rights of kings, and the strongest argument that can be used in favor of the original and natural equality of mankind.* A Christian, I say again, cannot fail of being a republican, for every precept of the Gospel inculcates those degrees of humility, self-denial, and brotherly kindness, which are directly opposed to the pride of monarchy and the pageantry of a court. A Christian cannot fail of being useful to the republic, for his religion teacheth him, that no man "liveth to himself." And lastly, a Christian cannot fail of being wholly inoffensive, for his religion teacheth him, in all things to do others what he would wish, in like circumstances, they should do to him.[28] [emphasis added]

His biographer draws the following portrait: "Piety to God was an eminent trait in the character of Dr. Rush. In all his printed works, and in all his private transactions, he expressed the most profound respect and veneration for the great Eternal." Both by words and in deeds "he expressed his reverence for the Divine character. It was his usual practice to close the day by reading to his collected family a chapter in the Bible, and afterwards by addressing his Maker in prayer, devoutly acknowledging his goodness for favors received, and imploring his continued protection and blessing." His respect for Jehovah led him to respect His ministers, at least those who acted consistently with their high calling. "He considered their office of the greatest importance to society, both in this world and that which is to come." He strengthened their hand, and was always ready and willing to support them in building churches for propagating the gospel. In an address to ministers of every denomination Rush was very practical about religion: "If there were no hereafter, individuals and societies would be great gainers by attending public worship every Sunday. Rest from labor in the house of God winds up the machine of both soul and body better than anything else, and thereby invigorates it for the labors and duties of the ensuing week."²⁹

Of all the founders, however, the one who thought most deeply about the law, particularly the connection between the *legislation* passed by human assemblies and the *law* which the Creator intended for human communities – the law of nature, that is, the law for *humans* in nature, which is different from the law for other animals – was James Wilson of Pennsylvania. Wilson wrote well and at length about the law, particularly in its deeper dimensions in philosophy and religious thought. Like Blackstone, Wilson saw the Ten Commandments as the Ur-text from which the common law proceeds, and recognized that Anglo-Saxon law shares the same assumptions about human liberty, individuality, and community as those set forth in the Holy Scriptures. He actually entered the seminary until his studies there were interrupted by his father's death, after which he turned to the law. Born a Presbyterian in Scotland, Wilson became an Anglican near the end of the War of Independence, as a kind of middle way between the strict emphasis on Scripture he had known as a boy and the emphasis on reason favored by the deists. The writings of Aquinas and Hooker on the sources of the law were especially dear to him.³⁰

The paintings in the Sistine Chapel systematically juxtapose four eras of legal history: the Greek and Roman lawgivers, the Law of the Torah, the New Law of Christ and the era of the Renaissance with which the paintings were contemporaneous. In accord with this tradition, like the rest of the founders, Wilson spontaneously understood the concept *law* as an analogous concept, with slightly different but related meanings in each of these cultural contexts. When the American people pay respect to the one word *law*, they do so with associations learned in all of these other contexts. These associations impose a heavy burden on human legislators, who in the writing of just and impartial laws labor to reconcile various competing moral demands. Just because a particular decree becomes by due process duly accepted *legislation*, it does not follow that it lives up to all the associations expected of *law* in its many rich and various contexts of reflection. Where a particular decree falls short, legislators must expect criticism and resistance. For instance, the arguments for American Independence rested on findings that the decrees of King George fell short of the due respect for law. Americans were thus quite critical about existing laws — some met their exacting tests, and some didn't. The distance between *legislation* and *law* is at least as great as that between intended aim and imperfect result.

Until recently, Wilson's work has been woefully understudied. Even in producing his new study of Wilson's thought, Mark David Hall was obliged to note how few earlier studies he found to fall back upon.[31] Moreover, some of the early modern, medieval and classical writers on whom Wilson drew are not as well known to contemporary scholars as they were to the founders. To grasp the full meaning of Wilson's allusions and citations would require of us the gradual recreation of that core knowledge.

7. *The Three Catholic Cousins*

No men and women in America had as much reason to be grateful for the Declaration and the Constitution as the Catholics of Maryland, led by Charles Carroll of Carrollton and his cousins Daniel and John of Rock Creek.[32] After the Glorious Revolution of British Protestants in 1688, the Marylanders who had founded Maryland as a Catholic colony with religious liberty for all found the last of their own rights stripped away from them. They were forbidden to hold public office, exercise the franchise, educate their children in the Catholic faith, and worship in public. For generations, therefore, the Carrolls had to send their sons to France for a Catholic education.

All these humiliating and restrictive covenants in Maryland dissolved with the new regime that entered after the Declaration. Through his writing in the newspapers, as well as through his great family wealth (perhaps the greatest in America) and his connections through marriage with the Carters and the Lees of Virginia, Charles Carroll was a friend to George Washington and during the War his ardent defender and important financial supporter of his troops. When Washington's men were low in morale at Valley Forge, Charles was the strongest voice at the Board of War for keeping Washington on, and turning aside the effort to replace him with General Horatio Gates. At another crucial moment, Washington sent Charles and John Carroll on a delegation (with Benjamin Franklin and Samuel Chase) to French Catholic Canada, seeking support for the American cause. The immediate effort failed, but the fame of Franklin and the rapport of the Carrolls with their Catholic confreres helped to establish the warm relations that led to assistance from the French fleet in later years.

Charles was a signer of the Declaration – the only one identified thereon by his property's name, "Charles Carroll of Carrollton" – and Daniel was a signer of the Constitution, along with another Catholic, Thomas FitzSimons of Pennsylvania. The top priority that Charles Carroll voiced in his conversations with Washington about the form of government that the colonies ought to form was "no religious test" for public office. He had been mightily irked that even with his talents and energy he had long been barred from public service, as had many other Catholics. Charles lived until 1832, the last of the signers of the Declaration to die, and full of honors at the ripe age of 95.

It was Daniel, at the constitutional convention, who formulated the presumption that the powers not formally delegated to the federal government were reserved to the people, and who helped put in words the limitation of the powers of the federal government. He was elected to the First Congress of the United States and to the Senate of Maryland, and President Washington appointed him one of the three governors of the new Federal City, later named Washington, D.C. Daniel's brother John became a Jesuit, was ordained a priest in Europe, and was then elected by the relatively few priests in the territory of the United States the first American-born bishop, and given the See of Baltimore (which in those days embraced a very large territory, including what is now the District of Columbia). In 1789, he founded the first college of Georgetown University. When the Vatican, according to the protocols required in Europe, asked the consent of the new American government to the imminent designation of John Carroll as Archbishop of Baltimore, U.S. officials were at first flummoxed. Finally, though, when they returned the request to the Vatican, they stated that there was no office in the United States empowered to consider such an issue, since on this side of the ocean the free exercise of religion prevails. The Vatican was pleasantly shocked, and took note.[33]

Catholics seldom receive credit for the regime of religious liberty they established in Maryland at its founding in 1634, nor notice for the abrogation of their rights under Protestant arms in 1649 and 1689, after the imposition of the new repression in Britain. Nonetheless, by 1776, the Carrolls had already achieved a certain fame for their strong convictions about religious liberty and the rights of conscience, both in private actions and in public worship, and also for their strong convictions about the consent of the governed as the sole legitimate source of political power. On these points, they had such writers as Thomas Aquinas, the medieval canonists described by Brian Tierney in his recent studies, and Francisco Suárez to draw upon – sources antedating Sidney and Locke.[34] No regime in Europe had yet found a way to realize the full force of these principles in practical institutions. But as the Carrolls saw it, such principles were rooted in a soundly elaborated philosophy of human nature and destiny, and had been gathering strength and precision from bitter experiences and energetic arguments during many centuries.

8. *George Mason*

George Mason of Virginia was steeped in the history and philosophy of British liberties, rights, and the common law. In England these grew out of the same soil as the Roman Catholic tradition, with the advantage of separation from the rest of the Continent, outside the orbit of ancient Roman Law which was abstract and logical. The common law (and the English habit of mind) had a distinctive love for the concrete, the tried and true, the tacit and the commonsensical. Just as the Latin tradition favored the abstract, the general, the clear and distinct idea, geometric logic, and argument from the top down, so the Continental mind loves the clarity of general principles. By contrast, the English mind proceeds rather like Sherlock Holmes and a large fictional universe of similarly sleuthing detectives in close search for the unique circumstance and the singular clue. In the Anglo-Saxon spirit, "Mason knew the strengths and weaknesses of the ancient republics as well as he knew the strengths and weaknesses" of his own field hands, writes his biographer. "He had charted his way so thoroughly through English constitutional history that every significant precedent was recorded in his mind as a guidepost for future reference. He had become convinced, as hours and days had melted into months of study, that there was a kind of *natural* law at work in this world that, if made a matter of practice, would surely put an end to the bondage" of the past.[35]

It was time, Mason believed in the early 1770s, to push the British Constitution beyond its previous limits and bring it closer to the ideal already emerging more clearly precedent by precedent, experience by experience, from the recesses in which it had been written in nature. For Mason, the true shape of law is an ideal form, an *ought*, which dwells inside the seed, shoots forth inside the tender shoot, expands in the first young plant, and blooms in the maturing and carefully pruned and nurtured bush, which the skilled gardener slowly brings to its highest form of perfection. But of course no metaphor taken from other departments of nature ever quite expresses the full complexity of *human* nature. For *each* human being has been endowed by its Creator with an inalienable capacity for *reflecting* and *choosing*. Each human being has an internal *self*-determining principle. This unique capacity of human nature evokes awe, wonder, and respect. It is not too much to speak of its interior space for action as *sacred*.

Ought, says his biographer, is Mason's key word, which runs through his draft of the Virginia Declaration of Rights. Governments *ought* to respect the unique capacities, responsibilities, dignities and rights of individuals. Individuals are the *ends*. Thus, Mason's declaration opens with a strong statement: All men are by nature free and have certain basic rights that cannot be tampered with, including "the enjoyment of life and liberty, with the means *of acquiring and possessing* property, and pursuing and obtaining happiness and safety" (emphasis added).[36] Protecting these is the true end of government.

The spirit and even the phrasing of Algernon Sidney and John Locke seep through many lines of Mason's declaration. But it is also true that he goes beyond them, as when Mason goes beyond Locke's stress on the mere *ownership* of property to mention a distinctively American experience: the experience (and the right) of *acquiring* property, especially on the part of those not well-born. In this Mason even anticipates, by some months, Adam Smith's identification of that natural law in the human breast by which humans yearn to "better their condition." This capacity had been overlooked for centuries even by very great philosophers of nature. In the land of opportunity, the unfolding of this capacity was a powerful reality.

But it is no doubt in its emphasis on the first of all rights, the right to liberty of conscience, the right which a man experiences in the presence of the Almighty, that Mason's declaration achieves its deepest originality. The American experience begins in a profound respect for the space not occupied by an established church, in the inviolable and inalienable arena of the decision-making of the individual soul before

God. As such, this experience leads beyond the virtue of *tolerance* to a more profound virtue, as President Washington was later to point out in his letter to the Hebrew congregation of Newport: not just to tolerate, but to *respect* the consciences of others.[37] As God respects every individual conscience, so must we.

In much of its phrasing, Mason's declaration anticipates the Declaration of Independence and the Constitution. This fact helps to verify Jefferson's confession that his own Declaration was not original but stated the common sense of the matter as it was widely understood in all the colonies.[38] Mason's biographer points out how much of Mason's language grew out of the earlier English heritage and a newer American vexation with abuses of power. "Colonial householders had seen their doors forced open by Crown agents who arrested and ransacked without legal authority. High-handed army officers had contemptuously flouted civil authority. Some of these grievances Virginians had personally experienced," while others they knew from the press and from letters that arrived from friends in sister colonies.[39] George Mason receives all too little credit for his originality, forcefulness, and intellectual leadership. His ideas are far too little studied, especially in our current understanding of constitutional principles.

9. *Thomas Paine*

Yet it was not only Catholics or devout Anglicans who saw the source of rights of conscience in God; this was true also of those few, like Tom Paine, who rejected the Bible and the common doctrines of Christianity and was therefore often called an atheist, but who believed devoutly in God and even in some form or other of eternal punishment or reward. So strongly did Paine believe this that he rushed to France after 1789, where, appalled by the rivers of blood flowing from the guillotine, and at the cost of being sent to prison himself, he campaigned vigorously against atheism. Paine could not see how one could deny the existence of God without taking away the foundation of human rights. In the libertinism with which the atheistic Jacobins violated the most basic rights of tens of thousands of their victims, he saw proof of the connection between atheism and the disappearance of rights.

"In my publications on religious subjects," Paine wrote some years after the prison term in France during which he completed *The Age of*

Reason, "my endeavors have been directed to bring man to a right use of the reason that God has given him; to impress on him the great principles of divine morality, justice, and mercy, and a benevolent disposition to all men, and to all creatures; and to inspire in him a spirit of trust, confidence and consolation in his Creator, unshackled by the fables of books pretending to be the word of God."[40]

From this passage, one can see, in retrospect, how much of Judaism and Christianity lingers in Paine's *Theophilanthropy*, as he called his new credo, his "Love of God and man." *The Age of Reason* was denounced by orthodox Protestant preachers in America because of its renunciation of the Bible, but Catholics, although dismayed by its simplistic attack on biblical literalism, found in it a familiar, if flawed, attempt at "natural theology," that is, that part of knowledge of God which can be discovered through reason alone (a branch of philosophy dear to many Jesuits of that era). Deist societies throughout America distributed Paine's manifesto broadly and with enthusiasm.

"I believe in one God, and no more," Paine wrote smartly at the beginning of *The Age of Reason*, "and I hope for happiness beyond this life. I believe in the equality of man; and I believe that religious duties consist in doing justice, loving mercy, and endeavoring to make our fellow-creatures happy." Then, lest one begin to think that Paine is really still a Protestant Christian, as these words about justice and mercy and fellow-feeling suggest, he immediately clarifies: "I do not believe in the creed professed by the Jewish Church, by the Roman Church, by the Greek Church, by the Turkish Church, by the Protestant Church, nor by any church that I know of. My own mind is my own church."[41]

Some years later, Paine described his philosophy this way: "The study of natural philosophy is a divine study, because it is the study of the works of God in the creation. If we consider theology upon this ground, what an extensive field of improvement in things both divine and human opens itself before us!" He goes on: "All the principles of science are of divine origin. It was not man that invented the principles on which astronomy, and every branch of mathematics, are founded and studied."[42] By 1797, Paine's battle against biblical Christians was known worldwide, but his new battle, as he told the Paris Society of Theophilanthropists, was against atheism:

> Religion has two principal enemies, fanaticism and infidelity, or that which is called atheism. The first requires to be combated by reason and morality,

the other by natural philosophy…. The existence of a God is the first dogma of the Theophilanthropists…. The universe is the bible of a true Theophilanthropist…. It is there that he reads of God. It is there that the proofs of his existence are to be sought and found.[43]

In 1807, Paine published another pamphlet, in which he included a short passage entitled *My Private Thoughts on a Future State*, which began as follows:

I have said, in the first part of *The Age of Reason*, that "I hope for happiness after this life." This hope is comfortable to me, and I presume not to go beyond the comfortable idea of hope, with respect to a future state. I consider myself in the hands of my Creator, and that He will dispose of me after this life consistently with His justice and goodness. I leave all these matters to Him, as my Creator and friend, and I hold it to be a presumption in man to make an article of faith as to what the Creator will do with us hereafter.[44]

Paine hardly seems to be aware of how much of his new credo he owes, not to reason, but to the words of Jesus Christ. Neither the Greeks nor Romans of the ancient world knew of "the Creator," nor of a divine justice and mercy, nor of eternal life, nor that God called them to be His friends. Far more than he recognized, Paine relied still on a Christian metaphysics, a Christian view of the cosmos and human destiny.

In real life, he certainly preferred to turn with robust hope toward assisting his fellow citizens to build up a more civilized city of reason, liberty, and rights. He knew from painful experience that the city he aspired to would be a modest city, no doubt faulty, even if true to its own best intuitions. In this vision, Paine participated willy-nilly in a Jewish and Christian hope in the friendliness of the Creator and Governor of all things, Who gave humans reason, and placed them in a time of suffering and trial. His own many afflictions Paine endured bravely, and died in poverty and without any monument to his name, in 1809. No one can deny Paine's commitment to liberty and rights, and his consistency in throwing his own safety against abuses of rights, whether by revolutionaries or kings. Not long before his death, he had fondly quoted Pope: "He can't be wrong whose life is in the right."[45]

Paine signed neither the Declaration nor the Constitution. Yet no one can deny him an important role among those who inspired the birth of this new republic. Through his eagerly read books, he awakened many to their rights. If nearly all of the other top one hundred founders more expressly employed biblical words and phrases in doing so, Paine spoke most eloquently of the lift provided by the other wing of the eagle, the lift provided by reason or, as he preferred, common sense. His is an important, if minority, voice in the American story.

10. *John Adams*

Like James Wilson, John Adams undertook a number of studies in the history of law and the history of constitutions, which offer us a glimpse into the depth of knowledge available to the founding generation. One can only stand in some awe of Adams' readings in classical, early Anglo-Saxon, continental, feudal and canon law, sections of which are now available in two recent collections.[46] No single man is more responsible for the Fourth of July, and the independence for which it stands, than John Adams. Jefferson supplied the words of the Declaration, but Adams begat the deed. Benjamin Rush said the consensus of the generation of 1776 was that Adams possessed more "learning probably, both ancient and modern, than any man who subscribed to the Declaration of Independence."[47] Independence, Richard Stockton wrote, was more owed to Adams than to any other.[48]

British forces occupied Adams' beloved Boston at the time, and the whole moral force of the Union (he knew) must be united behind the Declaration. Knowing full well the glory that would attach to the author of those words, and having all his life prepared for and coveted such glory, in a great act of self-abnegation Adams judged it more prudent that a man from Massachusetts not be their author, and stood aside for his rival from Virginia.

Well before his arrival at the opening meeting of the First Continental Congress in September 1774, Adams had reached the point in his own mind, against the self-interests of his family, that independence from Great Britain was essential. The price otherwise was obsequiousness, servility, and the fawning pursuit of parliamentary favors. Ever since 1688, Parliament had been gaining powers over the Crown and, faced with the heavy expenses of Empire a century later, had begun to squeeze the colonies for revenue and to exercise expedient but illegitimate power over them.

During the twenty years before 1776, no young lawyer in the colonies worked harder to master the law and the ideas of statesmanship

than John Adams. On a rigorous schedule worthy of his Puritan forebears (his father had been a modestly successful farmer south of
Boston), the young Adams roused himself at 6 a.m. to begin a long day
of studying Latin, Greek, and classic texts of several strategic sorts. Shy
and without social graces, Adams felt he had been born to greatness
but would have to work harder for it than others. He forced himself to
go deeper and to range more broadly than his peers. The King's agents
tapped him as the outstanding lawyer in the younger set, the perfect
choice to supervise the King's affairs in Massachusetts. Financial security and honor were his simply for remaining loyal to the king.

Yet more than partisanship, Adams loved justice. At enormous
risk to his reputation among the growing band of partisans of independence, he had decided in early 1770 to undertake the legal defense of the
young British soldiers who had excitedly opened fire on an angry Boston
mob, killing five. Adams himself believed that the integrity of the law
and the system of justice demanded his services. Independence, he was
certain, must not be won through mob action. "Where there is no law,
there is no liberty," was one of the sayings for which he was already
known. His brilliant and beautiful wife Abigail feared for his safety.
Despite public demonstrations against him, he won acquittal for the
frightened young men, rightly, according to the law, without dema-
goguery or tricks, and secured his reputation for both moral courage
and respect for law.

Yet Adams' daily observations showed him that the Crown was
more and more out of touch with realities in America, and that Parliament was more and more treating the colonists not as free Englishmen,
but as vassals for whom decisions could be taken without their consent.
Adams did not interpret America's cause as a "tax revolt" but as a
demand for dignity. The real villainy in the minor tax imposed by the
Stamp Act of 1765 was its underlying usurpation of consent and rights.
Unprotested, such usurpations would swell into full-fledged slavery.
No self-respecting free man could endure that prospect. The logic of
the Stamp Act imposed the duty of independence. Otherwise, a long
train of parliamentary abuses of the colonists would flow from that logic
until their weight became unendurable.

Day and night upon his arrival in Philadelphia in 1774, Adams
toiled to persuade his fellow congressmen of the necessity of independence. As much as possible, he did so outside the public eye, preferring

one-to-one arguments and small dinners. Union was the indispensable object, full support for independence from Carolina to Pennsylvania and New York. All an astute monarch had to do was sow division; that George III had not, only proved how out of touch with American reality he was. The two middle states, composed of the stolid Quakers of Pennsylvania and the ambitious New Yorkers, were also the most reluctant to declare independence, and mounted formidable obstacles against the aims of John Adams. They were also keystones in the arch of Union; their dissent portended the most fatal division.

Even in 1776, when the tide was clearly running toward the utter necessity of independence – and when potential allies like France might support an independent nation, but not a domestic rebellion – Adams bore the brunt of the deeply contested argument as the clear leader of the independence party. In the final debate, Jefferson was in Virginia and Adams singlehandedly brought the issue to a vote and, after powerful arguments against the motion by Pennsylvania, was obliged to give the decisive summation *ex tempore*, in what many recalled years later as the most brilliant political argument they ever heard. The night after the vote, he wrote to Abigail that the deed – including *his* role in the deed – would be remembered among free peoples forever, as few statesmen in all human history have been remembered.

The honor of being a constitutional lawgiver for his own Commonwealth, a "Solon or Lycurgus," was in his mind the greatest glory of his life. He could imagine no greater gift to a people than a good foundation in the law. Nonetheless, Adams was also the first man in America to suggest, as early as 1776, the method whereby a people might write their own constitution, a deed virtually never seen before in human history: first summon a convention, then establish a process of popular ratification. He gave reasons why a constitution ought to be written down, and what it ought not to write down. He himself practically wrote the Constitution of 1780 for Massachusetts, which became the model for nearly all the other states (after 1776, all needed new constitutions). All the participants in the federal Constitutional Convention of 1787 were urged by leading lawyers to master Adams' book on U.S. constitutions. His influence in the ratification fight after 1787 was pervasive because of his earlier writings, and in Massachusetts – in a close vote – it was indispensable.

Later, as George Washington's Vice President, Adams was no

match for the political guile of Thomas Jefferson, who did not scruple to spread untruths about Adams in order to undermine his reputation among the voters. Jefferson baldly denied to President Washington that he had libeled Vice-President Adams, but the evidence of his guilt was available in writing, both private and public; Washington did not stoop to answering him. Adams won the Presidency after Washington's term, but four years later fell to the plotting Jefferson in his reelection bid. He did not forgive Jefferson's slanders against his patriotism for many years.

Nonetheless, Adams had a largeness of mind that permitted the two to renew their friendship in later years, carrying on an extraordinary correspondence. Their deaths occurred, minutes apart on July 4, 1826, exactly fifty years to the day after their greatest mutual glory. No other social revolution of the next two centuries was to bring its grateful people so deep a respect for law and religion, and so orderly and prosperous a liberty. An outpouring of love and honor for both of them swept across the land in July of 1826.[49]

It remains odd that nearly all the important writings of Adams have, until recently, been inaccessible and are almost totally unknown to the general reader.[50] Odd, because from his youth, Adams had loved historical research (it was to run in the Adams family for another hundred years), and had made himself master of Anglo-Saxon law, canon law, the laws of the Germanic tribes, classical Greek and Latin authors, and of course the laws of Great Britain. Many esteemed him the most learned man in America in those conceptual and empirical questions that lie behind law and statecraft.

Despite the fact that so many historians and philosophers of government live and work in Boston, most general histories pay scant attention to the most important of all Bostonians, Adams. Perhaps the reason is that Jefferson, particularly, more easily suits the predilection of academics for a secular touch, whereas Adams is far more religious in his convictions – not an orthodox Christian, but utterly convinced of the importance of religion to the American form of government: "Our constitution was made only for a moral and religious people. It is wholly inadequate for the government of any other."[51]

For instance, in the debate over the Massachusetts Constitution of 1780, Adams argued against much opposition for an article mandating religious schools in every jurisdiction of the Commonwealth, paid for by the state treasury if necessary. Against the argument that such payments infringed on religious liberty, Adams argued that the article compelled no one's belief. Further, since experience shows that republics need virtue, and that virtue needs religion, such schools are an indispensable foundation of the free society, and all who benefit by the good habits they produce in the citizenry ought by right to pay for them. On this question, Adams is far more typical of the founding generation (and many state constitutions) than Jefferson and Madison, whose views of a few years later were at a far extreme on the spectrum of opinion.

From his youth through his old age, Adams was unusually thoughtful about religion. An inveterate annotator of his own books, Adams late in life came down hard on Condorcet for atheistical boastings. When Condorcet exclaimed that the "natural equality of mankind" is the foundation of all morality, Adams tartly retorted in the margin: "There is no such thing without a supposition of God. There is no right and wrong in the universe without the supposition of a moral government and an intellectual and moral governor."[52] When Condorcet asserted that genius had been suppressed by religious superstition, Adams retorted: "But was there no genius among the Hebrews? None among the Christians, nor Mahometans? I understand you, Condorcet. It is atheistic genius alone that you would honor or tolerate."[53] When Condorcet praised the ancient Greeks, Adams wrote in the margin: "As much as I love, esteem, and admire the Greeks, I believe the Hebrews have done more to enlighten and civilize the world. Moses did more than all their legislators and philosophers."[54]

Without the existence of an all-knowing moral Governor of the universe, the Divine Judge and Arbiter, Adams argued, there can be no right or wrong, only subjective opinion, whim, and desire. Turning from God is a recipe for a moral chaos in which no appeal to reason is efficacious, a world in which brute power decides right and wrong. The Hebrew recognition of one God – Creator, Governor and Judge – brings moral light into this darkness, teaches humans to respect each other as rational inquirers and free men, and, by insisting on fidelity to truth, frees humans striving for liberty from the shackles of brute power. For Adams, it is the pursuit of truth that gives men liberty. And this relation of freedom to truth we owe to Moses:

I will insist that the Hebrews have done more to civilize men than any other nation. If I were an atheist, and believed in blind eternal fate, I should still believe that fate had ordained the Jews to be the most essential instrument for civilizing the nations. If I were an atheist of the other sect, who believe or pretend to believe that all is ordered by chance, I should believe that chance had ordered the Jews to preserve and propagate to all mankind the doctrine of a supreme, intelligent, wise, almighty, sovereign of the universe, which I believe to be a great essential principle of all morality, and consequently of all civilization.[55]

As a young man, Adams often reflected on the "infinite variety of bodies" within the arc of his own vision, in a two-mile radius, and then tried to contemplate how many such small arcs there are on this huge planet – and then on other planets and other stars. The immensity of creation sank into his consciousness, and awe at the order and intelligence suffusing the whole, and maintaining it in existence, crept over him. His conviction of God's existence he drew primarily from the extraordinary variety and beauty of the observable world – "the amazing harmony of our solar system...the stupendous plan of operation" designed by God to act a particular role "in this great and complicated drama."[56] In the same vein, his contemplation of human progress through history – leveling mountains, digging out channels for canals, diverting rivers, clearing lands and cultivating new growth of seeds, mastering the arts of navigation and sailing – made him marvel at God's providential knowledge of this entire panorama. Adams also reflected on the new and amazing human ability to detect bodies in the heavens through the telescope, otherwise as invisible to the naked eye as those "innumerable millions of animals that escape the observation of our naked sight," until we look at them through the microscope. Yet God had known of all these possibilities from the beginning, outside time, in all eternity.[57]

Such reflections led Adams beyond the thinking of Jefferson. Jefferson's concept of reason was too narrow to allow for the possibility of miracles. Adams had a more robust view of reason, as Page Smith narrates, quoting directly from Adams:

"What now can preserve this prodigious variety of species and this inflexible uniformity among the individuals," he asked, "but the continual and vigilant providence of God?" Such a God could "easily suspend those laws whenever His Providence sees sufficient reason for such suspension. This can be no objection, then to the miracles of Jesus Christ." Ancient philoso-

phers, wise as they might have been, had been unable to overcome "preju-
dice, custom, passion, and bigotry." But God through Christ awakened
men to the truth. [58]

The necessity of answering to his Judge on the Last Day pushed
Adams to demand constant moral reform of his own character – a fear
of God that went hand-in-hand with his own ambition to prepare himself
for greatness. Smith records quotations from the young man's diaries:

"Oh!" he wrote, "that I could wear out of my mind every mean and base
affection; conquer my natural pride and self conceit, expect no more deference from my fellows than I deserve, acquire that meekness and humility
which are the sure mark and characters of a great and generous soul, and
subdue every unworthy passion.... How happy should I then be in favor and
good will of all honest men and the sure prospect of a happy immortality." [59]

In another entry, Adams asked himself: "What is the proper business of life?" His answer was that such pursuits as "honor, wealth, or
learning" would lead inevitably to disillusionment. He proposed for
himself more solid and lasting aims:

Contemplation of God, "habits of love and compassion...habits of temperance, recollection, and self-government" were the things that would afford
"real and substantial pleasure" and give "the prospect of everlasting felicity." [60]

In a similar vein, Adams came to appreciate the value of a large
institutional presence of religion throughout society, both in itself and as
a necessary support for republican experiments:

One great advantage of the Christian Religion is that it brings the great Principle of Law of Nature and Nations, Love your Neighbor as yourself, and do
to others as you would that others should do to you, – to the Knowledge,
Belief and Veneration of the whole People. Children, Servants, Women and
Men are all Professors in the science of public as well as private Morality. No
other Institutions of Education, no kind of political Discipline, could dif-
fuse this kind of necessary Information, so universally among all Ranks
and Descriptions of Citizens. The Duties and Rights of The Man and the Citizen are thus taught from early Infancy to every Creature. [61]

These convictions fortified Adams' commitment to the centrality of
liberty in human affairs – liberty constituted by the sound habits of self-
government, rooted in honesty. They also fortified his respect for
institutions, through which brotherly correction inspires the perfecting

of personal character, and truth is more diligently pursued. Study led him to believe that mistakes in the design of institutions are common, and that getting the design of institutions right is an art and science in itself.

In the subtlety of his understanding of custom, habits, and institutions, Adams is far more like Burke than like Locke. Examining customs and precedents, Adams, more fully than anyone, laid out the legal arguments that undergirded the long train of indictments against the abuses of king and Parliament in the Declaration of Independence. His arguments showed unambiguously that the original legal foundations for the several colonies rested on personal grants by the monarch, not on acts of Parliament. When Parliament later wrested more power from the monarch, it strayed beyond the grants of law establishing the colonies, despite the fact that no member of Parliament represented the votes of anyone in the colonies. Not only abuses by the monarch, therefore, but also those by a usurping Parliament were legal grounds for dissolving ties.

Against the Governor of Massachusetts who asserted that the struggle for independence could only be lost, Adams replied that even if that struggle ended in death, that would be a gain, not a loss, since death is better than slavery. Until encountering such passages from Adams, many people today will not really have *felt* how keenly the Americans had come to love their native freedom and how keenly they were jealous of every jot and tittle of it.

So far-reaching was Adams' early thought that he developed an articulated political architecture to guide *founders* (to Adams, a breathtaking concept at that time) and law*givers*, through the thickets of history, human nature, and political science. Adams took literally the idea that the American system is an experiment, to be tested as any other experiment and amended in the light of failures. However, he showed how well-grounded in past experience the main lines of the new experiment already were. He explained in an original way the fundamentals of republican government, the "art" of getting the architecture right.

Adams was a bold and original thinker, a fate ill-fortuned in democracies, since the favorite weapon of majorities is open mockery of minorities. For instance, Adams feared that the offices of a democracy would fall under the control of wealthy elites, generating a new aristocratic order. As a remedy he proposed the option of allowing states to elect senators either for very long terms or for life, as a way of institutionalizing a kind of natural aristocracy in one house. His aim was both to confine the will-to-power of the wealthy and to give it a safe channel. This shrewd proposal Jefferson (and later historians) leapt upon as un-American and anti-democratic. Adams saw clearly the irrepressible ability of the wealthy few, such as Jefferson, to win and stay in office. To keep the nation democratic, he feared, would require more than pretending that a natural aristocracy does not exist. In the two centuries since he made this argument, the persistent emergence of wealthy senators has confirmed his foresight.

Few today think so deeply about the architecture of American government as Adams did, and Adams did so *before* there was an American government. Without Adams, neither independence nor the Constitution nor its ratification would have seen reality. More deeply than his peers, he thought through the principles of the Republic to which we this day pledge allegiance.

There is ample reason, further, to believe that this century will at last be the Adams century. The return to religious and moral education as a *sine qua non* of the survival of the Republic is as finally apparent to many as it once was to him. The intellectual and legal bankruptcy of the extreme Jefferson/Madison position on church and state has been exposed. But the deepest reason of all is that no other founder – not Washington, not Jefferson, not Madison – delved so profoundly into the practical necessities of republican governance. Alongside these three, Adams certainly deserves to be listed as one of the four giants of the founding.

11. *Benjamin Franklin*

If the godly among the signers normally faced intellectual crises in their beliefs, so too did the less religious among them, as we have already seen in the case of Tom Paine, and might observe also in Benjamin Franklin. When men like Franklin made lists of the virtues they wanted to acquire by force of habit, they often listed a mix of biblical and ancient virtues, sometimes with a new virtue or two proper to the new world of experience in America, such as enterprise and initiative. It was the same with the vices they wanted to avoid and to strengthen their resolve against:

a mixture of the biblical, the ancient, and the new. But those who tried to accomplish this with as little an admixture of orthodox Christian doctrine as they could typically found themselves wrestling over and over with what they *did* believe. A few weeks before he died, Franklin explained his faith (once again) to the President of Yale, Ezra Stiles:

> Here is my creed. I believe in one God, Creator of the Universe. That He governs it by His providence. That He ought to be worshipped. That the most acceptable service we render him is doing good to His other children. That the soul of man is immortal, and will be treated with justice in another life respecting its conduct in this. These I take to be the principal principles of sound religion, and I regard them as you do in whatever sect I meet with them. As to Jesus of Nazareth, my opinion of whom you particularly desire, I think the system of morals and his religion, as he left them to us, the best the world ever saw or is likely to see; but I apprehend it has received various corrupt changes, and I have, with most of the present dissenters in England, some doubts as to his divinity; though it is a question I do not dogmatize upon, having never studied it, and think it needless to busy myself with it now, when I expect soon an opportunity of knowing the truth with less trouble. I see no harm, however, in its being believed, if that belief has the good consequence, as probably it has, of making his doctrines more respected and better observed; especially as I do not perceive that the Supreme [Being] takes it amiss, by distinguishing the unbelievers in His government of the world with any peculiar marks of His displeasure.[62]

Franklin was, of course, an estimable man, even a great man, but his creed is marked by a certain insouciance. Clearly, he was a freerider on Hebrew and Christian beliefs, and he certainly did not take time to think through the difference it might make to the texture of history if Jesus Christ *is* God, a question about which he did not busy himself. Yet he went on assuming that much of Christianity remained true, either way. One remembers that on a day of great crisis at the Constitutional Convention, when the two sides almost walked out on each other, it was Franklin – the supposed Deist – who moved that the Convention stop for a day of prayer to Divine Providence, for guidance through the impasse.[63]

A habit of easy tolerance towards views different from one's own may imperceptibly degenerate into intellectual indifference. Carelessness in belief feeds moral decline. Thus, the momentum of moral entropy is hastened by the cyclical decline from moral seriousness into insouciance, from which only periodic Awakenings have been known to offer a cure.

That it has historically been the habit of republics to sink into moral decay – that, too – was a constant theme of the founders. Even Ben Franklin himself, as the Convention ended, wondered whether the new republic faced a rising or a setting sun.

12. *The Price They Paid*

When the signers of the Declaration put down on the table their surety for their words, they pledged "Our Lives, our Fortunes and our Sacred Honor." They knew their daring words could cost them dearly. This is the price they paid:

Soldier sons taken captive:
Abraham Clark (F, 47)
John Hart (E, 356)
John Morton

Commercial property and/or ships burned:
John Hart
Carter Braxton
Joseph Hewes
John Hancock

Homes physically occupied:
Thomas Jefferson (Elk Hill)
John Witherspoon
Richard Stockton
John Hancock (E, 356)
John Hopkinson
Arthur Middleton
Philip Livingston

Prisoners of war:
Edward Rutledge (F, 128)
Arthur Middleton (F, 104)
Charles Pinckney (nara)
Richard Stockton (G)
George Walton (F, 141)
David Brearly (nara)
Jonathan Dayton (nara)
James McHenry (nara)
Thomas Heyward (F, 76)

Homes and/or property confiscated:
Lyman Hall (F, 66)
Philip Livingston (F, 95)
Thomas McKean (E, 356)

Homes damaged:
George Clymer (F, 50)
William Floyd (F, 54)
John Hart (F, 72)

Homes destroyed:
William Ellery (F, 52)
Lyman Hall (F, 66)
Thomas Heyward (F, 76)
William Hooper (F, 78-79)
Frances Lewis (F, 95)
Philip Livingston (F, 95)
Lewis Morris (F, 105)
Thomas Nelson (F, 111,112)
Richard Stockton (F, 134,35)

*Wife died in captivity or forced
separation:*
Francis Lewis (F, 95)

Soldier son(s) died in war:
John Witherspoon
John Morton

*Died of illness contracted on
 recruiting mission:*
Thomas Lynch, Jr. (F, 100)

Based on John Eidsmoe, *Christianity and the Constitution: The Faith of Our Founding Fathers* (Grand Rapids, Mich: Baker Book House, 1987) [E]; Robert G. Ferris and Richard E. Morris, *The Signers of the Declaration of Independence* (Arlington, VA: Interpretive Publications, 1982) [F]; Rev. Charles A. Goodrich, *Biographies of the Signers of the Declaration of Independence*, 1829 [G]; and the National Archives and Records Administration on line: www.nara.gov [nara].

Author's Note: *I am grateful to Erik Nelson, a graduate student in political science at Catholic University, who volunteered a day a week to help with the initial groundwork for this Appendix.*

Acknowledgments

The idea for this book first began germinating in 1964, when in my first book (published when I was a graduate student) I declared my intention to write a theology and philosophy that, at last, incorporated the new knowledge gained through the American experiment in religious liberty. The first actual attempt at this book got underway late in 1987. In the autumn of that year, I was honored to hold the Welch Chair in American Studies at the University of Notre Dame, and was invited to present six lectures in honor of the 200th anniversary of the Constitutional Convention in Philadelphia. The aim of those lectures was to spell out the "new science of politics" worked out by the drafters of the Constitution, beyond the horizons of a European classical education. My working title was *How to Make a Republic Work*.

At a low level, my task was that of Alexis de Tocqueville: To explain America to Catholic Europe. Like Tocqueville, I was brought up Catholic and was greatly inspired by the American adventure. I wanted to explain the newness of the American experiment to the "old world," especially those in Eastern Europe, Latin America, and among the growing millions of Christians in Africa and Asia. Such reflections might even assist American Protestants to see their achievements in a new way.

My aim in the Notre Dame lectures had been to bring the Catholic tradition and the American tradition together in greater detail than John Courtney Murray had in his classic text, *We Hold These Truths*. I tried to add an economic dimension to the political dimension stressed by Murray. Most of all, though, where Murray was strong on the Catholic side of the story, and rather cursory in his study of American documents, I wanted to emphasize the latter.

Catching wind of those earlier efforts, the Kansas State University *Law Review* proposed a digest of *How to Make a Republic Work*, and after much effort compressed its main argument into a substantial article, which was published in 1991. Later, most of the individual chapters from the Notre Dame lectures appeared elsewhere. But one perplexity I had not had a chance to address in the Notre Dame lectures continued to preoccupy me.

In this book, I have at last been free to concentrate on that large religious and philosophical issue: *Was the American founding anti-religious? Did it render religion irrelevant? Or did it depend on religion, as an eagle on one of its wings?*

Thanks to a joint grant from the Bradley Foundation and the Olin Foundation, the Catholic University of America was able to invite me to present four lectures on the American Founding at the Columbus Law School, during the busy and memorable election year of 2000. In a remarkable show of campus cooperation, the lectures were jointly sponsored by the departments of Philosophy, Religious Studies, Political Philosophy, and the Law School. On each occasion, distinguished commentators such as U.S. Supreme Court Justice Clarence Thomas, Assistant Secretary of State Richard J. Schifter, prize-winning author and journalist E. J. Dionne, and my renowned American Enterprise Institute colleague Walter Berns raised questions and difficulties. (The Honorable R. Sargent Shriver and Judge Robert H. Bork, who would have honored the occasion by their presence, also agreed to act as commentators, but unexpected family health crises prevented first one, then the other, from taking part.) Their questions were followed by questions from selected scholars in each of the sponsoring schools: Raymond Sokolowski, David Walsh, Robert Destro, and Joseph Komonchak. On each occasion, there also followed a dinner for some thirty-five invited students, professors, and guests for another two hours of questions and extended comments. Four student "Novak Fellows" from the respective departments – Molly McGrath, Daniel Ferris, Russell Fox, and John Gilman – helped to compile a list of the best questions posed throughout the lectures and dinners, which formed the nucleus of Chapter Five. The manuscript was also read in earlier stages of its development by three distinguished historians – James Hutson, Barry Shain, and Martin Marty – who saved me from many small errors and suggested important improvements; and also by the distinguished political theorist, Michael Zuckert, who did the same.

My debts of gratitude for the original inspiration go back very far, then, and leap ahead to the very recent present: To Peter Lombardo, who made the lectures at the University of Notre Dame in 1987 memorable for his hospitality at the Hesburgh Center; and to Father Kurt Pritzl, O.P., chairman of the Department of Philosophy and general organizer of the lecture series at Catholic University in 2000; and to all those others at both institutions who contributed time, efforts and a generous spirit to the accompanying events.

Thanks, too, to the trustees of the Lynne and Harry Bradley Foundation and the Olin Foundation for their grants to the Catholic University of America, which made this book possible.

Thanks as well to Robert J. Goldwin and Walter Berns, whose stimulus – always kindly and fraternal – has prodded me for these past twenty-some years, since I first came under their good influence at AEI in 1978.

And thanks to my agent Loretta Barrett and my publisher and editor Peter Collier at Encounter Books, for much sound advice, assistance, and friendship.

For the friendship provided by my wife Karen, and for the home suited to creativity which she has sustained over so many years, at much cost to herself, there are no sufficient words of gratitude.

Finally, over the years the revolving members of the John Courtney Murray Seminar who meet bi-monthly at the American Enterprise Institute to discuss such topics as those taken up in this book have given me incalculable stimulation and advice; I am deeply grateful to them, and to the Coca-Cola Foundation for the aid that has made our dinners possible. Matt Spalding provided extraordinary assistance in guiding my readings in the history of the founding, and Thomas West helped early and late. Brian Anderson made some key literary suggestions. To Graham Walker, Russell Hittinger; and (over the years) to Cornelis Heesters, Derek Cross, Erica Carson Walter and other researchers at the American Enterprise Institute, as well as interns such as Thomas Kilroy, Martin Wauck, Erik Nelson, and Louis Dezseran, my warmest thanks for suggestions and corrections on earlier versions of this manuscript, and for remarkable research assistance. First Cathie Love and then Laurel Cornell and Heba Abedin made everything happen in the office that needed to happen for the production of the manuscript and the organizing of the rest of us.

My warmest thanks to all!

Michael Novak

25 May 2001

Notes

Chapter One: Jewish Metaphysics at the Founding

[1] See the influential histories of Vernon Parrington, *Main Currents in American Thought* (New York: Harcourt, Brace, 1927); Louis Hartz, *The Liberal Tradition in America: An Interpretation of American Political Thought Since the Revolution* (New York: Harcourt, Brace, 1955); Charles Beard, *An Economic Interpretation of the Constitution of the United States* (New York: Free Press, 1965); and also such influential political philosophers as Leo Strauss, in *Natural Right and History* (Chicago: University of Chicago Press, 1953), pp. 244-251; Thomas L. Pangle, *The Spirit of Modern Republicanism: The Moral Vision of the American Founders and the Philosophy of Locke* (Chicago: University of Chicago Press, 1988); and D. G. Hart, "The Failure of American Religious History" in *The Journal of the Historical Society* (Boston University), vol. 1, no. 1 (Spring 2000). One astute historian has described the current situation in these words:

> It would seem wildly implausible to report that American historical scholarship has largely neglected the study of religion. Yet it is sadly true. Aside from a handful of moments in American history, notably the founding of New England, where mention of the religious dimension is unavoidable, precious little in the story of American history that survives in our standard textbooks even hints at the strong and abiding religiosity of the American people. It is not clear whether this fact reflects a commitment to philosophical secularism, or merely to methodological secularism, among the overwhelming majority of academic historians. But it does indicate an enormous gap between such historians and the rest of the American people, given that public-opinion polls indicate with numbing regularity that an overwhelming majority of Americans, usually in excess of 90 percent, claim to believe in a personal God and in the veracity of the Bible.

Wilfred M. McClay, *A Student's Guide to U.S. History* (Intercollegiate Studies Institute, 2000), p. 7.

[2] Walter Berns, "Religion and the Founding Principle," in Robert H. Horwitz, ed., *The Moral Foundations of the American Republic.* 3rd ed. (Charlottesville: University Press of Virginia, 1986), p. 214.

[3]   American-style constitutional government is the best actual, and probably the best possible, form of government in the modern world. Yet the theoretical groundwork of American constitutionalism was the political philosophy of Locke.

    Under the Constitution, the United States has enjoyed tremendous success. Many millions have appreciated the blessings of liberty and prosperity that we somehow owe to it. The United States led the forces that finally defeated Nazism and the beginning of the end of Communism. The vitality of the Constitution is certainly due in part to the conviction that its principles are just. Lincoln, King, and Reagan appealed to the principles of the Declaration which are the principles of Locke's *Second Treatise.* These men understood these also to be the principles of the Constitution.

Tom West, "John Locke, Philosopher of the Founding *And Why We Should Be Glad He Was*" (unpublished paper for the John Courtney Murray lecture), October 4, 2000.

[4]   The Pilgrim Code of Law (1636), for example, listed a number of values and rights within the body of what is otherwise a constitution, including the right to trial by jury and a commitment to equal taxation. The 1638 Act for the Liberties of the People set out for the Maryland legislature both prohibitions and goals. The most extensive was the Massachusetts Body of Liberties, though it was followed shortly by similar efforts in other colonies, to the south as well as to the north.

    Through these codifications and lists of rights, we see the foundation element of self-definition being differentiated into bills of rights. However, the colonists viewed a bill of rights as a virtual celebration of the people's fundamental values. The limitation on government was, as we have seen, that certain actions were not acceptable.

Donald S. Lutz, *The Origins of American Constitutionalism* (Baton Rouge: Louisiana State University Press, 1988), p. 61.

[5] E.g., Elisha Williams, "The Essential Rights and Liberties of Protestantism" in Ellis Sandoz, ed., *Political Sermons of the American Founding Era: 1730–1805* (Indianapolis: Liberty Press, 1991), pp. 51-118, especially pp. 56-69.

[6] Some scholars see in the founders' reasoning a form of the ancient *phronesis* or "practical wisdom." See Terence E. Marshall, "A French-American Dialogue: The Problem of Human Rights for Constitutional Government," *Crisis*, May 1994 (also published as an essay in *The Legacy of the French Revolution*, Rowman & Littlefield, 1996). In an argument presented to French scholars, Terence Marshall suggests that the American Founders employed the classical tradition of *phronesis* rather than the modern tradition of rationalism, preferred by the French Revolutionaries:

[T]he Madisonian synthesis of rights and prudence derives finally from another source than Montesquieu or Hume, Locke or Voltaire. An attentive reading of *The Federalist* reveals that the practical reason it manifests is founded not on a passion for security but on a concern for the disposition of soul requisite to a just or reasonable deliberation of public affairs.
Marshall, p. 49.

[7] Donald S. Lutz has carefully weighted what he describes as "The Relative Influence of European Writers on Late Eighteenth-Century American Political Thought," *The American Political Science Review*, vol. 78, 1983, pp. 185-197. Of the total number of citations from a comprehensive list of political writings, 34 percent were to the Bible; 22 percent to the Enlightenment; 18 percent to the Whigs; 11 percent to the Common Law; 9 percent to the Classics, 4 percent to peers, and 2 percent "others." In a total of 3,154 citations, Montesquieu was cited most (8.3 percent), followed closely by Blackstone (7.9 percent), third Locke (2.9), and fourth Hume (2.7). The fifth most cited thinker was the classic historian Plutarch (1.5 percent).

[8] Russell Kirk, *The Conservative Constitution* (Washington, D.C.: Regnery Gateway, 1990), p. 71.

[9] In Jefferson's May 8, 1825 letter to Henry Lee, he writes:
Not to find out new principles, or new arguments, never before thought of, not merely to say things which had never been said before; but to place before mankind the common sense of the subject, in terms so plain and firm as to command their assent, and to justify ourselves in the independent stand we are compelled to take. Neither aiming at originality of principle or sentiment, nor yet copied from any particular and previous writing, it was intended to be an expression of the American mind, and to give to that expression the proper tone and spirit called for by the occasion. All its authority rests then on the harmonizing sentiments of the day, whether expressed in conversation, in letters, printed essays, or in the elementary books of public right, as Aristotle, Cicero, Locke, Sidney &c. The historical documents which you mention as in your possession, ought all to be found, and I am persuaded you will find, to be corroborative of the facts and principles advanced in that Declaration.
Merrill D. Peterson, ed., *Jefferson: Writings* (NY: Library of America, 1984), p. 1501.

[10] Lutz, 1988, op cit., pp. 119-120.

[11] Ibid., p. 11. Later, Lutz writes:
Saying that English common law had relatively little impact on American constitutional design does not imply a lack of effect on the legal system. English common law was used in all colonies by 1776 as the basis for court procedures, methods of appeal, legal definitions, and other key aspects.

Again, however, it was selectively appropriated and blended with the colonists' principles and practices.

It is important to distinguish between the impact of common law upon the American legal system and upon American constitutional design. In England the common law was the primary means of limiting governmental power, whereas in America the means was different. The *idea* of limited government does in part derive from it. But in the American constitutional tradition, what *replaced* common law was a new political technique, the written constitution. No matter how important common law was for the operation of the American legal system, the written constitution that framed the system sprang from ideas, principles, and practices evolved primarily in America.

Pp. 62-63.

[12]   The Law is not merely the decree of a monarch who may pretend to divine powers – that the Israelites learned. The Law is not merely a body of convenient customs and usages that men have developed for themselves. The Law is not the instrument of oppression by a class or a hierarchy. For the true law is derived from the Covenant that God has made and reaffirmed with his people. The Law is revealed to save man from self-destruction; to redeem man from sin and its consequences; to keep man from becoming a Cain, his hand against every man's; to enable man to resemble the God in whose image he was created.

Kirk, op. cit., p. 28.

[13] Ibid., p. 29.

[14] John Adams, in a letter to Thomas Jefferson. See Reinhold Niebuhr, *The Irony of American History* (New York: Charles Scribner's Sons, 1952), p. 21.

[15] Robert N. Bellah, *The Broken Covenant: American Civil Religion in Time of Trial* (New York: Crossroad Books, 1975), pp. 12-13.

[16] Irving L. Thomson, "Great Seal of the United States," *Encyclopedia Americana*, XIII (1967), p. 362.

[17] Ezra Stiles, "The United States Elevated to Glory and Honour" (1783), in Conrad Cherry, ed., *God's New Israel* (Englewood Cliffs, NJ: Prentice Hall, 1971), p. 83.

[18] George W. Carey, ed., *The Political Writings of John Adams* (Washington, D.C.: Regnery Publishing, 2000), p. 3. John Adams, *Works* I.66.

[19] *The Federalist Papers* (New York: New America Library, 1961), *No. 1*, p. 33.

[20] The phrase comes from *Federalist No. 9*. Tocqueville attributed to the founders "a new political science," p. 12.

[21] *The Federalist Papers* (New York: New America Library, 1961), *No. 14*, pp. 104-105.

[22] T. R. Glover, as cited by Russell Kirk, expresses this well:

> "The Hebrew prophets kept the personality of God – kept it triumphantly, and abolished all other claimants to Godhead," T. R. Glover says. "God is personal, and God is one; God is righteous, and God is king – they are four great tenets on which to base any religion, and they were not lightly won. They were the outcome of experience, hard, bitter, and disillusioning – a gain required by the loss of all kinds of hopes and beliefs, national and personal, tested in every way that man or devil can invent for the testing of belief.... They made righteousness a thing no more of ritual and taboo but of attitude and conduct and spirit. They set religion free from ancient follies and reviving horrors."

The Roots of the American Order (Washington, D.C.: Regnery, 1991), p. 30.

[23] *A Summary View of the Rights of British America, 1774,* in Merrill D. Peterson, op. cit., p. 122.

[24] See Robert Alter, *The Art of Biblical Narrative* (New York: Basic Books, 1981).

[25] John Adams, "A Dissertation on the Canon and Feudal Law," in George W. Carey, ed., *The Political Writings of John Adams* (Washington, D.C.: Regnery, 2000), p. 19.

[26]
> Nor would I have you to mistake in the point of your own *liberty*. There is a *liberty* of corrupt nature, which is affected by *men* and *beasts* to do what they list; and this *liberty* is inconsistent with *authority*, impatient of all restraint; by this *liberty*, *Sumus Omnes Deteriores*, 'tis the grand enemy of *truth* and *peace*, and all the *ordinances* of God are bent against it. But there is a civil, a moral, a federal *liberty*, which is the proper end and object of *authority*; it is *liberty* for that only which is *just* and *good*; for this *liberty* you are to stand with the hazard of your very *lives*.... This *liberty* is maintained in a way of subjection to *authority*; and the *authority* set over you will in all administrations for your good be quietly submitted unto, by all but such as have a disposition to *shake off the yoke*, and lose their true *liberty*, by their murmuring at the honour and power of *authority*.

Tocqueville, op. cit., p. 46.

[27] John Perkins, "A Well-Wisher to Mankind" in Charles S. Hyneman and Donald S. Lutz, eds., *American Political Writing During the Founding Era: 1760–1805* (Indianapolis: Liberty Press, 1983), p. 151.

[28] Carey, op. cit., pp. 18-19.

[29] Herbert Butterfield, *The Whig Interpretation of History* (New York: AMS Press, 1978). But see also Michael Novak in the chapter on "The Catholic Whig:"
> Among Hayek's favorite exemplars of the Whig tradition are [Thomas Aquinas], Alexis de Tocqueville and Lord Acton. It is noteworthy that all three of Hayek's models are Catholic, and to his list other names can readily be added: Jacques Maritain, Yves R. Simon, and John Courtney Murray.

In important ways, all these thinkers go beyond the usual position of "liberal." For example, they have a respect for language, law, liturgy, and tradition that, in some sense, marks them as "conservative." Still, they believe in some human progress, and they emphasize human capacities for reflection on alternatives and free choices – characteristics that mark them as realistic progressives. With the liberals, they locate human dignity in liberty, but *ordered* liberty (just as, for Aquinas, practical wisdom is *recta ratio*). The Catholic Whigs, then, present a distinctive mix: conservative, progressive, liberal, and realistic.
On Cultivating Liberty (Lanham, MD: Rowman & Littlefield, 1999), pp. 145-146.

[30] Samuel Langdon, "The Republic Of The Israelites An Example To The United States," in Cherry, op. cit., pp. 98-99.

[31] John Adams to Abigail Adams, quoted in William J. Federer, ed., *America's God and Country* (Coppell, TX: FAME Publishing, 1994), p. 137. I have relied on the Federer account throughout.

[32] Jeffrey Hays Morrison, "John Witherspoon and 'The Public Interest of Religion,'" *Journal of Church and State*, vol. 4 (Summer 1999), p. 553.

[33] Thus, Witherspoon on Providence:

> While we give praise to God the supreme disposer of all events, for his interposition in our behalf, let us guard against the dangerous error of trusting in, or boasting of an arm of flesh.... If I am not mistaken, not only the holy scriptures in general, and the truths of the glorious gospel in particular, but the whole course of providence, seem intended to abase the pride of man, and lay the vain-glorious in the dust. How many instances does history furnish us with, of those who after exulting over, and despising their enemies, were signally and shamefully defeated. The truth is, I believe, the remark may be applied universally, and we may say, that through the whole frame of nature, and the whole system of human life, that which promises most, performs the least. The flowers of finest colour seldom have the sweetest fragrance. The trees of quickest groweth or fairest form, are seldom of the greatest value or duration. Deep waters move with least noise. Men who think most are seldom talkative. And I think it holds as much in war as in any thing, that every boaster is a coward.

Sandoz, op. cit., pp. 533-535. It is fascinating to compare this and other passages from Witherspoon's sermon to passages in Book III (On Providence) in the *Summa Contra Gentes*, or, say, this passage in Thomas Aquinas' *Summa Theologica*:

> There are three hoary errors on the subject of prayer. Some maintain that human affairs are not ruled by divine providence, and consequently to worship and pray to God is silly. Others maintain that everything happens of necessity, whether from the immutability of providence or from cosmic determinism or from the system of interacting causes; they also rule out the usefulness of prayer. A third group is of the opinion that while human affairs

are indeed ruled by providence and are not the result of necessity, nevertheless the disposition of divine providence is variable and can be swayed by petitions and suchlike. All these postulates we have already disproved. In urging the importance of prayer we should neither load the course of human events with necessity nor yet reckon that the dispositions of the divine plan can be changed. The matter will be made clearer if we consider that divine providence settles not merely what effects shall come about, but also in what manner and from what causes. Human acts should be numbered among the operative factors. Man must needs act, not in order to change the divine dispositions, but in order to execute them according to the order arranged. The situation is very much the same with respect to natural causes. Such is the case with prayer; we do not pray in order to change the divine disposition, but that we may ask for that which God has arranged to be granted through prayer.

Thomas Gilby, trans., *Saint Thomas Aquinas: Philosophical Texts* (New York: Oxford University Press, 1960), pp. 350-351, *Summa Theologica*, 2a-2ae, lxxxiii.2.

[34] Sandoz, op. cit., p. 547.

[35] Witherspoon's fuller quote:

It extends not only to things beneficial and salutary, or to the direction and assistance of those who are the servants of the living God; but to things seemingly most hurtful and destructive, and to persons the most refractory and disobedient. He overrules all his creatures, and all their actions.... Or, to apply it more particularly to the present state of the American colonies, and the plague of war, the ambition of mistaken princes, the cunning and cruelty of oppressive and corrupt ministers, and even the inhumanity of brutal soldiers, however dreadful, shall finally promote the glory of God, and in the mean time, while the storm continues, his mercy and kindness shall appear in prescribing bounds to their rage and fury....

It would be a criminal inattention not to observe the singular interposition of Providence hitherto, in behalf of the American colonies.... The signal advantage we have gained by the evacuation of Boston, and the shameful flight of the army and navy of Britain, was brought about without the loss of a man. To all this we may add, that the counsels of our enemies have been visibly confounded, so that I believe that I may say with truth, that there is hardly any step which they have taken, but it has operated strongly against themselves, and been more in our favor, than if they had followed a contrary course....

True religion is nothing else but an inward temper and outward conduct suited to your state and circumstances in providence at any time. And as peace with God and conformity to him, adds to the sweetness of created comforts while we possess them, so in times of difficulty and trial, it is in the man of piety and inward principle, that we may expect to find the uncorrupted patriot, the useful citizen, and the invincible soldier. God grant that in America true religion and civil liberty may be inseparable, and that the unjust attempts to destroy the one, may in the issue tend to the support and establishment of both.

Sandoz, op. cit., pp. 533, 535, 546-547, 557-558.

[36] Of the remaining twenty-two sermons, nine use citations from the New Testament as the text of the day, and others use Fourth-of-July motions, pamphlets on civil and religious subjects, and the like.

[37] Sandoz, op. cit., frontispiece. Here is how Witherspoon brought the moral force of biblical faith to the cause of independence:

> If your cause is just – you may look with confidence to the Lord and intreat him to plead it as his own. You are all my witnesses, that this is the first time of my introducing any political subject into the pulpit. At this season however, it is not only lawful but necessary, and I willingly embrace the opportunity of declaring my opinion without any hesitation, that the cause in which America is now in arms, is the cause of justice, of liberty, and of human nature. So far as we have hitherto proceeded, I am satisfied that the confederacy of the colonies, has not been the effect of pride, resentment, or sedition, but of a deep and general conviction, that our civil and religious liberties, and consequently in a great measure the temporal and eternal happiness of us and our posterity, depended on the issue. The knowledge of God and his truths have from the beginning of the world been chiefly, if not entirely, confined to those parts of the earth where some degree of liberty and political justice were to be seen, and great were the difficulties with which they had to struggle from the imperfection of human society, and the unjust decisions of usurped authority. There is not a single instance in history in which civil liberty was lost, and religious liberty preserved entire. If therefore we yield up our temporal property, we at the same time deliver the conscience into bondage.

Sandoz, p. 549.

[38] Lutz, op. cit., pp. 22-23.

[39] Ibid., p. 121.

[40]   Congress...also added two references to God, which were conspicuously missing in Jefferson's drafts, where God appeared only as the author of nature's laws and the endower of natural rights, and honor alone was "sacred." At the start of the final paragraph Congress inserted an appeal "to the supreme judge of the world" to affirm "the rectitude of our intentions," which echoed similar provisions in several state and local resolutions on Independence, and nearer the end of the document it also referred to the delegates' "firm reliance on the protection of divine providence." Americans held strong religious beliefs in 1776, and the Declaration was meant to state the convictions of the country's "good people."

Pauline Maier, *American Scripture: Making the Declaration of Independence* (New York: Knopf, 1997), pp. 148-149. Incidentally, prior to Jefferson's draft, more than 320 localities had published their own declarations of independence. Most echoed similar themes (pp. 48-49).

[41] Richard Hooker (1553-1600) offers a taxonomy of the many meanings of *eternal law* and *natural law* in use for centuries:

> I am not ignorant that by "law eternal" the learned for the most part do understand the order, not which God hath eternally purposed himself in all his works to observe, but rather that which with himself he hath set down as expedient to be kept by all his creatures, according to the several conditions wherewith he hath endowed them.... Now that law which, as it is laid up in the bosom of God, they call Eternal, receiveth according unto the different kinds of things which are subject unto it different and sundry kinds of names. That part of it which ordereth natural agents we call usually Nature's law; that which Angels do clearly behold and without any swerving observe is a law Celestial and heavenly; the law of Reason, that which bindeth creatures reasonably in this world, and with which by reason that may most plainly perceive themselves bound; that which bindeth them, and is not known but by special revelation from God, Divine law; Human law, that which out of the law either of reason or of God men probably gathering to be expedient, they make it a law. All things therefore, which are as they ought to be, are conformed unto this second law eternal; and even those things which to this eternal law are not conformable are notwithstanding in some sort ordered by the first eternal law.... Wherefore to come to the law of nature; albeit thereby we sometimes mean that manner of working which God hath set for each created thing to keep; yet forasmuch as those things are termed most properly natural agents, which keep the law of their kind unwittingly, as the heavens and elements of the world, which can do no otherwise than they do; and forasmuch as we give unto intellectual natures the name of Voluntary agents, that so we may distinguish them from the other; expedient it will be, that we sever the law of nature observed by the one from that which the other is tied unto.

Ecclesiastical Polity (Great Britain: Carcanet Press, 1990), Book I, pp. 40-41.

[42] "Fast Day Proclamation of the Continental Congress, December 11, 1776," Worthington C. Ford, Gaillard Hunt, et al., eds., *The Journals of the Continental Congress, 1774–1789* (Washington, D.C.: Government Printing Office, 1904-37), vol. 6, p. 1022.

[43] John Perkins, a pamphleteer writing in 1771, observed that if God had designed human beings to do His will automatically then every person:

> would have been a cold unspirited lump of absurdity; such only as Lucretian genius, or materializing projector would have had the credit of devising – No! Infinite wisdom laid a nobler plan, in which the rational creature, by the

use of moral powers, with Liberty, might approve himself to his maker in a suitable and determin'd degree; with attention to whose laws, providential dispensations, and by the assistance provided for him, he should obtain the happiness his nature was made capable of.

Hyneman and Lutz, op. cit., vol. I, p. 155.

44 William J. Bennett, *Our Sacred Honor* (New York: Simon & Schuster, 1997), p. 394. See also Matthew Spalding and Patrick Garrity, *A Sacred Union of Citizens*:

Over the first six months of the war Washington reorganized the existing forces under his command with the intent of creating a disciplined army. "Men accustomed to unbounded freedom, and no controul [sic]," Washington averred, "cannot brook the Restraint which is indispensably necessary to the good order and Government of an Army; without which, licentiousness, and every kind of disorder triumphantly reign." General Washington's initial orders are especially instructive, for in them he laid out the rules by which he "expected and required" his army to act and around which the new army would by built. The orders make clear that, for Washington, moral as well as physical discipline was necessary for good order. First he expected all geographic distinctions to be laid aside "so that one and the same Spirit may animate the whole." The Continental Congress had placed the troops of the several colonies under their pay and service, making them the army of "the United Provinces of North America." The only competition between various individuals and states should be over who would render the most essential service to "the great and common cause in which we are all engaged." Second, he expected that exact discipline and due subordination be observed, the failure of which would lead to "shameful disappointment and disgrace." Third, he expected a "due observance" of the rules that forbade profane cursing, swearing, and drunkenness. Fourth, he expected all officers and soldiers not on actual duty punctually to attend divine services "to implore the blessings of heaven upon the means used for our safety and defense." Fifth, he expected his officers to pay attention to the neatness and cleanliness of the soldiers.

(New York: Rowman & Littlefield, 1996), p. 14.

45 "To Walk Humbly with Thy God," Circular Address to the States, June 8, 1783. Bennett, op. cit., pp. 379-380. See also Spalding and Garrity, op. cit., pp. 19-23.

46 An early historical account of the battle includes the following passage:

The field artillery, tents, baggage, and about 9,000 men were conveyed to the city of New-York over East River, more than a mile wide, in less than 13 hours, and without the knowledge of the British, though not six hundred yards distant. Providence, in a remarkable manner favoured the retreating army. For some time after the Americans began to cross the state of the tide, and a strong north-east wind made it impossible for them to make use of their sail boats, and their whole number of row boats was insufficient for completing the business, in the course of the night. But about eleven o'clock, the wind died away, and soon after sprung up at south-east, and blew fresh, which rendered the sail boats of use, and at the same time made the passage from the island to the city, direct, easy and expeditious. Towards morning an extreme thick fog came up, which hovered over Long-Island, and by concealing the Americans, enabled them to complete their retreat without interruption, though the day had begun to dawn some time before it was finished. By a mistake in the transmission of orders, the American lines were evacuated for about three quarters of an hour, before the last embarkation took place, but the British though so near, that their working parties could be distinctly heard, being enveloped in the fog knew nothing of the matter. The lines were repossessed and held till six o'clock in the morning, when every thing [sic] except some heavy cannon was removed. General Mifflin, who commanded the rear guard left the lines, and under the cover of the fog got off safe. In about half an hour the fog cleared away, and the British entered the works which had been just relinquished. Had the wind not shifted, the half of the American army could not have crossed, and even as it was, if the fog had not concealed their rear, it must have been discovered, and could hardly have escaped.

David Ramsay, *The History of the American Revolution* (Indianapolis: Liberty Classics, 1990; originally published in 1789), pp. 283-284.

[47] George Washington to Samuel Langdon, September 28, 1789: "The man must be bad indeed who can look upon the events of the American Revolution without feeling the warmest gratitude towards the great Author of the Universe whose divine interposition was frequently manifested in our behalf." Bennett, op. cit., p. 400.

[48] *Federalist Nos. 2, 37, 43*. From France, Alexis de Tocqueville also took up this theme in *Democracy in America* (New York: Anchor Books, 1969), p. xi: "The gradual development of the principle of equality is a providential fact. It has all the chief characteristics of such a fact: it is universal, it is durable, it constantly eludes all human interference, and all events as well as all men contribute to its progress."

[49] *Thanksgiving Day Proclamation of October 20, 1779*, as cited by Jeffrey Hays Morrison, op. cit., *Journal of Church and State*, vol. 4 (Summer 1999), p. 565.

[50] Worthington and Hunt, op. cit., vol. 21, p. 1074.

[51]   In revealing the councils of our enemies, when the discoveries were seasonable and important, and the means seemingly inadequate or fortuitous; in preserving and even improving the union of the several States, on the breach of which our enemies placed their greatest dependence; in increasing the number and adding to the zeal and attachment of the friends of Liberty; in granting remarkable deliverances, and blessing us with the most signal success, when affairs seemed to have the most discouraging appearance; in raising up for us a powerful and generous ally, in one of the first of the Euro-

pean powers; in confounding the councils of our enemies, and suffering them
to pursue such measures as have most directly contributed to frustrate their
own desires and expectations; above all, in making their extreme cruelty to
the inhabitants of these States, when in their power, and their savage devastation of property, the very means of cementing our union, and adding
vigor to every effort in opposition to them.

And as we cannot help leading the good people of these States to a retrospect on the events which have taken place since the beginning of the war,
so we recommend in a particular manner to their observation, the goodness
of God in the year now drawing to a conclusion; in which the Confederation
of the United States has been completed; in which there have been so many
instances of prowess and success in our armies; particularly in the Southern States, where, notwithstanding the difficulties with which they had to
struggle, they have recovered the whole country which the enemy had overrun, leaving them only a post or two on or near the sea; in which we have
been so powerfully and effectually assisted by our allies; in which in all the
conjunct operations the most perfect harmony has subsisted in the allied
army; in which there has been so plentiful a harvest, and so great abundance
of the fruits of the earth of every kind, as not only enables us easily to supply
the wants of the army, but gives comfort and happiness to the whole people;
and in which, after the success of our allies by sea, a General of the first
Rank, with his whole army, has been captured by the allied forces under
the direction of our Commander in Chief...with grateful hearts, to celebrate
the praise of our gracious Benefactor; to confess our manifold sins; to offer
up our most fervent supplications to the God of all grace, that it may please
Him to pardon our offences, and incline our hearts for the future to keep
all his laws; to comfort and relieve all our brethren who are in distress or
captivity; to prosper all husbandmen, and give success to all engaged in lawful commerce; to impart wisdom and integrity to our counsellors, judgment
and fortitude to our officers and soldiers; to protect and prosper our illus-
trious ally, and favor our united exertions for the speedy establishment of a
safe, honorable and lasting peace; and bless all seminaries of learning; and
cause the knowledge of God to cover the earth, as the water covers the seas.
Thanksgiving Day Proclamation of October 26, 1781, in *The Journals of the Continental Congress 1774–1789*, eds. Ford and Hunt, op. cit., pp. 1074-1076.

[52] *Thanksgiving Day Proclamation of October 11, 1782*, in ibid., p. 647.

[53] Bennett, op. cit., p. 387.

[54] This thought is provoked in Jefferson's mind by the consideration of slavery,
and its effect upon the souls of slaves and slaveholders alike. The fuller passage
is:

And can the liberties of a nation be thought secure when we have removed
their only firm basis, a conviction in the minds of the people that these lib-

erties are of the gift of God? That they are not to be violated but with his
wrath? Indeed I tremble for my country when I reflect that God is just: that
his justice cannot sleep for ever.

"Notes on the State of Virginia," in Peterson, op. cit., p. 289.

[55] The verse is the final stanza of "America," about which Professor West
observes:

> Sidney's (and Locke's) overall argument gave to political obligation a new
> basis consistent with Christianity's universal claim but independent of any
> particular religious sect. The God of all mankind could now be the God of a
> particular political community. For if natural liberty and natural law come
> from God, only one kind of community will satisfy God's law: a consent-
> based republic protecting the equal liberty of all. *The final stanza of
> "America" shows that this argument is no mere logical inference but a tenet
> of faith* for the political community that established a representative democ-
> racy dedicated to the proposition that all men are created equal [emphasis
> added].

For context, see Thomas G. West, ed., "Introduction," in Algernon Sidney, *Discourses Concerning Government* (Indianapolis: Liberty Fund, 1996), p. xxii.

Chapter Two: Two Beat as One

[1] Mary Ann Glendon has assembled a list of passages appealing to such qualities
as these in "Philosophical Foundations of the Federalist Papers: Nature of Men,
Nature of Law," *Harvard Journal of Law and Public Policy*, vol. 16, no. 1 (Winter 1993), pp. 23-32. For instance:

> The *Federalist Papers* are not just an appeal to reason over passion. They
> are also a shrewd appeal to certain kinds of passion. Much of their persua-
> sive power comes from the way they speak directly to what Abraham Lincoln
> in his *First Inaugural* was to call "the better angels of our nature." Con-
> sider the passage in which Madison describes his ideal readers: "These
> papers are not addressed to persons [who are biased or without a spirit of
> moderation]. They solicit the attention of those only who add to a sincere
> zeal for the happiness of their country, a temper favorable to a just esti-
> mate of the means of promoting it." Though *The Federalist Papers'* authors
> repeatedly profess their skepticism about the ability of human reason to
> master passion, they frame their arguments to appeal to the human capac-
> ity to do precisely that. They call for "correct and unprejudiced minds," and
> they reach out to "sincere and disinterested advocate[s] for good govern-
> ment.

The best evidence of this point is the structure and style of the papers themselves – the way they state the questions, weigh the evidence, and seriously consider
arguments pro and con. The papers are a virtuoso performance of the exhorta-
tion in *The Federalist No. 71* to consider the ideas in all their aspects and to trace

them out to all their consequences. Thus, the human person, as envisioned by Hamilton, Jay, and Madison, seems to be much more than just a rational calculator. He is also a knower and a chooser, the kind of person who might just possibly be capable of "establishing good government from reflection and choice."
Pp. 29-30. Incidentally, the first appearance of the word "responsibility" in English occurred in *Federalist No. 63* (*Oxford English Dictionary*, *s.v.* "Responsibility"). Charles Kesler was the first to draw attention to this.

[2] See Eric Foner, ed., *Thomas Paine: Complete Writings* (New York: Library of America, 1995); also introduction to the chapter on Paine in *In God We Trust: The Personal Philosophy of the Founding Fathers*, selected and edited with commentary by Norman Cousins (New York: Harper & Row, 1988), pp. 389-393.

[3] "The Snare Broken," in Ellis Sandoz, ed., *Political Sermons of the American Founding Era, 1730–1805* (Indianapolis: LibertyPress, 1991), p. 258.

[4] Ibid.

[5] For other examples, see the texts referred to in notes 22, 24, 32, 33, and 34 infra. *The Jefferson Bible* (New York: Henry Holt & Company, 1995), introduction by Douglas Lurton, pp. ix-x.

[6] See infra, footnote 37.

[7] St. George Tucker, called "the American Blackstone" because he edited an important edition from Blackstone's *Commentaries*, cited in *The Founders' Constitution*, Philip B. Kurland and Ralph Lerner, eds. (Chicago: University of Chicago Press, 1987), vol. 5, p. 98.

[8] William Ellery Channing in 1820, as cited by James Hutson in an unpublished paper, "The Great Doctrine of Retribution: The Founders' Views on the Social Utility of Religion," presented to the John Courtney Murray Seminar at the American Enterprise Institute, 6 June 2000. A revised version of this paper can be found in James Hutson, *Forgotten Features of the Founding: The Recovery of Religious Themes in the Early American Republic* (Lanham, MD: Lexington Books, 2003).

[9] W. B. Allen, ed., *George Washington* (Indianapolis: LibertyClassic, 1988), p. 521.

[10] George Washington, "Farewell Address" in W. B. Allen, ed., *George Washington: Collection* (Indianapolis: Liberty Classics, 1988), p. 521.

[11]   Reason and common sense agreed on the basic elements of morality, and any religion that did not inculcate such a morality was unworthy of the name and deserved no following. Beyond that, however, it was obvious to common sense and to every rational being that a Creator, Preserver, and Supreme Ruler of the universe existed, "the author of all the relations of morality, and of the obligations these [imply]."
Edwin S. Gaustad, *Sworn on the Altar of God: A Religious Biography of Thomas Jefferson* (Grand Rapids: William B. Eerdmans Publishing, 1996), p. 163.

[12] From Rev. Ethan Allen's handwritten history "Washington Parish, Washington City" in the Library of Congress MMC Collection, 1167, MSS, as quoted in James H. Hutson, *Religion and the Founding of the American Republic* (Washington, D.C.: Library of Congress, 1998), p. 96. According to the most sustained study of Jefferson's religious convictions, it is probably more accurate to say that Jefferson was a Unitarian rather than a Christian. He disbelieved in miracles and other evidences of the workings of grace beyond the natural order. But he did believe that Protestant Christianity – as distinct from "monkish superstition" – is crucial to the American Republic, and for this reason he kept his own heterodoxies private and gave biblical Christianity public support. His letters show that he also believed in a divine Judge and, provisionally, in eternal life. The chronicler of his religious journey concludes that:

> Jefferson assumed an ordered, theocentric world; chaos was not king. He also affirmed that ours was and is a moral universe; unrestrained libertinism did not, must not, rule. In addition, he believed that free men and women could not find ultimate satisfaction in a religion devoid of Reason; phantoms and fanaticisms must not drive Reason from its proper place. And finally, Thomas Jefferson knew that he was not God. A large measure of perspective, a considerable degree of humility, arose from the keen sense that he, too, was only one of God's creatures. He, along with all other human beings, did not enter into the world booted and spurred, to mount the backs of those less fortunate. Rather, he, like all women and men, was bound in a bundle with the living, called and challenged to elevate, educate, liberate, and introduce lasting reforms in politics, morality, and religion.

Gaustad, op. cit., p. 228.

[13] Church services were held in the House of Representatives and the Supreme Court as soon as the government moved to Washington in 1800. Jefferson also allowed the War Office and the Treasury buildings to be used for church services. Ministers of all denominations preached at these services. Jefferson permitted members of the Marine Band (executive branch employees) to play in House church services. See Hutson, 1998, op. cit., pp. 84-97; see also, James H. Hutson, "Forum - Thomas Jefferson's Letter to the Danbury Baptists: A Controversy Rejoined" *The William and Mary Quarterly*, vol. 56, no. 4 (1999), pp.775-790; and Daniel L. Dreisbach, "Thomas Jefferson and the Danbury Baptists Revisited" *The William and Mary Quarterly*, vol. 56, no. 4 (1999), pp. 805-816.

[14] Alexis de Tocqueville, *The Old Régime and the French Revolution* (New York: Doubleday, 1955), p. 153.

[15] Ibid., p. 153. Another important text of Tocqueville:

> I do not know if all Americans have faith in their religion – for who can read the secrets of the heart? – but I am sure that they think it necessary to the maintenance of republican institutions. That is not the view of one class or party among the citizens, but of the whole nation; it is found in all ranks.

In the United States, if a politician attacks a sect, that is no reason why the supporters of that very sect should not support him; but if he attacks all sects together, everyone shuns him, and he remains alone.

While I was in America, a witness called at assizes of the county of Chester (state of New York) declared that he did not believe in the existence of God and the immortality of the soul. The judge refused to allow him to be sworn in, on the ground that the witness had destroyed beforehand all possible confidence in his testimony. Newspapers reported the fact without comment.

Alexis de Tocqueville, *Democracy in America*, trans. George Lawrence and ed. J.P. Mayer (New York: Doubleday, 1969), pp. 292-293.

[16] Ibid., p. 295 and pp. 46-47.

[17] Jonathan Mayhew, "The Snare Broken," in Sandoz, op. cit., pp. 258-259.

[18] Ibid., p. 159.

[19] Gaillard Hunt, ed., *The Writings of James Madison* (New York: G. P. Putnam's Sons, 1900-1910) vol. 9, p. 230, as quoted in Hutson, *Religion and the Founding*, p. 96.

[20] "Notes on the State of Virginia," in Merrill D. Peterson, *Thomas Jefferson: Writings* (New York: Library of America, 1984), Query XVIII, p. 289.

[21] *The Constitution of the United States* (Lake Bluff, Ill.: Regnery Gateway, 1986), pp. 314-315.

[22] Benjamin Perley Poore, *The Federal and State Constitutions, Colonial Charters, and other Organizing Laws of the United States* (Washington, D.C.: Government Printing Office, 1878), p. 1409.

[23] Sir William Blackstone, *Commentaries on the Laws of England*, quoted by Verna M. Hall, *Christian History of the Constitution* (San Francisco: Foundation for American Christian Education, 1962, 1979), pp. 140-46. Most of the American founders were lawyers, and many would likely have spent more time with Blackstone than with Locke and gotten their Locke through Blackstone.

[24] *The Political Writings of John Adams* (Liberal Arts Press, 1954), pp. 19-20, as quoted in Stanton Evans, *The Theme is Freedom* (Washington, D.C.: Regnery Publishers, 1994), p. 239.

[25] Jon Butler, *Awash in a Sea of Faith: Christianizing the American People* (Cambridge: Harvard University Press, 1992), pp. 201-202.

[26] Sandoz, op. cit., frontispiece.

[27] Benjamin Rush, "Of the Mode of Education Proper to a Republic" (1798), cited in William J. Bennett, *Our Sacred Honor* (New York: Simon & Schuster, 1997), p. 412.

[28] Ibid.

[29] Ibid.

[30] The great John Witherspoon used the term "state of nature" to describe humans in this state, after the fall:

> I do not speak this only to the heathen, daring profligate, or grovelling sensualist, but to every insensible secure sinner; to all those, however decent and orderly in their civil deportment, who live to themselves and have their part and portion in this life; in fine to all who are yet in a state of nature, for "except a man be born again, he cannot see the kingdom of God."

Sandoz, op. cit., p. 546. What Christians mean by "original sin" – the inherited disorder of man's nature in which each of us is born – differs from what Locke intends by "state of nature." But both concepts put the brakes on utopian hopes. Saint Augustine's classic metaphor was that human nature left to itself, after the fall, continues as a gimpy knee; even when fully healed, every so often it is unreliable. Similarly, Witherspoon preaches:

> The fear of man may make you hide your profanity: prudence and experience may make you abhor intemperance and riot; as you advance in life, one vice may supplant another and hold its place; but nothing less than the sovereign grace of God can produce a saving change of heart and temper, or fit you for his immediate presence.

Ibid., p. 546.

[31] "The Farmer Refuted" (1775), in Harold C. Syrett, ed., *Papers* (New York: Columbia University Press, 1961), vol. 1, p. 87, as quoted by Thomas West, Salvatori lecture.

[32] In a letter dated May 8, 1825, to Henry Lee, Jefferson writes:

> All American whigs thought alike on these subjects. When forced, therefore, to resort to arms for redress, an appeal to the tribunal of the world was deemed proper for our justification. This was the object of the Declaration of Independence. Not to find out new principles, or new arguments, never before thought of, not merely to say things which had never been said before; but to place before mankind the common sense of the subject, in terms so plain and firm as to command their assent, and to justify ourselves in the independent stand we are compelled to take. Neither aiming at originality of principle or sentiment, nor yet copies from any particular and previous writing, it was intended to be an expression of the American mind, and to give to that expression the proper tone and spirit called for by the occasion. All its authority rests then on the harmonizing sentiments of the day, whether expressed in conversation, in letters, printed essays, or in the elementary books of public right, as Aristotle, Cicero, Locke, Sidney, &c. The historical documents which you mention as in your possession, ought all to be found, and I am persuaded you will find, to be corroborative of the facts and principles advanced in that Declaration.

Peterson, op. cit., p. 1500.

[33] The founders often pair together Algernon Sidney and John Locke, although they more often cite Locke. Sidney is religiously more orthodox than Locke, and closer to the traditions of Aristotle and Cicero in defining liberty and linking it to certain indispensable virtues. Both authors were, in their respective masterpieces, commenting on the same work of Filmer. However, Sidney gives a larger role to virtue in the definition of liberty; Locke tends to stress the natural equality of all and thus to see individuals as "equal," that is, denuded of the virtues that characterize them differentially. In this, Sidney is closer to the ancients, and Locke to the tendencies of modernity. On *these* matters (not all) Sidney is a better guide to what the founders actually said and did than Locke. But this is not the place for a long argument on the relative merits of Sidney and Locke. See Thomas West, Introduction, *Discourses*, by Algernon Sidney (Indianapolis: Liberty Fund, 1997).

Note also that by interpreting the American constitutional tradition in a Lockean way apart from Sidney, and thus detaching liberty from virtue, and virtue from religion, Lockean interpreters may have been nudging the country down the winding road to Gomorrah, into the decadence that has destroyed many nations. See Robert Bork's analysis of the three errors in liberal – *i.e.*, Lockean – presuppositions, in *Slouching Toward Gomorrah* (New York: Regan Books, 1996), pp. 53-54.

[34] Some followers of Leo Strauss argue that Locke used conventional Christian language in order to subvert it. (Locke never asserts such an intention.) But one does not suppose that those whose moves in chess end in disaster intended what they did not have the wit to foresee. Just so, one ought not to take as willful the unforeseen logical consequences of moves taken in the heat of play even by philosophers. Locke's logic might lead to crass materialism, for instance, but it would be difficult to show that Locke himself was a crass materialist. On the difficult terrain between philosophy and religion, thinkers are often led into trains of logic that were no part of their intention. It is altogether possible that, in good faith, Locke's philosophical equipment was not subtle enough to make all the distinctions his argument needed.

Besides, if it is legitimate to argue that Locke used Christian terms to subvert Christian premises, it is equally legitimate to hypothesize that many in the founding generation used Lockean terms for Christian purposes. It is true that "natural rights" are not mentioned in the Bible *in ipsis verbis* (but then neither is the "trinity"), and it is true that (among others) Locke supplied the term. Yet,the content which at least some founders gave to the term had more to do with what they learned from the Bible than with the content Locke gave to it, as shown in many of the citations above.

[35] Bennett, op. cit., p. 41.

[36] Ibid., p. 408: John Adams to Benjamin Rush, 2 February 1807.

[37] Ibid., p. 398 for this and the previous quotation. Noah Webster, "Advice to the Young," from *Value of the Bible and the Excellence of the Christian Religion, 1834.*

[38] Ibid., p. 406. For a more elaborate analysis, see Mark David Hall, *The Political and Legal Philosophy of James Wilson, 1742–1798* (Columbia: University of Missouri Press, 1957), Chapter 2, "James Wilson, Morality and Natural Law," pp. 35-67.

[39] Sandoz, op. cit., "A Sermon Given on the Day of the Commencement of the Constitution," October 25, 1780, pp. 631-656.

[40] Ibid., p. 637.

[41] Ibid., pp. 647-648.

[42] See Michael Novak, *God's Country: Taking the Declaration Seriously* (1999 Francis Boyer Lecture) (Washington, D.C.: AEI Press, 2000).

[43] James Walsh points out that "the mental and moral philosophy of these theses, the metaphysics and ethics as taught by the college presidents and tutors, were a direct heritage from the Scholastic philosophy of the medieval universities." He gives as one instance, "a pair of linked theses presented at the College of Rhode Island (Brown)":

> *Deus potest esse ergo est* (God can be, therefore He exists). Any "clerke of Oxenforde" or of Paris would have been able to take part handsomely in this disputation, could he have been translated to eighteenth-century Providence. For this is one form of the ontological argument for the existence of God first called to the attention of the Schoolmen by St. Anselm in the eleventh century.

James J. Walsh, *The Education of the Founding Fathers of the Republic; Scholasticism in the Colonial Colleges; a Neglected Chapter in the History of American Education* (New York: Fordham University Press, 1935), pp. 11-13.

[44]
> Our frame is contriv'd, as everything through universal nature is, with nothing wanting, nothing redundant. And our being endow'd with reason and understanding, instead of more instinctive powers, shows that we were ordain'd for self-direction, in conducting by the former: And in fact, we find that we determine frequently on action and conduct by consideration and reflection, without any instinctive impulse, further than self-love, which without the other, is blind in the human species.

John Perkins, in Charles Hyneman and Donald S. Lutz, eds., *American Political Writing During the Founding Era: 1769–1805*, 2 vols. (Indianapolis: Liberty Fund, 1983), vol. 1, p. 148.

[45] Peterson, op. cit., pp. 814-16, "Letter to Peter Carr, 19 August 1785."

[46] From "A Bill Establishing a Provision for Teachers of the Christian Religion," quoted in John Eidsmoe, *Christianity and the Constitution: The Faith of Our Founding Fathers* (Grand Rapids: Baker Books, 1987), p. 310.

[47] Tocqueville, *Democracy*, op. cit., vol. I, part II, 9, p. 292. It is here that Tocqueville calls religion "the first of their political institutions." A powerful phrase.

[48] Ibid.

[49] Ibid., p. 293.

[50] Ibid., vol. II, part I, 5, pp. 442-446.

[51] Ibid, part II, 15, pp. 542ff.

[52] Quoted by James Madison, *Notes of Debates in the Federal Convention of 1787* (New York: W.W. Norton, 1987), pp. 209-210.

[53] Tocqueville, *Democracy*, op. cit., p. 291.

[54] Philip B. Kurland and Ralph Lerner, eds., *The Founders' Constitution* (Chicago: The University of Chicago Press, 1987), vol. 1, pp. 166-169.

[55] William Lee Miller, *The Business of May Next* (Charlottesville: University of Virginia Press, 1992), p. 22.

[56] Hamden [Pseud.], "On Patriotism," *South Carolina Gazette* (Charleston), Nov. 29, 1773, in footnote 9, as cited in Lutz, op. cit., p. 77.

[57] Quoted by Rocco Pezzimenti, *The Open Society and its Friends* (Millennium Editrice: Roma, 1997, and Fowler Wright Books: Leominster, U.K.), p. 59.

[58] Professor Lutz summarizes as follows:

> Instead of viewing the community as antagonistic to individual interests, rights, and liberties, the Americans of that era saw it as the primary means for fulfilling individual goals. The conclusion followed from the first fundamental conviction discussed earlier – humans develop and maintain the highest levels of moral and material existence on Earth while living in communities. As Levi Hart wrote: "Civil society is formed for the good of the whole body of which it is composed. Hence the welfare and prosperity of the society is the COMMON GOOD, and every individual is to seek and find his happiness in the welfare of the whole, and everything to be transacted in society, is to be regulated by this standard."... Furthermore, the communitarian spirit resulted from and enhanced individual equality. "A state of society necessarily implies reciprocal dependence in all its members; and rational government is designed to realize and strengthen this dependence and to render it, in such equal in all ranks, from the supreme magistrate, to the meanest peasant, that each may feel himself bound to seek the good of the whole community." True self-interest was the pursuit of the common good of the community. Self-interest at odds with the community was mistaken, because it was short term. But the long-run interest of the individual invariably matched that of the entire community.

The Origins of American Constitutionalism (Baton Rouge: Louisiana State University Press, 1988), pp. 76-77.

[59] Israel Evans, "A Sermon Delivered at the Annual Election" (1791), Sandoz, op. cit., p. 1062.

[60] John Leland, "The Rights of Conscience Inalienable" (1791), ibid., p. 1085.

[61] Washington, Letter to Colonel Benedict Arnold dated 14 September 1775; quoted by John Eidsmoe, *Christianity and the Constitution: The Faith of Our Founding Fathers* (Grand Rapids: Baker Books, 1987), pp. 122-123.

[62] Miller, op. cit., p. 115.

[63] Hitchcock, "An Oration in Commemoration of the Independecne of the United States of America" (1793), Sandoz, op. cit., p. 1183.

[64] Tocqueville, *Democracy*, op. cit., pp. 46-47.

Chapter Three: Immoral Man, Moral Society...

[1]   Had no important step been taken by the leaders of the Revolution for which a precedent could not be discovered, no government established of which an exact model did not present itself, the people of the United States might at this moment have been numbered among the melancholy victims of misguided councils, must at best have been laboring under the weight of some of those forms which have crushed the liberties of the rest of mankind. Happily for America, happily, we trust, for the whole human race, they pursued a new and more noble course. They accomplished a revolution which has no parallel in the annals of human society. They reared the fabrics of governments which have no model on the face of the globe. They formed the design of a great Confederacy, which it is incumbent on their successors to improve and perpetuate. If their works betray imperfections, we wonder at the fewness of them.

The Federalist Papers (New York: New America Library, 1961), *No. 14*, pp. 104-5.

[2] I borrow much in this chapter from John T. Noonan, Jr., *The Lustre of Our Country* (Berkeley: University of California Press, 1998), especially from the chapter "JM's Original Insight," pp. 61-90.

[3] Ibid., quoting Witherspoon, p. 65.

[4] Ibid., p. 78.

[5]   My own opinion has always been in favor of a bill of rights; provided it be so framed as not to imply powers not meant to be included in the enumeration. At the same time I have never thought the omission a material defect, nor been anxious to supply it even by subsequent amendment, for any other reason than that it is anxiously desired by others.

Robert A. Goldwin, *From Parchment to Power* (Washington, D.C.: AEI Press, 1997), quoting Madison, p. 62.

   Madison was confident that this mistrust was unwarranted. But for a constitution establishing popular government, based on consent of the people and majority rule, with powers limited so as to secure the rights of the minority and of individuals – for such a constitution, he came to realize, it is not enough to have the allegiance of "the great mass of the people," of "the whole community." With such universal allegiance, the majority can be expected to restrain itself, by appeal to the Constitution, on those occasions when it is tempted to deny the rights of the minority by the exercise of abusive majority power.

Ibid., p. 73.

6 Ibid., p. 73.

7 See Goldwin for an account on how Madison introduced the proposals for the Bill of Rights, op. cit., pp. 105-108.

8 Ibid., p. 174.

9 Robert A. Rutland, *George Mason, Reluctant Statesman* (Baton Rouge: Louisiana State University Press, 1989), p. 93. See also Goldwin, "Fisheries, Post Roads, and Ratifications," op. cit., pp. 169-175.

10 Goldwin, op. cit., pp. 80-81.

11 Ibid., p. 62.

12 Ibid., pp. 162-163.

13 Wilfred Parsons, S.J., *The First Freedom: Considerations on Church and State in the United States* (New York: The Declan X. McMullen Company, 1948), pp. 30-49.

14 Quoted by V. Phillip Muñoz, "Religion and the Social Compact: James Madison's Principle of Religious 'Non-Cognizance'" (draft of a doctoral dissertation for Claremont Graduate School, on file with the author), p. 7.

15 James H. Hutson, *Religion and the Founding of the American Republic* (Washington, D.C.: The University Press of New England, 1998), pp. 96-97.

16 "Religious bondage shackles and debilitates the mind and unfits it for every noble enterprise, every expanded prospect." "Letter to William Bradford, 1 April 1774," in Robert S. Alley, ed., *James Madison on Religious Liberty* (Buffalo: Prometheus Books, 1985), p. 50.

17 A constitution protecting religious liberty, moreover, would encourage immigration, a point Madison makes in his "Memorial and Remonstrance," which undoubtedly would lead to an influx of even more sects. Enlarging the orbit of republican government could prevent the emergence of a single dominant religious majority. Minority sects could then check one another, as was done in Virginia, preventing any one sect from receiving preferential treatment. If properly arranged, diversity of religious opinion – which, hitherto, had been an impetus to religious oppression – could be transformed into the principal protection of religious liberty.

Muñoz, op. cit., p. 13.

[18] James Madison, "Memorial and Remonstrance Against Religious Assessments," in Philip B. Kurland and Ralph Lerner, eds., *The Founders' Constitution* (Chicago: University of Chicago Press, 1987), vol. 5, p. 82.

[19] Noonan, op. cit., pp. 72-73.

[20]   And Mr. Madison, stressing the students' need for "pretty full information," proceeded to reply with thoughtful deliberation until his friend pressed him for a quicker answer. His list for the university included a substantial number of the Fathers of the Church; the lights of the Dominican and Franciscan orders, Thomas Aquinas and Duns Scotus; Calvin, Socinius; later controversialists, among them the Jesuit Robert Bellarmine and the Protestant champion William Chillingsworth and the Jansenist Catholic Blaise Pascal; and the "celebrated work" of Samuel Clark, a theologian warmly recommended at Princeton by the Reverend Witherspoon and still reverently remembered by Mr. Madison. The choices were ponderous but discriminating. Not a single book of infidelity or skepticism, no Voltaire or Hume or Paine was listed, no works loose in their principles or "Enemies to religion."

Ibid., p. 86.

[21]   If men were angels, no government would be necessary. If angels were to govern men, neither external nor internal controls on government would be necessary. In framing a government which is to be administered by men over men, the great difficulty lies in this: you must first enable the government to control the governed; and in the next place oblige to control itself.

The Federalist Papers No. 51, op. cit., p. 322.

[22] "Letter to Edward Livingston, 10 July 1822," in Robert S. Alley, op. cit., p. 83.

[23] Sam Adams, "Letter to James Warren, 4 November 1775," in Kurland and Lerner, eds., op. cit., vol.1, pp. 668-669.

[24] Article III continues as follows:

And the people of this Commonwealth have also a right to, and do, invest their legislature with authority to enjoin upon all the Subjects an attendance upon the instructions of the public teachers aforesaid, at stated times and seasons, if there be any on whose instructions they can Conscientiously and conveniently attend – *PROVIDED, notwithstanding*, that the several towns, parishes, precincts, and other bodies politic, or religious societies, shall, at times, have the exclusive right of electing their public Teachers, and of contracting with them for their support and maintenance. –And all monies, paid by the Subject of the support of the public teacher or teachers of his own religious sect or denomination, provided there be any on whose institution he attends; otherwise it may be paid towards the support of the teacher or teachers of the parish or precinct in which the said monies are raised – And every denomination of Christians, demeaning themselves peaceably, and as good Subjects of the Commonwealth, shall be equally under the protection of the Law: And no subordination of any one sect or denomination to another shall ever be established by law.

"The Massachusetts Constitution of 1780, Article III," in Kurland and Lerner, op. cit., vol. 5, pp. 77-78.

[25] John Witte, Jr., finds six distinct objections to Article III's establishment of public religious institutions:

1. The charge that Article III's establishment of public religious institutions contradicted the liberties of private religions guaranteed in Article II.

2. The charge that the happiness of a people and the good order and preservation of civil government did not, as a matter of historical fact, depend on piety, religion, and morality.

3. An acknowledgment of the utility of piety, morality, and religion, but a fear that such an institutional establishment would jeopardize both religion and the state.

4. The charge that to institute even a mild establishment would inevitably lead to more odious forms.

5. An amplification of Isaac Backus' charge that Article III constituted another species of taxation without representation – now in the religious sphere.

6. The charge that Article III's final guarantee of the equality of all denominations simply contradicted the prior provisions on state tax support for some denominations.

See "'A Most Mild and Equitable Establishment:' John Adams and the Massachusetts Experiment," in James H. Hutson, *Religion and the New Republic: Faith in the Founding of America* (Lanham, MD: Rowman & Littlefield, 2000), pp. 23-24.

[26] Witte arranges the supporters in the following groups:

- One group of proponents, composed of congregationalist ministers, invoked traditional "theocratic" arguments for this institutional establishment.

- A second group thought such an institutional establishment was an inevitable and innocuous act of a political majority seeking to promote the common good and the personal happiness of all subjects.

- A third group argued that tithing and other forms of state support for religious institutions would ultimately serve to keep the state small and efficient. The congregationalist preacher Joseph McKeen put this well: "The more, therefore, that the principles of piety, benevolence, and virtues are diffused among a people, the milder may their government and laws be, and the more liberty are they capable of enjoying, because they govern themselves." In *A Sermon Preached on the Public Fast in the Commonwealth of Massachusetts* (Salem: Thomas C. Cushing, 1793), pp. 17-21.

- But the most thorough defense of the provisions in Article III was offered by Theophilus Parsons, who had already written the 1778 Essex Result and was now writing as chief Justice of the Massachusetts Supreme Juridical Court:

To object that this is a violation of conscience is to mistake man's conscience for his money. But as every citizen derives the security of his
property, and fruits of his industry, from the power of the state, so, as the
price of this protection, he is bound to contribute, in common with his fellow-
citizens.... The great error lies in not distinguishing between liberty of
conscience in religious opinions and worship, and the right of appropriat-
ing money by the state. The former is an unalienable right; the latter is
surrendered to the state, as the price of protection.... The object of public
religious instruction is to teach, and to enforce by suitable arguments, that
practice of a system of morals among the people, and form and cultivate
reasonable and just habits and manners; by which every man's person and
property are protected from outrage, and his personal and social enjoyments
promoted and multiplied. From these effects every man enjoys the most
important benefits; and whether he be, or be not, an auditor of any public
teacher, he receives more solid and permanent advantages from the public
instruction, than the administration of justice in courts of law can give him.
The like objection may be made by any man to the support of public schools.
Ibid., pp. 24-29.

27   My first venture in political philosophy, published in 1932, was entitled
Moral Man and Immoral Society. Its thesis was the obvious one, that collective self-regard of class, race, and nation is more stubborn and persistent
than the egoism of individuals. This point seemed important, since secular
and religious idealists hoped to change the social situation by beguiling the
egoism of individuals, either by adequate education or by pious benevolence.
A young friend of mine recently observed that, in the light of all the facts and
my more consistent "realism" in regard to both individual and collective
behavior, a better title might have been *The Not so Moral Man in His Less
Moral Communities.*
Reinhold Niebuhr, *Man's Nature and His Communities: Essays on the Dynamics
and Enigmas of Man's Personal and Social Existence* (New York: Scribner's,
1965), p. 22.

28 Barry A. Shain, *The Myth of American Individualism* (Princeton: Princeton
University Press, 1994), p. 278.

29 Ibid., p. 279. The internal quote is from Michael Kammen's *Spheres of Liberty*
(Madison: University of Wisconsin Press, 1986), pp. 21-22.

30 Ibid., p. 280. Shain is quoting from the *New-York Weekly Journal*, 7 July 1740.

31 "'Letter by J.,' in *The Boston Evening Post* for 23 May 1763," in Charles S.
Hyneman and Donald S. Lutz, eds., *American Political Writing During the Founding Era, 1760–1805*, 2 vols. (Indianapolis: Liberty Press, 1983), vol. 1, p. 23.

32 Lord Acton, cited in J. Rufus Fears, ed., *Essays in Religion, Politics, and
Morality; Selected Writings of Lord Acton* (Indianapolis: Liberty Classic, 1988),

p. 613. The full text is:

> The Catholic notion, defining liberty not as the power of doing what we like, but the right of being able to do what we ought, denies that general interests can supersede individual rights.

See also p. 491:

> The center and supreme object of liberty is the reign of conscience. Religion produced this force only in the seventeenth century – just as it redeemed slavery only in the nineteenth century, in the 30 years from 1833 to 1864.

[33] "On the cover page, Jefferson described the contents [of his revised New Testament] as 'an abridgement of the New Testament for the use of the Indians, unembarrassed with matters of fact or faith beyond the level of their comprehension.'" F. Forrester Church, "Introduction," *The Jefferson Bible: The Life and Morals of Jesus of Nazareth* (Boston: Beacon Press, 1989).

[34] Thomas Jefferson, *Jefferson's "Bible,"* with an introduction by F. Forrester Church and an afterword by Jaroslav Pelikan (Boston: Beacon Press, 1989). Introductions by William Murchison and Judd W. Patton (Grove City: American Book Distributors, 1996), pp. xiii-xvii.

[35]   The assertion of that *principle* [liberty], at *that time*, was the word, "fitly spoken," which has proved an "apple of gold" to us. *The Union*, and the *Constitution*, are the Picture of Silver, subsequently framed around it.

Roy P. Basler, ed., *The Collected Works of Abraham Lincoln* (New Brunswick, NJ: Rutgers University Press, 1953), vol. 4, p. 169.

[36] Hutson, 1998, op. cit., p. 15.

[37] See Hutson, ibid., for a useful summary, especially chapter 5.

[38] Ibid., pp. xiv and 18. Even worse, between 1659-1662, Quakers were hanged in Massachusetts and persecuted in Virginia.

[39] Incidentally, Carroll's top priority was that there be no religious test for office. Carroll's reflections continued:

> That hope was thus early entertained, because all of them joined the same cause, with few exceptions of individuals. God grant that this religious liberty may be preserved in these States, to the end of time, and that all believing in the religion of Christ may practice the leading principle of charity, the basis of every virtue.

"Letter to Rev. John Stanford, 9 October 1827," in Kate M. Rowland, ed., *The Life and Correspondence of Charles Carroll of Carrollton, 1737–1832*, 2 vols. (New York: G. P. Putnam & Sons, 1898), vol. 2, p. 358.

[40] John Carroll eulogized George Washington as follows:

> Religion and observation had taught him, that God's provident wisdom "reacheth from end to end mightily, and disposeth all things sweetly." This became the polar star, by which he was guided in his progress through life,

and in all his anxious solicitude for maintaining the liberty, perfecting the policy, preserving the peace, insuring the stability of his country on the foundations of order and morality, and guarding it against the turbulence of faction, licentiousness, foreign hostility and artifice.

John Carroll, "Eulogy on George Washington," in Julian L. Maline and Wilfred M. Mallon, et al., eds., *The Prose and Poetry of America* (Syracuse, NY: The L.W. Singer Company, 1949), pp. 428-429.

[41] Goldwin, op. cit., pp. 66-68.

[42]   But preachers in America are continually coming down to earth. Indeed they find it difficult to take their eyes off it. The better to touch their hearers, they are forever pointing out how religious beliefs favor freedom and public order, and it is often difficult to be sure when listening to them whether the main object of religion is to procure eternal felicity in the next world or prosperity in this.

Alexis de Tocqueville, *Democracy in America*, translated by George Lawrence and edited by J. P. Mayer (New York: Doubleday & Company, 1969), p. 530.

[43] The full text of the First Amendment is:
      Congress shall make no law respecting an establishment of religion, or prohibiting the free exercise thereof; or abridging the freedom of speech, or of the press, or the right of the people peaceably to assemble, and to petition the Government for a redress of grievances.

[44] For reformed Protestants, the ability of the saved individual (saint) to live voluntarily in accordance with the laws of God was an important indication to both the individual and the community that he or she was indeed truly reborn in Christ. Shain, op. cit., p. 125.

[45] See Hutson, op. cit., 1998, p. 96. See also James H. Hutson, "Forum – Thomas Jefferson's Letter to the Danbury Baptists: A Controversy Rejoined," *The William and Mary Quarterly*, vol. 56, no. 4 (1999): pp. 775-790, and, in the same issue, Daniel L. Dreisbach, "Thomas Jefferson and the Danbury Baptists Revisited," pp. 805-816.

[46] When, at the Constitutional Congress, Peter Sylvester of New York objected to the provision that "'no religion shall be established by law,' because 'it might be thought to have a tendency to abolish religion altogether,' Madison replied that he understood the language to mean merely that 'Congress should not establish *a* religion, and enforce the legal observation of it by law.'" *Annals of Congress*, 1:757 (August 15, 1789) as quoted in Walter Berns, "Religion and the Founding Principle," in Robert H. Horwitz, ed., *The Moral Foundations of the American Republic*, p. 209.

[47] James Hutson, "'Nursing Fathers:' the model for church-states relations in America from James I to Jefferson" (on file with author).

[48] See Daniel Dreisbach, *Thomas Jefferson and the Wall of Separation Between Church and State* (New York: University Press, forthcoming in 2002). Dreisbach presented a preview of his book to the John Courtney Murray Seminar at the American Enterprise Institute (May 2001). See also his *Real Threat and Mere Shadow* (Westchester, IL: Crossway Books, 1987), pp. 47-54, 125 ff. In his *William and Mary* article (fn. 45), Dreisbach reprints a facsimile of Jefferson's clear, easily legible, handwritten letter. The Library of American edition of Jefferson, incredibly, also still reprints the mistranscription.

[49] *The Federalist Papers*, op. cit., pp. 144-145.

[50] George Washington, "Farewell Address," in W. B. Allen, ed., *George Washington: A Collection* (Indianapolis: Liberty Classics, 1988), pp. 521-522.

[51] John Adams, "To the Officers of the First Brigade of the Third Division of the Militia of Massachusetts, October 11, 1798" in Bennett, *Our Sacred Honor* (New York: Simon & Schuster, 1997), p. 370.

[52] John Adams, "Letter to Zabdiel Adams, 21 June 1776" in William Bennett, op. cit., p. 371.

[53] George Washington, "First Inaugural Address," in George Allen, ed., op. cit., p. 462.

[54]   Whilst the last members were signing it Doctor Franklin looking towards the President's Chair, at the back of which a rising sun happened to be painted, observed to a few members near him, the Painters had found it difficult to distinguish in their art a rising from a setting sun. "I have," said he, "often and often in the course of the Session, and the vicissitudes of my hopes and fears as to its issue, looked at that behind the President without being able to tell whether it was rising or setting: But now at length I have the happiness to know that it is a rising and not a setting sun."
James Madison, *Notes of Debates in the Federal Convention of 1787* (New York: W. W. Norton and Company, 1966), p. 659.

[55] Max Farrand, ed., *The Records of the Federal Convention of 1787*, rev. ed., 4 vols. (New Haven, CT: Yale University Press, 1966), vol. 3, p. 85.

Chapter Four: A Religious Theory of Rights

[1] Alexis de Tocqueville, *Democracy in America*, ed. J. P. Mayer, trans. G. Lawrence (New York: Anchorbooks, 1969), p. 450.

[2] Hugh Nolan, ed., *Pastoral Letters of the United States Catholic Bishops*; vol. I: *1792–1940* (Washington, D.C.: United States Catholic Conference, 1983), p. 228.

[3]   If we regard the Bill of Rights as a verbal portrait of "the People of the United States," what do we see? Starting with the opening words of the First Amendment, we see that this is a people who takes religion very seriously,

seriously enough to insist that all Americans be free to choose how they will worship, if they choose to worship at all; who cannot be required to follow governmental or any other sort of dictate in matters of religion, or be denied the right to follow ancient religious practice, if that is their choice; who will not seek to impose their religious beliefs or practices on others, or allow others to impose their beliefs on them. This is a people who will insist that their voices be heard, in speech and print; who will not hesitate to broadcast their own opinions, however unpopular, or to hear them from others, no matter how unwelcome they many be; who expect to have much to say about the governing of their nation; and who will gather together, if and when they so choose, to let the government know, peaceably but unmistakably, when they have grievances.

Robert A. Goldwin, *From Parchment to Power* (Washington, D.C.: AEI Press, 1997), pp. 180-181.

[4] Letter "To Henry Lee" (8 May 1825) in Merrill D. Peterson, *Jefferson: Writings* (New York: Library of America, 1984), p. 1502.

[5] John Adams, "A Dissertation on the Canon and Feudal Law," in George W. Carey, ed., *The Political Writings of John Adams* (Washington, D.C.: Regnery Publishing, 2000), p. 19.

[6] Ibid.

[7]   Instead of establishing religion, the founders *established* religious freedom, and the principle of religious freedom derives from a non-religious source. Rather than presupposing a Supreme Being, the institutions they established presuppose the rights of man, which were discovered by Hobbes and Locke to exist prior to all government – in the state of nature to be precise. To secure these rights, men must leave the state of nature, which they do by giving their consent to civil government. Nevertheless, the rights presuppose the state of nature, and the idea of the state of nature is incompatible with Christian doctrine. According to Christian doctrine, "the first and great commandment" is to love God, and the second, which is like unto it, is to love one's neighbor as oneself. In the state of nature, however, man is not obliged to love anyone, but merely to preserve himself and, what is more to the point, "to preserve the rest of mankind [only] when his own preservation comes not in competition."

Walter Berns, "Religion and the Founding Principle," in Robert H. Horwitz, ed., *The Moral Foundations of the American Republic* (Charlottesville: University Press of Virginia, 1986), pp. 204-229, at 215.

[8] Michael Zuckert, *The Natural Rights Republic* (Notre Dame: University of Notre Dame Press, 1996).

[9] Michael Zuckert, "Founder of the Natural Rights Republic," in Thomas S. Engeman, *Thomas Jefferson and the Politics of Nature* (Notre Dame: Notre Dame University Press, 2000), pp. 11-58.

[10] Ibid., p. 17.

[11] Thucydides, *The Peloponnesian Wars* (New York: Modern Library, 1951), p. 331.

[12] Quoted in Forrest McDonald, *Novus Ordo Seclorum: The Intellectual Origins of the Constitution* (Lawrence: University of Kansas, 1985), p. 9.

[13] Tocqueville, op. cit., p. 288.

[14] John Locke, *Second Treatise of Government*, chap. II, para. 6.

[15] Zuckert, 1996, op. cit., pp. 119-122.

[16] Ibid., pp. 13-39.

[17] Ibid., pp. 151-152.

[18] Zuckert discusses the research by Alice Baldwin, *The New England Clergy and The American Revolution* (Durham, NC: F. Ungar, 1958) and Claude Newline, *Philosophy and Religion in Colonial America* (New York: Greenwood Press, 1962). He argues that these scholars suggest that Locke's influence, especially as regards the political message of the preachers, was overwhelming. He cites Baldwin, who wrote that "all through the New England colonies the ministers were helping to spread the theories of the philosophers and to give them religious sanctions." This caused a dramatic new openness to "Natural Religion," which was philosophical more than scriptural. More recent scholarship comes to a similar conclusion, which Zuckert summarizes as follows:

> Dworetz finds [in *Unvarnished Doctrine: Locke, Liberalism, and the American Revolution* (Durham: Duke University Press, 1990)] that the ministers came early to Locke – well before 1763 – and their constant preaching of him made his political ideas thoroughly familiar to the American public, regardless of whether the latter had read Locke or not. "Most Americans before and after 1763, and especially in New England, 'absorbed' Lockean political ideas *with* the Gospel."

Ibid., p. 151.

[19] Ibid., pp. 156-157. See John Locke, *Two Treaties of Government* (New York: The New American Library, 1963), pp. 179 and 184, for references to Bellarmine. There is reason to believe Locke was familiar with Suárez's work. See the introduction by W. von Leyden to John Locke, *Essays on the Law of Nature* (Oxford: Clarendon Press, 1954), pp. 36-37.

[20] I am not ignorant that by "law eternal" the learned for the most part do understand the order, not which God hath eternally purposed himself in all his works to observe, but rather that which with himself he hath set down as expedient to be kept by all his creatures, according to the several conditions wherewith he hath endued them. They who thus are accustomed to speak apply the name of law unto that only rule of working which superior

NOTES TO CHAPTER FOUR   211

authority imposeth; whereas we somewhat more enlarging the sense thereof term any kind of rule or canon, whereby actions are framed, a law. Now that law which, as it is laid up in the bosom of God, they call *Eternal*, receiveth according unto the different kinds of things which are subject unto it different and sundry kinds of names. That part of it which ordereth natural agents we call usually *Nature's* law; that which Angels do clearly behold and without any swerving observe is a law *Celestial* and heavenly; the law of *Reason*, that which bindeth them, and is not known but by special revelation from God, *Divine* law; *Human* law, that which out of the law either of reason or of God men probably gathering to be expedient, they make it a law. All things therefore, which are as they ought to be, are conformed unto *this second law eternal*; and even those things which to this eternal law are not conformable are notwithstanding in some sort ordered by *the first eternal law*. For what good or evil is there under the sun, what action correspondent or repugnant unto the law which God hath imposed upon his creatures, but in or upon it God doth work according to the law which himself hath eternally purposed to keep; that is to say, the *first law eternal?* So that a twofold law eternal being thus made, it is not hard to conceive how they both take place in all things.

Wherefore to come to the law of nature: albeit thereby we sometimes mean that manner of working which God hath set for each created thing to keep; yet forasmuch as those things are termed most properly natural agents, which keep the law of their kind unwittingly, as the heavens and elements of the world, which can do no otherwise than they do; and forasmuch as we give unto intellectual natures the name of *Voluntary* agents, that so we may distinguish them from the other; expedient it will be, that we sever the law of nature observed by the one from that which the other is tied unto.

Richard Hooker, *Ecclesiastical Polity* (Great Britain: Carcanet Press, 1990), Book I, pp. 40-41.

[21] Acton summarizes as follows:

Gregory VII had begun the disparagement of civil authorities by saying that they are the work of the devil; and already in his time both parties were driven to acknowledge the sovereignty of the people, and appealed to it as the immediate source of power.

Two centuries later this political theory had gained both in definiteness and in force among the Guelphs, who were the Church party, and among the Ghibellines, or Imperialists. Here are the sentiments of the most celebrated of all the Guelphic writers: "A king who is unfaithful to his duty forfeits his claim to obedience. It is not rebellion to depose him, for he is himself a rebel whom the nation has a right to put down. But it is better to abridge his power, that he may be unable to abuse it. For this purpose, the whole nation ought to have a share in governing itself; the Constitution ought to combine a limited and elective monarchy, with an aristocracy of merit, and such an admixture of democracy as shall admit all classes to office, by popular election. No government has a right to levy taxes beyond the limit determined by the people. All political authority is derived from popular suffrage, and all laws must be made by the people or their representatives. There is no security for us as long as we depend the will of another man."

This language, which contains the earliest exposition of the Whig theory, is taken from the works of St. Thomas Aquinas, of whom Lord Bacon says that he had the largest heart of the school divines. And it is worthwhile to observe that he wrote at the very moment when Simon de Montfort summoned the Commons; and that the politics of the Neapolitan friar are centuries in advance of the English statesman's.

From "The History of Freedom in Christianity," in *The History of Liberty*, Rufus J. Fears, ed., (Indianapolis: Liberty Classics, 1985), p. 34.

[22] St. Thomas writes:

If to provide itself with a king belongs to the right of a given multitude, it is not unjust that the king be deposed or have his power restricted by that same multitude if, becoming a tyrant, he abuses the royal power.

Ibid., p. 27.

[23] Person signifies what is noblest in the whole of nature (*Summa Theologica* Ia.xxix.2).

Among substances the individual merits a special name, and so is termed *hypostasis, suppositum, or first substance.* Particular individuals have a still more special and perfect existence in rational substances who are masters of their own activity and act of themselves, unlike other things which are acted upon. Therefore singular rational substances receive the special name of *persons* (*Summa Theologica* Ia.xix.I).

An individual who is governed for the sake of the species is not governed because of any inherent worth. But human persons come under divine providence in their own right, for the activities of rational creatures alone are divinely directed for the sake of the individual as well as of the species (III *Contra Gentes*, 113).

St. Thomas Aquinas, Philosophical Texts, trans. Thomas Gilby (New York: Oxford University Press, 1960), pp. 389, 392. The historical emergence of personal dignity was beautifully treated by Jacques Maritain with respect to the arts in *Creative Intuition in Art and Poetry*, Bollinger Series (New York: Pantheon Books, 1953); and with respect to politics in *The Person and the Common Good*, trans. John J. Fitzgerald (New York: Charles Scribner's Sons, 1947).

[24] "It is lawful for a man to hold private property; and it is also necessary for the carrying on of human life." *Summa Theologica* 2a–2ae, Q. lxvi, art. 2.

[25] *Contra Impugnantes, Dei cultum at religionem* (Paris, September-October 1256).

[26] "Although the judgment of an erring reason is not derived from God, yet the erring reason puts forward its judgment as being true, and consequently as being derived from God, from Whom is all truth." *Summa Theologica* I-II, Q.19, art. 5. And also Question 17, art. 4 in *De Veritate*: In the Fourth Article We Ask: Does A False Conscience Bind? James McGlynn, S.J., trans., *The Disputed Questions on Truth* (Chicago: Henry Regnery Company, 1953), p. 329.

[27] Donald Lutz, *The Origins of American Constitutionalism* (Baton Rouge: Louisiana State University Press, 1988), p. 118.

[28] Michael Novak, "The Catholic Whig Revisited," in Brian Anderson, ed., *On Cultivating Liberty: Reflections on Moral Ecology by Michael Novak* (Lanham: Rowman & Littlefield, 1999), pp. 145-60.

[29] See especially the books by Jacques Maritain, *Reflections on America* (New York: Scribner, 1958) and R. L. Bruckberger, *Image of America* (New York: Viking Press, 1959).

[30] The twenty-six papers given at the conference displayed a great deal of self-confidence, even boastfulness. They are reprinted in the special volume, William H. Hughes, *Souvenir Volume: Three Great Events in the History of the Catholic Church in the United States* (New York: Arno Press, 1978).

> Our American constitution is the only philosophical, or dialectic, constitution the world has ever known. It has not only eliminated the barbarism of the Greco-Roman civilization, abolished all privileged and slave classes, and extended equal rights to all, but it is founded in a living principle. All life is based on unity in diversity; on extremes, with a medium of reconciliation. Unity without diversity is stagnation or death; diversity without unity is discord. The first results in centralized despotism; the second, in anarchy. Our constitution, by the providential events which gave it birth, rather than by human counsel, is not only democratic, but, by the division of the powers of government between the general and the state governments, each acting in its own sphere, is founded in truth and in reality, has in it the principle of life, and so long as it is preserved in its essential character, cannot die.
>
> The American system is also anti-Protestant, and must either reject Protestantism or be overthrown by it. Based on natural law and justice, our institutions are incompatible with a religion claiming to be revealed, but which fails to harmonize the natural and the supernatural, reason and revelation, calls reason "a stupid ass," and says nature is totally depraved.

H. F. Browson, "Lay Action in the Church," p. 29.

[31] This mixture of the ancient and the new is not unique to the founding generation of Americans. It was altogether typical of Renaissance Rome. The Sistine Chapel, for instance, draws deliberately on a sense of analogs from the Torah, the ancient Greeks and Romans, and the New Law of Christ.

> The violet cloud against which the Creator stretches out a creative finger to Adam is in the shape of the human cortex: a vivid rendering of the *Imago Dei.* Not unlike Michelangelo, the founding generation admired Greece and Rome, Jerusalem and the Christian past, and in their case the common law of London and the economic insights of Adam Smith's Edinburgh. The logic of the liberty they erected into "a new model for the ages" has many roots. See James Madison in *Federalist #14.*
>
> Is it not the glory of the people of America that, whilst they have paid a decent regard to the opinions of former times and other nations, they have not suffered a blind veneration for antiquity, for custom, or for names, to overrule the suggestions of their own good sense, the knowledge of their own situation, and the lessons of their own experience? To this manly spirit posterity will be indebted for the possession, and the world for the example, of the numerous innovations displayed on the American theater in favor of private rights and public happiness.

The Federalist Papers (New York: New America Library, 1961), p. 104.

[32] Carey, op. cit., p. 19.

[33] Hamilton, in *The Federalist Papers*, op. cit., p. 33. See also Mary Ann Glendon, "Philosophical Foundations of the Federalist Papers: Nature of Men, Nature of Law," *Harvard Journal of Law and Public Policy*, vol. 16, no. 1 (Winter 1993), pp. 23-32.

[34] "Summary View of the Rights of British America," in *Thomas Jefferson: Writings*, ed. Merrill D. Peterson (New York: Library of America, 1984), p. 122.

[35] Quoted in Russell Kirk, *The Conservative Constitution* (Washington, D.C.: Regnery, 1990), ch. 6, p. 81.

[36] On the power of this theme, see Matthew Spalding and Patrick J. Garrity, *A Sacred Union of Citizens* (Lanham: Rowman & Littlefield, 1996).

[37]   Washington...believed that the formation of character – whether of a man or a nation – was the first and most important step toward independence and greatness. "[T]he first transactions of a nation, like those of an individual upon his first entrance into life," Washington wrote at the time of the ratification of the Constitution, "make the deepest impression, and are to form the leading traits in its character." The success of the American experiment in self-government would require good laws and good citizens, and Washington set out to establish a nation of both. The way to do so, he concluded, was to establish rightly from the very beginning not only a sense of character as a nation but also a nation of character.

Ibid., pp. 10-11. See also ch. 1 "Remembering Washington's Legacy," pp. 3-4, and ch. 2, "Establishing the National Character."

[38] James Madison, *Notes of Debates in the Federal Convention of 1787* (New York: W. W. Norton & Co., 1987), p. 209.

[39] In the classic phrase of Aquinas, they may be *actus hominis*, but they cannot be *actus humanus*. They may be actions "of a man" (like twitching one's toes inadvertently while lying on the beach), but not "human actions." The distinguishing mark of the latter is that, to the question, 'What are you doing?' the answer would not be, 'Nothing' – as it would be in the case of the inadvertent twitching – but something like 'I'm trying to…,' expressing conscious purpose.

Aquinas: "Of the actions done by man those alone are properly called human which are proper to man insofar as he is a man – only those actions which proceed from deliberate will are properly called human actions." (ST I-II, Q. 1, Art. 1).

[40] Harry Jaffa rightly goes beyond Locke to Aristotle:

> Lincoln's morality then extends the full length of Jefferson's, but it also goes further. Jefferson's horizon, with its grounding in Locke, saw all commands to respect the rights of others as fundamentally hypothetical imperatives: *if* you do not wish to be a slave, then refrain from being a master. Lincoln agreed, but he also said in substance: he who wills freedom for himself must simultaneously will freedom for others. Lincoln's imperative was not only hypothetical; it was categorical as well. Because all men by nature have an equal right to justice, all men have an equal duty to do justice, wholly irrespective of calculations as to self-interest. Or, to put it a little differently, our own happiness, our own welfare, cannot be conceived apart from our well-doing, or just action, and this well-doing is not merely the adding to our own security but the benefiting of others. Civil society, for Lincoln as for Aristotle and Burke, is a partnership "in every virtue and in all perfection." And, while our duties to friends and fellow citizens take precedence over duties to those who are not friends or fellow citizens, the possibility of injustice exists in every relationship with every other human being. Indeed, if it was not possible to do justice to non-fellow citizens, the possibility of justice and friendship with fellow citizens would not exist. For civil society is the realization of a potentiality which must exist whenever man encounters his fellow, or it is not a potentiality anywhere. And that potentiality, for Lincoln, found its supreme expression in the proposition that "all men are created equal."

Harry V. Jaffa, *The Crisis of the House Divided: An Interpretation of the Issues in the Lincoln-Douglas Debates* (Chicago: University of Chicago Press, 1959), p. 327. In a recent essay, Jaffa wrote

> That the Founding, which Lincoln inherited, was dominated by an Aristotelian Locke – or a Lockean Aristotle – has been a conspicuous theme of my writing since 1987…. My critics, friendly and unfriendly, may ask why it took me so long to see the purloined letter on the mantelpiece. The reason is that I took for granted that the account of the Hobbesian Locke in Leo Strauss's *Natural Right and History* represented the Locke that informed the American founding. That rights were prior to duties, that duties were derived from rights, that civil society arose from a contract solely for mutual self-preservation, and that the goods of the soul were subordinated in all

> decisive respects to the goods of the body, were conclusions of Strauss's interpretation. Strauss himself never said that this Locke was the Founders' Locke, but the spell cast by his book led many of us to apply it to the Founders. Many former students of Strauss, to this day, regard it as heresy to think that Strauss's chapters on Hobbes and Locke do not constitute the authoritative account of the philosophic foundations of American constitutionalism…. Strauss also taught us that the authors of the past – and this certainly included political men no less than philosophers – were to be understood as they understood themselves, before the attempt was made to understand them differently or better. It was, and is, an anachronism to assume that the Founders read Locke through the eyes of Strauss!

"Aristotle and Locke in the American Founding," *Claremont Review*, Winter 2001, p. 10.

[41] For a defense of Locke against the charges of flatness and insipidity, see Thomas G. West, "John Locke, Philosopher of the Founding *And Why We Should Be Glad He Was*" (unpublished paper presented at American Enterprise Institute at the John Courtney Murray lecture), October 4, 2000.

[42] Our contemporaries are naturally little disposed to belief, but once they accept religion at all, there is a hidden instinct within them which unconsciously urges them toward Catholicism. Many of the doctrines and customs of the Roman Church astonish them, but they feel a secret admiration for its discipline, and its extraordinary unity attracts them.

Tocqueville, op. cit., p. 450.

[43] James Wilson, "Oration on the Fourth of July," in Colleen A. Sheehan and Gary L. McDowell, eds., *Friends of the Constitution: Writings of the "Other" Federalists, 1787–1788* (Indianapolis: Liberty Fund, 1998), pp. 502-503.

[44] G. K. Chesterton, "The Blue Cross," *The Father Brown Stories* (London: The Folio Society, 1996), vol. 1, p. 21.

[45] *Fides et Ratio*, encyclical of John Paul II, September 14, 1998, in *Origins*, vol. 28, no. 19 (October 22, 1998), pp. 317-348.

[46] Quoted by A. S. Will, *Life of Cardinal Gibbons, Archbishop of Baltimore*, vol. I (New York: E. P. Dutton & Company, 1922), pp. 309-310.

[47] Michael Novak, "St. Thomas in Motion," *Downside Review*, 78 (1960), 293-302.

[48] See Jacques Maritain, *Existence and the Existent*, Lewis Galantiere and Gerald Phelan, trans. (New York: Image Books, 1956). See especially chapter 1, "Being," pp. 20-51.

[49] Two points should be observed concerning the healthy constitution of a state or nation. One is that all should play a responsible part in the governing: this ensures peace, and the arrangement is liked and maintained by all. The other concerns the type of government; on this head the best arrangement

for a state or government is for one to be placed in command, presiding by authority over all, while under him are others with administrative powers, yet for the rulers to belong to all because they are elected by and from all. Such is the best polity, well combined from the different strains of monarchy, since there is one at the head; of aristocracy, since many are given responsibility; and of democracy, since the rulers are chosen from and by the people. (*Summa Theologica*, Ia-2ae, cv. I.)

Thomas Gilby, op. cit., p. 382.

[50] On the historical development of the term see my "Thomas Aquinas, 'The First Whig,'" in *This Hemisphere of Liberty* (Washington, D.C.: AEI Press, 1992), pp. 107-123.

[51]   The history of natural rights theories can best be seen as a series of creative responses to a variety of past experiences.... But I do not want to argue that the whole story of natural rights is just a chapter of historical accidents. The point is rather that, once the idea that all persons possess rights had grown in to existence, it displayed a remarkable vitality and adaptability and proved relevant to a variety of emerging problems.... The medieval idea that liberty is a natural right led on to effective movements for the abolition of slavery only when it was reinforced by the humanitarian impulses of the late Enlightenment.

Brian Tierney, *The Idea of Natural Rights* (Grand Rapids: Wm. B. Eerdmans Publishing, 1997), p. 345.

[52] Fears, op. cit., p. 508.

[53] *Contra Impugnantes, Dei Cultum at Religionem* (Paris, September-October 1256).

[54] James A. Weisheipl, O.P., *Friar Thomas D'Aquino: His Life, Thought and Works* (Garden City, NY: Doubleday & Company, 1974), pp. 32-33.

[55] Saint Ambrose (339-397), Archbishop of Milan, prevented the Emperor Theodosius from entering Milan Cathedral. The saint banned Theodosius from the cathedral after the massacre of a subject population in Thessalonica, an action long considered the origin of the practice of sancturay. In the words of Ambrose:

They claim that everything is legal for the emperor since everything belongs to him. To this I reply: Think not, Caesar, that you have imperial authority over divine things. Make no such claim, and if you wish for a long reign, make your submission to God. It is written: 'To God what is God's; to Caesar what is Caesar's.' To the emperor the palace, to the priest the churches. Your rights extend to the public buildings, not to sacred ones.

Newman C. Eberhardt, *A Summary of Catholic History*, vol. I (St. Louis: B. Herder, 1961), p. 164.

[56] Reprinted in *First Things*, April 1998, as "John Paul II on the American Experiment," pp. 36-37.

Chapter Five: Ten Questions About the Founding

[1] Wilfred M. McClay, *A Student's Guide To U.S. History* (Wilmington, DE: Intercollegiate Studies Institute, 2000), pp. 73-74.

[2] For an "unscientific" sampling of prayers, see Josiah Benjamin Richard, ed., *God of Our Fathers* (Reading, PA: Reading Books, 1994). For example, this version of The Lord's Prayer from Benjamin Franklin's personal papers (1779):

> Heavenly Father, may all revere thee and become thy dutiful children and faithful subjects. May thy laws be obeyed on earth as perfectly as they are in Heaven. Provide for us this day as thou has hitherto daily done. Forgive us our trespasses and enable us likewise to forgive those that offend us. Keep us out of temptation, and deliver us from evil.

Richard, p. 70.

[3] In *Federalist No. 2*:

> It has often given me pleasure to observe that independent America was not composed of detached and distant territories, but that one connected, fertile, widespreading country was the portion of our western sons of liberty. *Providence* has in a particular manner blessed it with a variety of soils and productions and watered it with innumerable streams for the delight and accommodation of its inhabitants. A succession of navigable waters forms a kind of chain round its borders, as if to bind it together; while the most noble rivers in the world, running at convenient distances, present them with highways for the easy communication of friendly aids and the mutual transportation and exchange of their various commodities.
>
> With equal pleasure I have as often taken notice that *Providence* has been pleased to give this one connected country to one united people – a people descended from the same ancestors, speaking the same language, professing the same religion, attached to the same principles of government, very similar in their manners and customs, and who, by their joint counsels, arms, and efforts, fighting side by side throughout a long and bloody war, have nobly established their general liberty and independence.
>
> This country and this people seem to have been made for each other, and it appears as if it was the *design of Providence that an inheritance so proper and convenient for a band of brethren, united to each other by the strongest ties,* should never be split into a number of unsocial, jealous, and alien sovereignties.

The Federalist Papers (New York: New America Library, 1961), p. 38.

[4] Alexis de Tocqueville, *Democracy in America*, trans. and ed. Harvey C. Mansfield and Delba Winthrop (Chicago: University of Chicago Press, 2000), pp. 505-506.

[5] Ibid., p. 501.

[6]   I doubt that men were more virtuous in aristocratic centuries than in others, but it is certain that the beauties of virtue were constantly spoken of then;

only in secret did they study the side on which it is useful. But as the imagination takes a less lofty flight and each man concentrates on himself, moralists become frightened at this idea of sacrifice and they no longer dare to offer it to the human mind; therefore they are reduced to inquiring whether the individual advantage of citizens would not be to work for the happiness of all, and when they have discovered one of the points where particular interest happens to meet the general interest and to be confounded with it, they hasten to bring it to light; little by little such observations are multiplied. What was only an isolated remark becomes a general doctrine, and one finally believes one perceives that man, in serving those like him, serves himself, and that his particular interest is to do good.... In the United States it is almost never said that virtue is beautiful. They maintain that it is useful and they prove it every day. American moralists do not claim that one must sacrifice oneself to those like oneself because it is great to do it; but they say boldly that such sacrifices are as necessary to the one who imposes them on himself as to the one who profits from them.

Ibid., pp. 500-501.

[7] Ibid., p. 502.

[8] The great security against a gradual concentration of the several powers in the same department, consists in giving to those who administer each department the necessary constitutional means and personal motives to resist encroachments of the others. The provision for defense must in this, as in all other cases, be made commensurate to the danger of attack. Ambition must be made to counteract ambition. The interest of the man must be connected with the constitutional rights of the place. It may be a reflection on human nature, that such devices should be necessary to control the abuses of government. But what is government itself, but the greatest of all reflections on human nature? If men were angels, no government would be necessary. If angels were to govern men, neither external nor internal controls on government would be necessary. In framing a government which is to be administered by men over men, the great difficulty lies in this: you must first enable the government to control the governed; and in the next place oblige it to control itself. A dependence on the people is, no doubt, the primary control on the government; but experience has taught mankind the necessity of auxiliary precautions. This policy of supplying, by opposite and rival interests, the defect of better motives, might be traced through the whole system of human affairs, private as well as public. We see it particularly displayed in all the subordinate distributions of power, where the constant aim is to divide and arrange the several offices in such a manner as that each may be a check on the other that the private interest of every individual may be a sentinel over the public rights. These inventions of prudence cannot be less requisite in the distribution of the supreme powers of the State.

Federalist No. 51, p. 321.

⁹ Tocqueville, Mansfield and Winthrop, op. cit., p. 505.

¹⁰ Three versions of *The Jefferson Bible* are available. The first is introduced by F. Forrester Church and has an afterword by Jaroslav Pelikan (Boston: Beacon Press, 1989); the second has a foreword by Judd W. Patton (Grove City: American Book Distributors, 1996); the third is introduced by Douglas Lurton (New York: Henry Holt & Co., 1995). These words of Jefferson were taken from the introduction by F. Forrester Church, p. viii.

¹¹ "Virginia Declaration of Rights" (12 June 1776), found in Philip B. Kurland and Ralph Lerner, eds., *The Founders' Constitution* (Chicago: University of Chicago Press, 1987), vol. I, p. 7.

¹²   But before we see how Congress's drafting committee and the committee's designated draftsmen put together the Declaration that Congress took up on July 2, it's worth our while to stop and examine the other "Declarations of Independence" that Americans in colonies (or, as they soon became, states) and localities adopted between April and July 1776, of which Virginia's was one among many. There are, in fact, at least ninety documents in that category, and perhaps still more waiting to be found. Most have been forgotten under the influence of our national obsession with "the" Declaration of Independence, although the bulk of them were published almost a century and a half ago, scattered through the pages of Peter Force's voluminous *American Archives*.

Pauline Maier, *American Scripture: Making the Declaration of Independence* (New York: Alfred A. Knopf, 1997), p. 48.

¹³ For Lonergan's view on common sense, see his Chapter VI, "Common Sense and Its Subject" and Chapter VII, "Common Sense as Object." The chapters contain a general discussion and finish with the treatment of its bias (weakness). He defines common sense as follows:

We have worked toward the notion of common sense as an intellectual development. Naturally enough, there will arise the question of the precise inventory of this public store. How does it define its terms? What are its postulates? What are the conclusions it infers from the premises? But if the question is obvious enough, the answer is more difficult. For the answer rests on one of those queer insights that merely grasps the false supposition of the question. Definitions, postulates, and inferences are the formulation of general knowledge. They regard, not the particular but the universal, not the concrete but the abstract. Common sense, unlike the sciences, is a specialization of intelligence in the particular and the concrete. It is common without being general, for it consists in a set of insights that remains incomplete, until there is added at least one further insight into the situation in hand and, once that situation has passed, the added insight is no longer relevant, so that common sense at once reverts to its normal state of incompleteness.... Common sense...clings to the immediate and practical, the concrete and particular. It remains within the familiar world of things for us.

Bernard J. F. Lonergan, *Insight: A Study of Human Understanding* (New York: Longmans, Green & Co., 1958), pp. 175, 179. Lonergan analyzes the "bias" in this fashion:

> To err is human, and common sense is very human. Besides the bias of the dramatic subject, of the individual egoist, of the member of a given class or nation, there is a further bias to which all men are prone. For men are rational animals, but full development of their animality is both more common and more rapid than a full development of their intelligence and reasonableness.... The lag of intellectual development, its difficulty and its apparently meagre [sic] returns bear in an especial manner on common sense. It is concerned with the concrete and the particular. It entertains no aspirations about reaching abstract and universal laws. It is easily led to rationalize its limitations by engendering a conviction that other forms of human knowledge are useless or doubtfully valid. Every specialist runs the risk of turning his specialty into a bias by failing to recognize and appreciate the significance of other fields. Common sense almost invariably makes that mistake; for it is incapable of analyzing itself, incapable of making the discovery that it too is a specialized development of human knowledge, incapable of coming to grasp that its peculiar danger is to extend its legitimate concern for the concrete and the immediately practical into disregard of larger issues and indifference to long-term results.

Ibid., pp. 225-226.

14   Enlightened by a benign religion, professed, indeed, and practiced in various forms, yet all of them inculcating honesty, truth, temperance, gratitude, and the love of man; acknowledging and adoring an overruling Providence, which by all its dispensations proves that it delights in the happiness of man here and his greater happiness hereafter – with all these blessings, what more is necessary to make us a happy and a prosperous people?

Merill D. Peterson, *Thomas Jefferson: Writings* (New York: Library of America, 1984), "Summary View of the Rights of British America," p. 494.

15 "Pastoral Letter issued by the Third Plenary Council of Baltimore, December 7, 1884," in Hugh Nolan, ed., *Pastoral Letters of the United States Catholic Bishops* (United States Catholic Conference, 1984), p. 228.

16   Our public discourse has been shaped, in ways we may be only dimly aware of, by the teachings, or the popular corruptions of the teachings, of the great thinkers of the modern age. Charles Darwin taught us, we suppose, that a person is the isolated product of a competition for survival among selfish genes coping with material circumstances; his or her morals are entirely utilitarian and self-centered. Sigmund Freud taught us, we suppose, that guilt is an unhealthy expression of a repressed impulse; to live well we must overcome guilt. Karl Marx taught us, we suppose, that we are driven entirely by economic impulses; the societies we produce are based simply on the power relationships that result from class warfare. Scholars who have studied these

thinkers know that their teachings were more complex and subtle than this
and, at least in the case of Darwin, quite different. No matter; the spirit of
the age will shape how any message is understood.
James Q. Wilson, *The Moral Sense* (New York: Free Press, 1993), p. viii.

[17] See Vernon Parrington, *Main Currents in American Thought* (New York: Harcourt, Brace and Company, 1927); Charles Beard, *An Economic Interpretation of
the Constitution of the United States* (New York: Free Press, 1965).

[18] See Leo Pfeffer, *Church, State, and Freedom* (Boston: Beacon Press, 1953),
and *God, Caesar, and the Constitution: The Court as Referee of Church-State
Confrontation* (Boston: Beacon Press, 1975).

[19] For a brief discussion of this "new class," see *The American Vision: An Essay on
the Future of Democratic Capitalism*:
> Since World War II, great changes in the American social order have altered
> the domestic balance of power. Even a short time ago there would have been
> widespread agreement with Calvin Coolidge's sentiment, "the business of
> America is business." Since World War II, a new social class has emerged
> whose main business is not business. The fact that there is such a class – the
> intellectual class, or more exactly, the class whose power base lies in "the
> knowledge industry" and in the State – is not new. But two powerful changes
> have recently raised the status of that class: (1) it has grown enormously in
> numbers, both in its leadership cadres and in the millions of citizens whose
> cause is linked with theirs; and (2) simultaneously, powerful instruments of
> social change have emerged which are perfectly suited to its own needs and
> purposes. These are the national media of communication, especially televi-
> sion and radio, but also the national news magazines, and the major national
> organs of daily news. These two changes have critically affected the nation's
> self-understanding. The "rules of the game" have been changed.

(Washington, D.C.: AEI Press, 1978), pp. 29ff.

[20] See Lionel Trilling, *Beyond Culture: Essays on Literature and Learning* (New
York: The Viking Press, 1968).
> Trilling's is the classic text identifying a specific "adversary culture" within
> U.S. culture, a culture that now governs the mainstream in the universities,
> the magazines, movies, and television. Coincident with its rise is the grad-
> ual collapse of the prestige of scientific and technical elites, and even of the
> idea of progress. This adversary culture celebrates the antibourgeois
> virtues. By its own innermost intention, it defines itself *against* the common
> culture. It has increasingly lost its connection with ordinary people, whom
> it is inclined to scorn. *They* are religious, but the adversary culture is not.
> More than 100 million Americans attend church or synagogue every week-
> end, but the so-called popular culture of Hollywood and television is
> ignorant of this powerful vein of popular life.

Michael Novak, *The Catholic Ethic and the Spirit of Capitalism* (New York: Free Press, 1993), p. 211.

[21] In a forthcoming study, "Ministers of Reform and the Gospel of Progress," Matthew Spalding argues that the Social Gospel Movement was less a justification of progressive reforms and more a deeply problematic and widely influential reinterpretation of theology that embraced the methods of the new social sciences, in particular the new economics (which tended socialist) and Social Darwinism (which undermined original sin, among other things), and was anti-capitalist, pro-statist and de-emphasized personal moral responsibility.

[22] Gordon Wood, *The Creation of the American Republic* (Chapel Hill: University of North Carolina Press, 1968), pp. 273-282.

[23] Catholics, in particular, highly value the emphasis on the human *duty* to worship God in the American approach to religious liberty. John Noonan in a chapter called "James [sic] Maritain Loves James Madison" describes how the French philosopher came to see that the "constitutional arrangements of the United States" are of "exceptional historic significance" and how Maritain's views came to influence the Catholic embrace of religious liberty. Noonan argues that the Second Vatican Council followed the analysis of the American arrangements advanced by Jacques Maritain and John Courtney Murray, S.J., in defining religious liberty quite carefully:

> Religious liberty, the report continued, does not entail "indifferentism," as though it makes no difference what one believes, nor freedom from the human obligation to God, nor the relativism of truth, nor *pessimissimus dilettantismus*, that one has a quasi-right to be content with one's uncertainty as to religious truth and no need to search and struggle to discover it. The Fathers of the Council were asked not to take religious liberty in any of these senses. What did the term mean? Two things: positively, "the right of the human person to the free exercise of religion according to the dictate of the person's conscience"; negatively, immunity from all external coercion in such matters. Affirming the existence of religious truth and the duty to seek it, the report asked the Council to assert the inviolability of the person in relationship to God.

The Lustre of Our Country (Berkeley: University of California Press, 1998), pp. 336-342.

[24] See, *e.g.*, Niebuhr's discussion on "Having, and Not Having, the Truth" in *The Nature and Destiny of Man* (New York: Macmillan, 1943). My own brief summary of this long passage in Niebuhr is as follows: "There is always some truth in the errors of others and some error in my truth. The standard of evidence is beyond all of us. We need to listen hard – even where we would rather not listen – to learn all that we might learn about reality, especially moral reality." *On Cultivating Liberty*, Brian Anderson, ed. (Lanham, MD: Rowman & Littlefield, 1999), p. 25.

25 James Madison, "Memorial and Remonstrance Against Religious Assessments" (20 June 1785), found in Philip B. Kurland and Ralph Lerner, eds., *The Founders' Constitution* (Chicago: University of Chicago Press, 1987), vol. 5, p. 82. Compare the Virginia Declaration of Rights in 1776:

> That Religion, or the *duty* which we owe to our *Creator*, and the manner of discharging it, can be directed only by reason and conviction, not by force or violence; and, therefore, all men are equally entitled to the free exercise of religion, according to the dictates of conscience; and that it is the mutual duty of all to practise Christian forbearance, love, and charity, towards each other. [emphasis on "duty" added]

Kurland and Lerner, op. cit., p. 7.

26   Only in freedom can man direct himself toward goodness. Our contemporaries make much of this freedom and pursue it eagerly; and rightly so, to be sure. Often, however, they foster it perversely as a license for doing whatever pleases them, even if it is evil.

    For its part, authentic freedom is an exceptional sign of the divine image within man. For God has willed that man remain "in the hand of his own counsel" so that he can seek his Creator spontaneously, and come freely to utter and blissful perfection through loyalty to Him. Hence man's dignity demands that he act according to a knowing and free choice. Such a choice is personally motivated and prompted from within. It does not result from blind internal impulse nor from mere external pressure.

    Man achieves such dignity when, emancipating himself from all captivity to passion, he pursues his goal in a spontaneous choice of what is good, and procures for himself, through effective and skillful action, apt means to that end. Since man's freedom has been damaged by sin, only by the help of God's grace can he bring such a relationship with God into full flower. Before the judgment seat of God each man must render an account of his own life, whether he has done good or evil.

Gaudium et Spes, in Walter Abbott, S.J., ed., *The Documents of Vatican II* (America Press, 1966), pp. 214-215, para. 17.

27   The Church values the democratic system inasmuch as it ensures the participation of citizens in making political choices, guarantees to the governed the possibility both of electing and holding accountable those who govern them, and of replacing them through peaceful means when appropriate. Thus she cannot encourage the formation of narrow ruling groups which usurp the power of the State for individual interests or for ideological ends.

    Authentic democracy is possible only in a State ruled by law, and on the basis of a correct conception of the human person. It requires that the necessary conditions be present for the advancement both of the individual through education and formation in true ideals, and of the "subjectivity" of society through the creation of structures of participation and shared responsibility. Nowadays there is a tendency to claim that agnosticism and skeptical relativism are the philosophy and the basic attitude which correspond to democratic forms of political life. Those who are convinced that they know the truth and firmly adhere to it are considered unreliable from a democratic point of view, since they do not accept that truth is determined by the majority, or that it is subject to variation according to different political trends. It must be observed in this regard that if there is no ultimate truth to guide and direct political activity, then ideas and convictions can easily be manipulated for reasons of power. As history demonstrates, a democracy without values easily turns into open or thinly disguised totalitarianism.

Nor does the Church close her eyes to the danger of fanaticism or fundamentalism among those who, in the name of an ideology which purports to be scientific or religious, claim the right to impose on others their own concept of what is true and good. *Christian truth* is not of this kind. Since it is not an ideology, the Christian faith does not presume to imprison changing sociopolitical realities in a rigid schema, and it recognizes that human life is realized in history in conditions that are diverse and imperfect. Furthermore, in constantly reaffirming the transcendent dignity of the person, the Church's method is always that of respect for freedom.

But freedom attains its full development only by accepting the truth. In a world without truth, freedom loses its foundation and man is exposed to the violence of passion and to manipulation, both open and hidden. The Christian upholds freedom and serves it, constantly offering to others the truth which he has known (cf. Jn 8:31-32), in accordance with the missionary nature of his vocation. While paying heed to every fragment of truth which he encounters in the life experience and in the culture of individuals and of nations, he will not fail to affirm in dialogue with others all that his faith and the correct use of reason have enabled him to understand.

Centesimus Annus (London: Catholic Truth Society, 1991).

28   Furthermore, in the course of this century the Popes, following in the footsteps of Leo XIII, systematically developed the themes of Catholic social doctrine, expounding the characteristics of a just system in the area of relations between labour and capital. We may recall the Encyclical *Quadragesimo Anno* of Pius XI, the numerous interventions of Pius XII, the Encyclicals *Mater et Magistra* and *Pacem in Terris* of John XXIII, the Encyclical *Populorum Progressio* and the Apostolic Letter *Octogesima Adveniens* of Paul VI. I too have frequently dealt with this subject: I specifically devoted the Encyclical *Laborem Exercens* to the importance of human labour, while in *Centesimus Annus* I wished to reaffirm the relevance, one hundred years later, of the doctrine presented in *Rerum Novarum*. In my Encyclical *Sollicitudo Rei Socialis* I had earlier offered a systematic reformulation of the Church's entire social doctrine against the background of the East-West confrontation and the danger of nuclear war. The two elements of the Church's social doctrine – *the safeguarding of human dignity*

and rights in the sphere of a just relation between labour and capital and *the promotion of peace* – were closely joined in this text. The Papal Messages of 1 January each year, begun in 1968 in the pontificate of Paul VI, are also meant to serve the cause of peace. [emphasis in original]
Tertio Millennio Adveniente (Pauline Books, 1994).

29 The widely debated symposium "The End of Democracy?" appeared in *First Things* in 1996. The original contributions and many responses have been published by Richard John Neuhaus, ed., *The End of Democracy?: The Celebrated* First Things *Debate, with Arguments Pro and Con and "The Anatomy of a Controversy"* (Dallas: Spence Publishing, 1997).

30 Alexis de Tocqueville, *Democracy in America*, translated by George Lawrence and edited by J. P. Mayer (New York: Doubleday, 1969), p. 681.

31 What appears to be happening is that the elite is becoming more secular. The secularization thesis holds that America is rapidly becoming a secular society. Research has shown this to be false. Americans are as religious as they have been in the past, perhaps more so. See Richard John Neuhaus, *Unsecular America* (Grand Rapids: William B. Eerdmans Publishing Co., 1986). Peter Berger captures this in his famous aphorism that if India is the most religious country in the world, and Sweden the least religious, then America is a nation of Indians ruled by Swedes.

32 See "Thomas Aquinas, the First Whig," in Michael Novak, *This Hemisphere of Liberty* (Washington, D.C.: AEI Press, 1992), pp. 107-123.

33 Aquinas as translated by Thomas Gilby, *St. Thomas Aquinas, Philosophical Texts* (New York: Oxford University Press, 1960), p. 392: "Person signifies what is noblest in the whole of nature."

34   Divine providence extends to all things. Yet a special rule applies where intelligent creatures are involved. For they excel all others in the perfection of their nature and the dignity of their end: they are masters of their activity and act freely, while others are more acted on than acting. They react to their destiny by their own proper activity, that is by knowing and loving God, whereas other creatures show only some traces of this likeness.... To begin with, rational creatures are governed for their own benefit, whereas other creatures are governed for the sake of men. Men are principals, not merely instruments.... But rational creatures have an affinity to the whole, for, in a sense, each is all. They are not made for anyone's utility. Providence directs rational creatures for the welfare and growth of the individual person, not just for the advantage of the race.
Ibid., pp. 355-356.

35 Lord Acton quotes a text he attributes to Aquinas and appends his own comments as follows:

"A king who is unfaithful to his duty forfeits his claims to obedience. It is not rebellion to depose him, for he is himself a rebel whom the nation has a right to put down. But it is better to abridge his power that he may be unable to abuse it. For this purpose, the whole nation ought to have a share in governing itself; the Constitution ought to combine a limited and elective monarchy, with an aristocracy of merit, and such an admixture of democracy as shall admit all classes to office, by popular election. No government has a right to levy taxes beyond the limit determined by the people. All political authority is derived from popular suffrage, and all laws must be made by the people for their representatives. There is no security for us as long as we depend on the will of another man." This language, which contains the earliest exposition of the Whig theory of revolution, is taken from the works of St. Thomas Aquinas, of whom Lord Bacon says that he had the largest heart of the school of divines. And it is worthwhile to observe that he wrote at the very moment when Simon de Montfort summoned the Commons; and the policies of the Neapolitan friar are centuries in advance of the English statesman's.

"The History of Freedom in Christianity," in Lord Acton, *Essays on Freedom and Power*, selected and with a new introduction by Gertrude Himmelfarb (New York: Meridian Books, 1955), p. 88.

[36] Brian Tierney, *The Idea of Natural Rights* (Grand Rapids: Wm. B. Eerdmans Publishing, 1997).

[37]   [A]lthough Thomas himself did not choose to develop a doctrine of subjective rights, there was nothing in his work that necessarily excluded such a concept. One can add now that the principles of Thomist philosophy and the idea of subjective rights were not only theoretically impossible; they actually coexisted in the work of Hervaeus Natalis. Moreover this was not just a rare aberration. The combination of a professed Thomism with an acceptance of a rights language derived ultimately from medieval jurisprudence was characteristic of the greatest thinkers of the Spanish "second scholasticism," whose works provide the principal link between medieval and modern rights theories.

Ibid., p. 108.

[38]   The idea of natural rights grew up – perhaps could only have grown up in the first place – in a religious culture that supplemented rational argumentation about human nature with a faith in which humans were seen as children of a caring God. But the idea was not necessarily dependent on divine revelation, and later it proved capable of surviving into a more secular epoch. The disinclination of some Enlightenment skeptics to regard God's law as a sufficient ground for moral behavior, and the widespread tendency, after Hume, to doubt whether reflecting on human inclinations could yield moral insights, raised new problems about the justification of rights that are still

matters of dispute. But the appeal to natural rights became more prominent than ever in the political discourse of the eighteenth century. The doctrine of rights shaped by the experience of previous centuries turned out to be still of value in addressing the problems of a new era. The proponents of the secularized rights theories of the Enlightenment had often forgotten the remoter origins of the doctrines they embraced; but their rhetoric about the rights of man becomes fully intelligible only when it is seen as the end product of a long process of historical evolution.

Perhaps it would be more satisfying if the idea of natural rights had entered Western political thought with a clatter of drums and trumpets in some resounding pronouncement like the American Declaration of Independence or the French Declaration of the Rights of Man and the Citizen. In fact, though, this central concept of Western political theory first grew into existence almost imperceptibly in the obscure glosses of the medieval jurists. One might say that, in the works of the early Decretists, a distinctive mutation of thought and language occurred which gave rise to a whole new species of ideas, the species of natural rights theories. Individual examples of the species came to vary widely after a few generations, shaped by the experience of changing environments. In some later historical environments natural rights theories could not survive at all. Sometimes the seed fell on stony ground. Sometimes the theories that grew up were stunted and deformed.

Ibid., pp. 343-344.

[39] Tierney writes, for instance:

Current writings on the rights theories of the sixteenth-century Spanish authors often assume, either that they found a doctrine of natural rights in Aquinas and simply appropriated it, or that they "betrayed" Aquinas by adopting a doctrine that was opposed to his teachings and that was derived ultimately from Ockham's nominalism and voluntarism. Both views seem simplistic. Ockham did not invent the concept of natural rights; it had deeper roots in medieval jurisprudence. And the doctrine of subjective rights did not formally contradict anything that Aquinas wrote. It remains true, though, that the earlier Dominican master had chosen to exclude this meaning from the several definitions of the word *ius* that he presented in the *Summa theologiae*. The Spanish Dominicans were intent on reviving and propagating the teachings of the greatest master of their Order. They might have decided to follow his example in this matter also. But, in the context of their times, they *needed* a doctrine of natural rights, above all to cope with the moral problems raised by the Spanish conquests in America. Accordingly, they chose to associate a doctrine of rights with Thomist principles that they professed. The result was that, when new problems arose in the early modern era, a theory of natural rights was very widely diffused and was readily available for use by future generations of jurists and philosophers.

There is one further point. The Spanish Dominicans were inevitably influenced by an underlying Christian attitude that animated all the scholastic disciplines, an attitude that attributed a unique value to individual persons as children of God, made "in his image." In this connection they often quoted scripture, especially the first chapter of Genesis; but, by drawing on a juridical tradition that derived natural rights and natural law from human rationality and free will, and by appealing to Aristotelian philosophy (when it suited their purpose), they also showed how a doctrine of natural rights might be constructed without any overt dependence on Christian revelation.

Ibid., pp. 286-287.

40   The history of natural rights theories can best be seen as a series of creative responses to a variety of past experiences. I have been emphasizing that, in discussing this history, we need to consider a sequence of changing contexts, sets of contingent circumstances that no one planned or foresaw. But I do not want to argue that the whole story of natural rights is just a chapter of historical accidents. The point is rather that, once the idea that all persons possess rights had grown into existence, it displayed a remarkable vitality and adaptability and proved relevant to a variety of emerging problems.... The medieval idea that liberty is a natural right led on to effective movements for the abolition of slavery only when it was reinforce by humanitarian impulses of the late Enlightenment.

Ibid., p. 345.

41 Ibid., pp. 343-344.

42 See Friedrich Hayek, "Why I Am Not a Conservative," in *The Constitution of Liberty* (Chicago: Henry Regnery, 1960), pp. 397-411.

43 In a letter to Henry Lee, in Adrienne Koch and William Peden, eds., *The Life and Selected Writings of Thomas Jefferson* (New York: The Modern Library, 1972), p. 719.

44 Quoted in Ronald Reagan's "First Inaugural Address," January 20, 1981, *Speaking My Mind: Selected Speeches* (New York: Simon & Schuster, 1989), p. 64. Regarding Joseph Warren's role at Bunker Hill, I have learned much from Catherine Drinker Bowen, *John Adams and the American Revolution* (Boston: Little, Brown, 1950); David Ramsay, *The History of the American Revolution* (1789), Lester H. Cohen, ed. (Indianapolis: LibertyClassics, 1990); and Benson Bobrick, *Angel in the Whirlwind* (New York: Simon & Schuster, 1997).

Epilogue: How Did the Virginians Ground Religious Rights?

[1]Consider these two passages:

> Instead of establishing religion, the Founders established religious freedom, and the principle of religious freedom derives from a nonreligious source. Rather than presupposing a Supreme Being, the institutions they established presuppose the rights of man, which were discovered by Hobbes and Locke to exist prior to all government – in the state of nature to be precise. To secure these rights, men must leave the state of nature, which they do by giving their consent to civil government. Nevertheless, the rights presuppose the state of nature, and the idea of the state of nature is incompatible with Christian doctrine. According to Christian doctrine, "the first and great commandment" is to love God, and the second, which is like unto it, is to love one's neighbor as oneself. In the state of nature, however, man is not obliged to love anyone, but merely to preserve himself and, what is more to the point, "to preserve the rest of mankind [only] when his own preservation comes not in competition."

* * *

> The origin of free government in the modern sense coincides and can *only* coincide with the solution of the religious problem, and the solution of the religious problem consists in the subordination of religion.

Walter Berns, "Religion and the Founding Principle," in Robert H. Horwitz, ed., *The Moral Foundations of the American Republic*, 4th ed. (Charlottesville: University of Virginia Press, 1986), pp. 215, 223.

[2] Two quotes from Berns display the framework:

> ...by separating the spiritual from the temporal, Jesus not only provided the basis for the subsequent separation of church and state, but, even before the advent of the liberal state, he made it impossible for a Christian to be a patriotic citizen in the classical sense. From this time forward, Athenians and all other Europeans would have two masters – one civil, the other ecclesiastical – and, to quote Jean-Jacques Rousseau (who, of course, was speaking before the advent of the United States), "no people has ever been able to figure out whom it was obliged to obey, the ruler or the priest."

* * *

> Two powers, two sovereigns, and a never-ending dispute over jurisdiction – there was much in this history to confirm Rousseau's judgment that a sound constitution was impossible in a Christian state.

Walter Berns, *Making Patriots* (Chicago: University of Chicago Press, 2001), pp. 24, 26.

[3] Berns does credit John Witherspoon with recognizing that religion makes better citizens:

> The point has to be made – in fact, it has to be emphasized – that the Founders did not attempt to discourage religious belief; on the contrary,

within the limits imposed by their Lockean principles, they intended to promote or protect it. They did so because they had reason to believe that, in certain important respects, the religious make better citizens than do the irreligious.... This was surely the judgment of John Witherspoon, who, by any fair reckoning, deserves to be numbered among the Founders of this country.

Ibid., pp. 39-40.

4 Maritain preceded his praise for the American Constitution with the following:
Paradoxically enough, and by virtue of the serious religious feelings of the Founding Fathers, it appeared, at a moment of unstable equilibrium (as all moments in time are) in the history of ideas, as a lay – even, to some extent rationalist – fruit of the perennial Christian life-force, which despite three centuries of tragic vicissitudes and spiritual division was able to produce this momentous temporal achievement at the dawn of the American nation: as if the losses suffered by human history in the supreme domain of the integrity and unity of faith, and in the interest in theological truth, had been the price paid....

Man and the State (Chicago: University of Chicago Press, 1951), pp. 183-184.

In an earlier work, Maritain had found one of the Constitution's Christian forerunners: "Its structure owes little to Rousseau, if I am to believe some Dominican friends of mine that this Constitution has rather some relation to ideas which presided in the Middle Ages at the constitution of St. Dominic's Order." *Scholasticism and Politics* (New York: Macmillan Co., 1940), p. 91.

5 Jacques Maritain, *Reflections on America* (New York: Charles Scribner's Sons, 1958), pp. 180-181, citing Peter Drucker, "Organized Religion and the American Creed," in the *Review of Politics*, July 1956.

6 Ibid., p. 181.

7 Ibid., pp. 182-183.

8 Jacques Maritain, *Christianity and Democracy* (San Francisco: Ignatius Press, 1986), chapter 4. Emphasis added.

9 *Man and the State*, pp. 182-183. Emphasis added.

10   To say that Jefferson advocated religious freedom and the separation of church and state, and to leave it at that, is to miss what was then the truly radical character of his views on religion. Americans, he suggests, no more than the immediate addressees of Locke's writing, are not going to accept a policy of freedom and separation, or of toleration (and Jefferson made copious notes and significant use of Locke's *Letter Concerning Toleration*), until they can be persuaded to accept the ground of this toleration, and the ground of this toleration is the opinion that traditional Christian doctrine is false. When it is shown to be false, and when the truth of this falseness is, "by

the light of science," spread among the mass of mankind, it will be possible for men to attach themselves more firmly to the god of the Declaration of Independence – "Nature's God" – and the religious problem will be solved and free government secure. But Jefferson circulated these opinions only among a few of his correspondents.

Berns, "Religion and the Founding Principle," pp. 221-222.

[11] "Upon the subsidence of Revolution, and with piety becoming outspoken, Patrick Henry, well aware of his ascendancy in the House of Delegates, found it seasonable to press for common support; and, late in May, 1784, he broached his proposal with customary eloquence." Marvin K. Singleton, "Colonial Virginia As First Amendment Matrix: Henry, Madison, and Assessment Establishment," *James Madison on Religious Liberty*, ed. Robert S. Alley (Buffalo, NY: Prometheus Books, 1985), p. 161. See also John T. Noonan, Jr., who reproduces James Madison's notes from the Virginia debates in *The Lustre of Our Country* (Los Angeles, CA: The Regents of the University of California, 1998), pp. 61-65.

[12]   Jefferson thought that true religious liberty required both the disestablishment and the free exercise of religion. The state, he insisted, should give no special aid, support, privilege, or protection to any religion ... should refrain "from intermeddling ... with religious institutions, their doctrines, discipline, or exercises ..." [and] should respect the liberty of conscience and free exercise of all its subjects.

Adams thought that true religious liberty required the state to balance the establishment of one "Publick religion" with the freedom of many private religions. On the one hand, he said, every polity must establish by law some form of public religion, some image and ideal of itself, some common values and beliefs to undergird and support the plurality of private religions. The notion that a state and society could remain neutral and purged of any religion was, for Adams, a philosophical fiction.

John Witte, Jr.: "A Most Mild and Equitable Establishment of Religion" in *Religion and the New Republic* (Lanham, MD: Rowman & Littlefield, 2000), pp. 2-3.

[13]   The *Body Politic* or the *Political Society* is the whole. The *State* is a part – the topmost part – of this whole. *Political Society*, required by nature and achieved by reason, is the most perfect of temporal societies. It is a concretely and wholly human reality, tending to a concretely and wholly human good – the common good. It is a work of reason, born out of the obscure efforts of reason disengaged from instinct, and implying essentially a rational order; but it is no more Pure Reason than man himself. The body politic has flesh and blood, instincts, passions, reflexes, unconscious psychological structures and dynamism – all of these subjected, if necessary by legal coercion, to the command of an Idea and rational decisions. Justice is a primary condition for the existence of the body politic, but Friendship is its very life-giving form. It tends toward a really human and freely achieved com-

munion. It lives on the devotion of the human persons and their gift of themselves. They are ready to commit their own existence, their possessions and
their honor for its sake. The civic sense is made up of this sense of devotion
and mutual love as well as of the sense of justice and law.

In contrast, "The *State* is only that part of the body politic especially concerned with the maintenance of law, the promotion of the common welfare
and public order, and the administration of public affairs."
Maritan, *Man and the State*, pp. 11, 12.

[14] "That no free government, or the blessings of liberty, can be preserved to any
people but by a firm adherence to justice, moderation, temperance, frugality, and
virtue and by frequent recurrence to fundamental principles." *The Virginia Declaration of Rights*, p. 15.

[15] These four texts are to be found in Philip B. Kurland and Ralph Lerner, eds.,
The Founders Constitution (Chicago: University of Chicago Press, 1987), vol. 5,
pp. 3, 77, 82, 84 respectively.

[16]   Although general assessment laws were enacted in Massachusetts, Connecticut, and New Hampshire, and passed by both houses in Maryland and
Georgia, scholars and jurists, in seeking to describe the emerging sentiment
in the new American republic about the relationship between church and
state, have focused on the one state in which efforts to pass a general assessment plan failed – the Commonwealth of Virginia.
James Hutson, *Religion and the Founding of the American Republic* (Washington, D.C.: Library of Congress, 1998), p. 66.

[17] Hutson provides several examples of presidential support, by each of the first
four presidents:

As commander of the Continental Army, Washington frequently invoked
God's assistance for the American cause, often in words that made a deep
impression on his fellow citizens. They especially cherished his circular to
the chief executives of the thirteen states, June 8, 1783, announcing his
intention to resign his command and praying that God would "most graciously be pleased to dispose us all, to do Justice, to love mercy, and to
demean ourselves with that Charity, humility and pacific temper of mind,
which were the Characteristicks of the Divine Author of our blessed Religion, and without an humble imitation of whose example in these things, we
can never hope to be a happy Nation."

* * *

Washington's successor, John Adams, who unapologetically called himself
a "church going animal," continued his predecessor's policy of offering
strong rhetorical support for religion. "Statesmen," Adams contended, "may
plan and speculate for Liberty, but it is Religion and Morality alone, which
can establish the principles upon which Freedom can securely stand." In
his inaugural address, Adams used a well-known phrase from the Declara-

tion of Independence to inform his countrymen that "a decent respect for Christianity [was] among the best recommendations for public service."

* * *

Jefferson permitted executive branch employees under his direct control, members of the Marine Band, to participate in House church services.... The assistance of the Marine Band was a modest contribution to religion in the capital compared to Jefferson's decision to let executive branch buildings, the War Office and the Treasury, be used for church services....

During Jefferson's administration, church services were conducted in the Supreme Court's chambers – both Cutler and Adams describe them – which is not surprising, since Chief Justice John Marshall, who must have approved the services in the Court, had voted for a general religious tax as a member of the Virginia Assembly in 1784 and later served as vice-president of the American Bible Society.

* * *

James Madison's actions as president show that his attitude was also within the Founding consensus. On June 7, 1812, Foster, the British minister, reported seeing him leaving church services in the Capitol in a coach and four – Jefferson always came on horseback – and, during the War of 1812, a Navy chaplain preached on Matthew 5:9, "blessed are the peacemakers," while he was in the congregation – thus symbolically signaling his approval for public support of religion. Madison also reverted to the earlier policy of Washington, Adams, and the Continental Congress, proclaiming on four occasions between 1812 and 1815 national days of thanksgiving.

Ibid., ch. 6, especially pp. 80, 81, 89, 91, 96.

[18] Kurland and Lerner, p. 77. Emphasis added.

[19] William Penn, *Some Fruits of Solitude*, in *Reflections and Maxims Relating to the Conduct of Human Life* (Bedford, MA: Applewood Books, 1996), p. 34. First published in London in 1693.

[20] In the *Fundamental Constitutions of Pennsylvania*, Penn wrote:

Considering that it is impossible that any People or Government should ever prosper, where men render not unto God, that which is God's, as well as to Caesar, that which is Caesar's;

and also perceiving that disorders and mischiefs that attend those places where *force is used* in matters of faith and worship, and seriously reflecting upon the tenure of the new and Spiritual government, and that both *Christ did not use force and that he did expressly forbid it in* his holy Religion, as also that the Testimony of his blessed Messengers was, that the weapons of the Christian warfare were not Carnall but Spiritual....

Therefore, in reverence to God the Father of lights and spirits, the Author as well as object of all divine knowledge, faith and worship, I do hereby declare for me and myn and *establish it for the first fundamental of the Government of my Country;*

> *that every Person that does or shall reside therein shall have and enjoy*
> *the Free Possession of his or her faith and exercise of worship towards God,*
> *in such way and manner as every Person shall in Conscience* believe is most
> acceptable to God and so long as every such Person useth not this Christian
> liberty to Licentiousness, that is to say to speak loosely and prophainly of
> God, Christ or Religion, or to Committ any evil in their Conversation [way
> of living], he or she shall be protected in the enjoyment of the aforesaid
> Christian liberty by the civill Magistrate.

Fundamental Constitutions of Pennsylvania, 1682, William Penn, The Historical
Society of Pennsylvania Collection, Philadelphia. Emphasis added.

[21] *Memorial and Remonstrance*, p. 1. Emphasis added.

[22] Is this not what Maritain meant by the American conception being affected by
the "yeast" of the gospels, working their subtle and mysterious way through human
thought and history?

[23] Ibid., p. 6. Emphasis added. The term "pre-existed" seems to allude to the
eternal knowledge and decision of the Creator, before the beginning of time, much
as the "eternal law" pre-existed the "natural law."

[24] Thomas Jefferson, *Rights of British America*, 1774, ME 1:211, Papers 1:135.

[25] Thomas Jefferson, *Autobiography*, in Kurland and Lerner, eds., vol 5, p. 85.

[26] *Reflections on America*, pp. 182-183.

[27] "Bill for Establishing Religious Freedom," section 1.

[28] Berns, "Religion and the Founding Principle," p. 215.

[29]

> Wherefore according to the order of natural inclinations, is the order of the
> precepts of the natural law. Because in man there is first of all an inclina-
> tion to good in accordance with the nature which he has in common with all
> substances: inasmuch as every substance seeks the preservation of its own
> being, according to its nature: and by reason of this inclination, whatever is
> a means of preserving human life, and of warding off its obstacles, belongs to
> the natural law.

Thomas Aquinas, *Summa Theologica* (Westminster, MD: Christian Classics, 1981),
I-II, Question 94, article 2.

[30]

> A man is said to love himself by reason of his loving himself with regard to his
> spiritual nature, so that accordingly, a man ought, out of charity, to love
> himself more than he loves any other person. This is evident from the very
> reason for loving: since, God is loved as the principle of good, on which the
> love of charity is founded; while man, out of charity, loves himself by rea-
> son of his being a partaker of the aforesaid good, and loves his neighbor by
> reason of his fellowship in that good. Now fellowship is a reason for love

according to a certain union in relation to God. Wherefore just as unity surpasses union, the fact that man himself has a share in the Divine good, is a more potent reason for loving than that another should be a partner with him in that share. Therefore man, out of charity, ought to love himself more than his neighbor.

Ibid., I-II, Question 26, article 4.

[31] Berns, *Making Patriots*, p. 32.

Appendix: The Forgotten Founders

[1] William Stevens Perry, D.D., *The Faith of the Signers of the Declaration of Independence* (Tarrytown, N.Y.: William Abbott, 1926), pp. 218-221.

[2] See http://www.nara.gov/exhall/charters/constitution/overview.html, visited April 16, 2001, 3:30 p.m.

[3] His lifelong friend Robert Troup wrote that "[Young Hamilton] was attentive to public worship, and in the habit of praying upon his knees both night and morning.... I have lived in the same room with him for some time, and I have often been powerfully affected by the fervor and eloquence of his prayers. He had read many of the polemical writers on religious subjects, and he was a zealous believer in the fundamental doctrines of Christianity.... I confess that the arguments with which he was accustomed to justify his belief, have tended in no small degree to confirm my own faith in revealed religion."

John Eidsmoe, *Christianity and the Constitution: The Faith of Our Founding Fathers* (Grand Rapids, MI: Baker Book House, 1987), p. 154.

[4] Ibid., p. 320.

[5] Rev. Charles A. Goodrich, *Biographies of the Signers to the Declaration of Independence* (New York: W. Reed, 1829).

[6] Ibid.

[7] James H. Hutson, in "James Madison and the Social Utility of Religion: Risks v. Rewards" (unpublished paper presented at the John Courtney Murray seminar at the American Enterprise Institute), notes that in *Federalist No. 10*, Madison asked how "the public good, and private rights" might be secured against tyrannical majorities. "We well know," Madison answered, "that neither moral nor religious motives can be relied on as an adequate control. They are not found to be such on the injustice and violence of individuals and lose their efficiency in proportion to the number combined together." These are extraordinary statements, Hutson concludes, "betraying a pessimism about the social value of religion so extreme that they separate Madison from all other Founders, Jefferson included."

[8] Eidsmoe, op. cit., p. 188.

[9] Have we not already seen enough of the fallacy and extravagance of those idle theories which have amused us with promises of an exemption from the

imperfections, weaknesses and evils incident to society in every shape? Is it not time to awake from the deceitful dream of a golden age, and to adopt as a practical maxim for the direction of our political conduct that we, as well as the other inhabitants of the globe, are yet remote from the happy empire of perfect wisdom and perfect virtue?

Federalist No. 6, in Clinton Rossiter, ed., *The Federalist Papers* (New York: Mentor, 1961), p. 59.

[10] "A letter to James A. Bayard, April 1802," Eidsmoe, op. cit., 146-147.

[11] *Federalist Papers*, op. cit., pp. 110-111.

[12] "The Farmer Refuted," 1776, cited in Eidsmoe, op. cit., p. 145.

[13] Joseph J. Ellis gives a dramatic account of this duel, with a clarifying discussion of the historical controversies to which it has given rise, in *Founding Brothers: The Revolutionary Generation* (New York: Knopf, 2000), pp. 20-47. His notes are particularly helpful.

[14] Christopher Yates, *Alexander Hamilton: How the Mighty Are Redeemed* (Washington, D.C.: Family Research Council, 2001), pp. 23-24.

[15] Letter to Mrs. Hamilton, July 10, 1804, quoted in Norman Cousins, *"In God We Trust": The Religious Beliefs and Ideas of the American Founding Fathers* (New York: Harper & Brothers, 1958).

[16] Matthew F. Rose, *John Witherspoon, An American Leader* (Washington, D.C.: Family Research Council, 1999), pp. 19-20.

[17] Ibid., p. 33.

[18] William Livingston assuredly had supporters among the liberal Christian ranks when he held that the more orthodox Calvinist erred in their insistence that "mankind are purely passive in their reformation from vice to virtue." From the progressive perspective, people were not wholly dependent on "a superior and irresistible agency" that reduced them to "mere machines void of intelligence and free volition."

Barry A. Shain, *The Myth of American Individualism* (New Jersey: Princeton University Press, 1994), pp. 129-130.

[19] In 1787 Livingston was selected as a delegate to the Constitutional Convention, though his gubernatorial duties prevented him from attending every session. He did not arrive until June 5 and missed several weeks in July, but he performed vital committee work, particularly as chairman of the committee that reached a compromise on the issue of slavery. He also supported the New Jersey Plan. Later, he spurred New Jersey's rapid ratification of the Constitution (1787). The next year, Yale awarded him an honorary doctor of laws degree.

[20] Robert Ernst, *Rufus King: American Federalist* (Chapel Hill, NC: University of North Carolina Press, 1968), p. 291.

[21] Letter to daughter Betsy, 20 August 1796, as quoted in Eidsmoe, op. cit., pp. 307-308.

[22] Dickinson to his father, 29 November 1754, in "Farmer's Letter," Paul L. Ford, ed., *The Writings of John Dickinson* (Philadelphia: The Historical Society of Pennsylvania, 1895), p. 265; ibid., p. 307.

[23] Cited by Page Smith, *John Adams* (Garden City, NY: Doubleday, 1962), p. 111.

[24] Dickinson cited by Stanton Evans, *The Theme is Freedom* (Washington, D.C.: Regnery Publishing, 1994), p. 239.

[25] Dickinson, op. cit., pp. 326-327.

[26] Working his way through published descriptions of other yellow fever epidemics, Rush found some cases of people who recovered after being given massive doses of laxative. He tried it on some of his own critical patients and became convinced as through a revelation that this cleansing of the bowels was one part of the one, only, and infallible cure. The other was bloodletting.... Sleepless, snatching mouthfuls of food when he could, Rush saw as many as 120 patients a day and beat off more who clutched at him and begged his help as he walked the somber streets. He came down with the fever himself but recovered, sturdily crediting his own treatment for his survival. Then he resumed his man-killing schedule. His visible courage as well as his persistent, if misguided, optimism at least helped to keep panic from spreading and deepening.
Bernard A. Weisberger, *America Afire* (New York: Harper Collins, 2000), pp. 81-82.

[27] Rush's tract continues:
In vain will you command your flocks to offer up the incense of faith and charity, while they continue to mingle the sweat and blood of Negro slaves with their sacrifices. – If the blood of Abel cried aloud for vengeance; – *If, under the Jewish dispensation, cities of refuge could not screen the deliberate murderer* – if even manslaughter required sacrifices to expiate it, – and if a single murder so seldom escapes with impunity in any civilized country, what may you not say against that trade, or those manufacturers *of laws, which destroy the lives of so many thousands of our fellow-creatures every year?* – If in the Old Testament "God swears by his holiness, and by the excellency of Jacob, that the earth shall tremble, and everyone mourn that dwelleth therein for the iniquity of those who oppress the poor and crush the needy," what judgments may you not denounce upon those who continue to perpetrate these crimes, after the more full discovery which God has made of the law of equity in the New Testament?.... Remember that *national crimes require national punishments*, and without declaring what punishment awaits this evil, you *may venture to assure them, that it cannot pass with impunity, unless God shall cease to be just or merciful.* [emphasis added]
"On Slavekeeping" (1773), in William Bennett, *Our Sacred Honor* (New York: Simon and Schuster, 1997), pp. 376-377.

[28] "Of the Mode of Education Proper in a Republic" (1798), in Bennett, op. cit., pp. 412-413.

[29]   Rush continues: "If there were no hereafter, individuals and societies would be great gainers by attending public worship every Sunday." Goodrich, op. cit.

[30]   Wilson, in his careful division of law into these categories, displayed his indebtedness to the Scholastic-Anglican tradition of Aquinas and Hooker. How closely he followed the Anglican theologian may be seen from the topical index of the first book of *Ecclesiastical Polity*. Where Hooker speaks of nature's laws and calls them the second law eternal, the law of "natural things," Wilson calls them simply the "laws of nature," but both terms comprehend the same category and stand in the same relation on the one hand to the eternal law by which God guides his own actions and, on the other, to human law.
Page Smith, *James Wilson: Founding Father* (Chapel Hill, NC: University of North Carolina Press, 1956), p. 330.

[31]   James Wilson is perhaps the most underrated founder. One of only six men to sign both the Declaration of Independence and the Constitution, his influence on the latter was second only to that of James Madison. Wilson also played a central role in the ratifying debates and was the moving force behind the Pennsylvania Constitution of 1790. Furthermore, as a law professor and Supreme Court justice, he produced some of the period's most profound commentary on the Constitution and American law. Yet, in spite of his many historic contributions, and the high quality of his political thought, Wilson has been largely overlooked by political scientists, historians, and academic lawyers alike. Of the few works on him, most are simply descriptive or too narrowly focused on one particular aspect of his thought.
Mark David Hall, *The Political and Legal Philosophy of James Wilson, 1742–1798* (Columbia, MO: University of Missouri Press, 1997), p. 1.

[32]   Ronald Hoffman, *Princes of Ireland, Planters of Maryland* (Chapel Hill, NC: Omohundro Institute, University of North Carolina Press, 2000). For Charles Carroll of Carrollton, see pp. 204-205, 265-266, 281-282, and 351-388; for Daniel Carroll, see pp. 125, 283, 332; for John Carroll, see p. 51.

[33]   Thomas W. Spalding, *The Premier See: A History of the Archdiocese of Baltimore, 1789–1989* (Baltimore: The Johns Hopkins University Press, 1989). See the Prologue, pp. 1-4. Spalding recounts: "Congress instructed Franklin to notify the papal nuncio in Paris that the Roman proposal, 'being purely spiritual, is without the jurisdiction and the powers of Congress, who have no authority to permit or refuse it'"(p. 10).

[34]   The language of subjective natural rights has become a central, characteristic theme of Western political discourse. It is important to know when and how the cluster of ideas it conveys grew into existence, what historical context made their articulation possible and their survival likely. The key concepts of the seventeenth-century rights theorists often had medieval origins. But in tracing out those origins it is not enough to look at Aquinas and Ockham…. There are relevant comments for instance in Olivi, Gerson, Summenhart, Vittoria, Suarez, and Grotius.

Brian Tierney, *The Idea of Natural Rights* (Atlanta: Scholar Press, 1997), pp. 88-89.

[35] Robert A. Rutland, *George Mason, Reluctant Statesman* (Baton Rouge: Louisiana State University Press, 1989), pp. 56-57.

[36] Ibid., pp. 59-60.

[37] It is now no more that toleration is spoken of as if it were the indulgence of one class of people that another enjoyed the exercise of their inherent natural rights, for, happily, the Government of the United States, which gives to bigotry no sanction, to persecution no assistance, requires only that they who live under its protection should demean themselves as good citizens in giving it on all occasions their effectual support.

"To the Hebrew Congregation in Newport" (August 1790), in W. B. Allen, ed., *George Washington, A Collection* (Indianapolis: Liberty Classics, 1988), p. 548. Compare the language by George Mason of the first draft of the Virginia Declaration:

That as Religion, or the Duty which we owe to our divine and omnipotent Creator, and the Manner of discharging it, can be governed only by Reason and Conviction, not by Force or Violence; and therefore that all Men shou'd enjoy the fullest Toleration in the Exercise of Religion, according to the Dictates of Conscience, unpunished and unrestrained by the Magistrate, unless, under Colour of Religion, any Man disturb the Peace, the Happiness, or Safety of Society, or of Individuals. And that it is the mutual Duty of all, to practice Christian Forbearance, Love and Charity towards Each other.

Daniel Dreisbach, "George Mason's Pursuit of Religious Liberty in Revolutionary Virginia," *The Virginia Magazine of History and Biography*, vol. 108, no. 1 (Spring 2000).

[38] In a letter to Henry Lee, Jefferson wrote not long before he died:

This was the object of the Declaration of Independence. Not to find out new principles, or new arguments, never before thought of, not merely to say things which had never been said before mankind the common sense of the subject, in terms so plain and firm as to command their assent, and to justify ourselves in the independent stand we are compelled to take. Neither aiming at originality of principle or sentiment, nor yet copied from any particular and previous writing, *it was intended to be an expression of the American mind*, and to give to that expression the proper tone and spirit called for by the occasion. All its authority rests then on the harmonizing sentiments of the day, whether expressed in conversation, in letters, printed essays, or in the elementary books of public rights, as Aristotle, Cicero, Locke, Sidney, &c. The historical documents which you mention as in your possession, ought all to be found, and I am persuaded you will find, to be corroborative of the facts and principles advanced in that Declaration. Be pleased to accept assurance of my great esteem and respect. [emphasis added]

Letter: "To Henry Lee" (Monticello, May 8, 1825), in Merrill D. Peterson, ed., *Jefferson: Writings* (New York: Library of America, 1984), p. 1501.

39 Rutland, op. cit., pp. 59-60.

40 Paine cited in Norman Cousins, ed., *In God We Trust* (New York: Harper & Brothers, 1958), pp. 393-394.

41 Ibid., p. 395.

42 Ibid., p. 423, "The Existence of God," 1797.

43 Ibid.

44 Ibid., p. 442, "My Private Thoughts on a Future State," 1807.

45 Ibid.

46 George W. Carey, ed., *The Political Writings of John Adams* (Washington, D.C.: Regnery Publishing, 2000); and C. Bradley Thompson, ed., *The Revolutionary Writings of John Adams* (Indianapolis: LibertyFund, 2001).

47 Benjamin Rush quoted in Joseph J. Ellis, *The Passionate Sage: The Character and Legacy of John Adams* (New York: W.W. Norton, 1994), p. 29.

48 Richard Stockton quoted in *The Works of John Adams, Second President of the United States*, ed. Charles Francis Adams, 10 vols. (Boston: Little, Brown, 1850-1856), 3:56.

49 Andrew Burstein, *America's Jubilees: How in 1826 a Generation Remembered Fifty Years of Independence* (New York: Alfred A. Knopf, 2001).

50 Interest in Adams is suddenly growing. Bradley Thompson recently brought us the first study of Adams' political thought, C. Bradley Thompson, *John Adams and the Spirit of Liberty* (Lawrence, KS: University of Kansas Press, 1998), plus a collection of Adams' writings, *The Revolutionary Writings of John Adams* (Indianapolis: LibertyFund, 2000). Among the solid biographies are Page Smith's two-volume study, *John Adams* (New York: Doubleday & Company, 1962); Catherine Drinker Bowen, *John Adams and the American Revolution* (Boston: Little, Brown, 1990), gives reliable biography a novelistic touch that brings key characters to life. Joseph J. Ellis, *Passionate Sage: The Character and Legacy of John Adams* (New York: W.W. Norton, 2001), tells a shorter version of the story.

51 Adams as cited by Eidsmoe, op. cit., p. 273.

52 Ibid., p. 281.

53 Ibid., p. 280.

54 Ibid.

55 Letter to F. A.Vanderkemp, 6 February 1809, as quoted by Russell Kirk, *The Roots of American Order* (Washington, D.C.: Regnery Publishing, 1991), p. 17.

56 Page Smith, op. cit., p. 30, quoting from *Adams' Papers* I, p. 22.

57 Ibid.

58 Ibid., quoting from *Papers* I, pp. 11, 39.

[59] Ibid., pp. 30-31, quoting *Papers* I, p. 8.

[60] Ibid., p. 31, quoting *Papers* I, p. 31.

[61] Adams quoted in Sidney Ahlstrom, *A Religious History of the American People* (New Haven: Yale University Press, 1972), p. 366.

[62] Cousins, op. cit., pp. 18-19.

[63] Franklin, the oldest delegate, invoked the Almighty:

> I have lived, Sir, a long time, and the longer I live, the more convincing proofs I see of this truth – that *God governs in the affairs of men.* And if a sparrow cannot fall to the ground without his notice, is it probable that an empire can rise without his aid? We have been assured, Sir, in the sacred writings, that "except the Lord build the House they labor in vain that build it." I firmly believe this; and I also believe that without his concurring aid we shall succeed in this political building no better than the Builders of Babel: We shall be divided by our little partial local interests; our projects will be confounded, and we ourselves shall become a reproach and bye word down to future ages. And what is worse, mankind may hereafter from this unfortunate instance, despair of establishing governments by Human Wisdom and leave it to chance, war and conquest. I therefore beg leave to move – that henceforth prayers imploring the assistance to Heaven, and its blessings on our deliberations, be held in this Assembly every morning before we proceed to business, and that one or more of the Clergy of this City be requested to officiate in that service.

Adrienne Koch, ed., *Notes on Debates in the Federal Convention of 1787 Reported by James Madison* (New York: W.W. Norton, 1966), pp. 209-210.

Bibliography

Acton, Lord, *Essays in Religion, Politics, and Morality: Selected Writings of Lord Acton*, 2 vols. (Indianapolis: Liberty Classic, 1988).

Adair, Douglass, *Fame and the Founding Fathers* (Indianapolis: Liberty Fund, 1998) (reprint, edited by Trevor Colbourn, with a personal memoir by Caroline Robbins and a bibliographical essay by Robert E. Shalhope).

Ahlstrom, Sydney E., *A Religious History of the American People* (New Haven: Yale University Press, 1972).

Allen, W. B., ed., *George Washington: A Collection* (Indianapolis: Liberty Classics, 1988).

Alley, Robert S., ed., *James Madison on Religious Liberty* (Buffalo: Prometheus Books, 1985).

Alter, Robert, *The Art of Biblical Narrative* (New York: Basic Books, 1981).

Amos, Gary T., *Defending the Declaration: How the Bible and Christianity Influenced the Writing of the Declaration of Independence* (Brentwood, Tennessee: Wolgemuth & Hyatt, 1989).

Appleby, Joyce, *Inheriting the Revolution: The First Generation of Americans* (Cambridge: Harvard University Press, 2000).

Aquinas, Thomas, *Contra Impugnantes, Dei Cultum at Religionem* (Paris, September–October 1256), in John Procter, S.T.M, ed., *An Apology for the Religious Orders, Being a Translation of Two of the Minor Works of the Saint* (St. Louis, MO: B. Herder, 1902).

——, *The Disputed Questions on Truth*, trans. James McGlynn, S.J. (Chicago: Henry Regnery Company, 1953).

——, *Saint Thomas Aquinas: Philosophical Texts*, trans. Thomas Gilby, O.P. (New York: Oxford University Press, 1960).

——, *Summa Contra Gentiles*, trans. by the English Dominican Fathers from the Latin (London, Burns, Oates & Washbourne, 1923).

——, *Summa Theologica*, 5 vols., transl. by Fathers of the English Dominican Province (Westminster, MD: Christian Classics, 1981).

Bailyn, Bernard, *Faces of the Revolution: Personalties and Themes in the Struggle for American Independence* (New York: Alfred A. Knopf, 1990).

Banning, Lance, *The Sacred Fire of Liberty: James Madison and the Founding of the Federal Republic* (Ithaca: Cornell University Press, 1995).

Barlow, J. Jackson, Leonard W. Levy, and Ken Masugi, eds., *The American Founding: Essays on the Formation of the Constitution* (New York: Greenwood Press, 1988).

Barton, David, ed., *Wives of the Signers* (Aledo: WallBuilder Press, 1989).

Basler, Roy P., ed., *The Collected Works of Abraham Lincoln* (New Brunswick, N.J.: Rutgers University Press, 1953).

Beard, Charles, *An Economic Interpretation of the Constitution of the United States* (New York: Free Press, 1965).

Becker, Karl L., *The Declaration of Independence: A Study of the History of Political Ideas* (New York: Vintage Books, 1998).

Bellah, Robert N., *The Broken Covenant: American Civil Religion in Time of Trial* (New York: Crossroad Books, 1975).

Bennett, William J., *Our Sacred Honor* (New York: Simon & Schuster, 1997).

Bercovitch, Sacvan, *The Puritan Origins of the American Self* (New Haven: Yale University Press, 1975).

Berns, Walter, *In Defense of Liberal Democracy* (Chicago: Gateway Editions, 1984).

——, *Making Patriots* (Chicago: University of Chicago Press, 2001).

——, "Religion and the Founding Principle," in Robert H. Horwitz, ed., *The Moral Foundations of the American Republic*, 3d ed. (Charlottesville: University Press of Virginia, 1987).

——, *The Writing of the Constitution of the United States* (Washington, D.C.: AEI Press, occasional paper, n.d.).

Biographical Directory of the America Congress 1774–1971 (Washington, D.C.: United States Printing Office, 1971).

Bloom, Allan, ed., *Confronting the Constitution* (Washington, D.C.: American Enterprise Institute, 1990).

Bowen, Catherine Drinker, *Miracle at Philadelphia* (Boston: Little, Brown & Co., 1966).

——, *John Adams and the American Revolution* (Boston: Little & Brown, 1950).

Bowers, Claude G., *The Young Jefferson* (Boston: Houghton Mifflin, 1945).

——, *Jefferson in Power: Jefferson's Years as President* (Boston: Houghton Mifflin, 1967).

Brookhiser, Richard, *Alexander Hamilton, American* (New York: Free Press, 1999).

——, *Founding Father: Rediscovering George Washington* (New York: Free Press, 1996).

Bruckberger, R. L., O.P., *Image of America* (New York: Viking Press, 1959).

Bryce, James, *The American Commonwealth* (New York: Macmillan & Co., 1895).

Burns, James MacGregor, *The Vineyard of Liberty* (New York: Vintage Books, 1983).

Butler, Jon, *Awash in a Sea of Faith: Christianizing the American People* (Cambridge: Harvard University Press, 1992).

——, *Becoming America* (Cambridge: Harvard University Press, 2000).

Butterfield, Herbert, *The Whig Interpretation of History* (New York: AMS Press, 1978).

Butterfield, Lyman H., ed., *Letters of Benjamin Rush*, 2 vols. (Philadelphia: The American Philosophical Society, 1951.).

Cappon, Lester J., *The Adams-Jefferson Letters* (New York: Simon & Schuster, 1959).

Carey, George W., *The Political Writings of John Adams* (Washington, D.C.: Regnery Publishing, 2000).

Carroll, Charles, *The Life and Correspondence of Charles Carroll of Carrollton, 1737–1832*, 2 vols., ed. Kate Mason Rowland (New York, 1898).

Carson, Clarence B., *A Basic History of the United States*, 2 vols. (Wadley: American Textbook Committee, 1984).

Casas, Bartolomé de las, *The Only Way*, trans. Helen Rand Parish, ed. Francis Patrick Sullivan, S.J., (Mahwah, NJ: Paulist Press, 1992).

Chafuen, A. A., *Christians for Freedom: Late-Scholastic Economics* (San Francisco: Ignatius Press, 1986).

Cherry, Conrad, ed., *God's New Israel* (Englewood Cliffs, N.J.: Prentice Hall, 1971).

——, *The Theology of Jonathan Edwards: A Reappraisal* (Bloomington: Indiana University Press, 1966); new introduction, 1990.

Chevalier, Michael, *Society, Manners, and Politics in the United States* (1839; New York: Augustus M. Kelley, 1966).

Church, F. Forrester, "Introduction," *The Jefferson Bible: The Life and Morals of Jesus of Nazareth* (Boston: The Beacon Press, 1989).

Clark, Harrison, *All Cloudless Glory: The Life of George Washington, from Youth to Yorktown* (Washington, D.C.: Regnery, 1995).

Clark, J. C. D., *The Language of Liberty 1660–1832: Political Discourse and Social Dynamics in the Anglo-American World* (Cambridge: Cambridge University Press, 1994).

Cohen, Bernard I., *Science and the Founding Fathers* (New York: W.W. Norton, 1995).

Colbourn, H. Trevor, *The Lamp of Experience: Whig History and the Intellectual Origins of the American Revolution* (Indianapolis: Liberty Fund, 1998).

Continental Congress, *The Journals of the Continental Congress, 1774–1789*, Worthington C. Ford, Gaillard Hunt, et al., eds., 34 vols. (Washington, D.C.: Government Printing Office, 1904–37).

Cooke, Jacob E., *Alexander Hamilton: A Biography* (New York: Scribner's, 1982).

Cousins, Norman, ed., *In God We Trust: The Personal Philosophies of the Founding Fathers* (New York: Harper & Row, 1988).

Craycraft, Kenneth R., *The American Myth of Religious Freedom* (Dallas: Spence, 1999).

Crèvecoeur, J. Hector St. John de, *Letters from an American Farmer* (New York: Viking Press, 1981).

Croly, Herbert, *The Promise of American Life*, with a foreword by Michael McGerr (Boston: Northeastern University Press, 1989).

Diamond, Martin and William B. Schambra, ed., *As Far As Republican Principles Will Admit* (Washington, D.C.: AEI Press, 1992).

Dietze, Gottfried, *The Federalist: A Classic on Federalism and Free Government* (Baltimore: The John Hopkins University Press, 1960, 1999).

Dolan, Jay P., *Heritage of '76* (Notre Dame, IN: University of Notre Dame Press, 1975).

Dreisbach, Daniel L., "George Mason's Pursuit of Religious Liberty in Revolutionary Virginia," *The Virginia Magazine*, vol. 108, no. 1 (2000), pp. 5-44.

——, *Real Threat and Mere Shadow* (Westchester, NY: Crossway Books, 1987).

——, *Thomas Jefferson and the Wall of Separation Between Church and State* (New York: New York University Press, 2002).

Edwards, Jonathan, *A Jonathan Edwards Reader*, edited by John E. Smith, Harry S. Stout, and Kenneth P. Minkema (New Haven: Yale University Press, 1995).

Eidsmoe, John, *Christianity and the Constitution: The Faith of Our Founding Fathers* (Grand Rapids, MI: Baker Books, 1987).

Ellis, Joseph J., *Founding Brothers: The Revolutionary Generation* (New York: Alfred A. Knopf, 2000).

——, *Passionate Sage: The Character and Legacy of John Adams* (New York: W.W. Norton, 1993).

Engeman, Thomas, *Thomas Jefferson and the Politics of Nature* (Notre Dame: University of Notre Dame Press, 2000).

Epstein, David F., *The Political Theory of the Federalists* (Chicago: University of Chicago Press, 1986).

Ernst, Robert, *Rufus King: American Federalist* (Chapel Hill: University of North Carolina Press, 1968).

Evans, M. Stanton, *The Theme Is Freedom: Religion, Politics, and the American Tradition* (Washington, D.C.: Regnery, 1994).

Farrand, Max, ed., *The Records of the Federal Convention of 1787*, rev. ed., 4 vols. (New Haven: Yale University Press, 1966).

Fears, J. Rufus, ed., *Essays in Religion, Politics, and Morality: Selected Writings of Lord Acton*, 2 vols. (Indianapolis: Liberty Classic, 1988).

Federer, William J., ed., *America's God and Country* (Coppell, TX: FAME Publishing, 1994).

Fehrenbacher, Don, ed., *Abraham Lincoln: Speeches and Writings, 1859–1865* (New York: Library of America, 1989).

Foner, Eric, ed., *Thomas Paine: Complete Writings* (New York: Library of America, 1995).

Franklin, Benjamin, *Autobiography and Other Writings*, ed. Russell B. Nye (Boston: Houghton Mifflin, Riverside Edition, 1958).

Freeman, Douglas Southall, *Washington*, abridged by Richard Harwell (New York: Charles Scribner's Sons, 1968).

Frisch, Morton J., ed., *Selected Writings and Speeches of Alexander Hamilton* (Washington, D.C.: AEI Press, 1985).

Gaustad, Edwin Scott, *A Religious History of America* (New York: Harper & Row, 1966).

——, *Sworn on the Altar of God: A Religious Biography of Thomas Jefferson* (Grand Rapids, MI: William B. Eerdmans Publishing Company, 1996).

Gilby, Thomas, O.P., trans., *Saint Thomas Aquinas: Philosophical Texts* (New York: Oxford University Press, 1960).

Glendon, Mary Ann, *A Nation Under Lawyers* (Cambridge: Harvard University Press, 1994).

——, "Philosophical Foundations of the Federalist Papers: Nature of Men, Nature of Law," *Harvard Journal of Law and Public Policy*, vol. 16, no. 1 (Winter 1993).

Goldwin, Robert A., *From Parchment to Power* (Washington, D.C.: AEI Press, 1997).

——, ed., *A Nation of States* (Chicago: Rand McNally, 1963).

Goodrich, Rev. Charles A., *Lives of the Signers to the Declaration of Independence* (New York: W. Reed & Co., 1829).

Greene, Jack P., *Colony to Nation, 1763–1789: A Documentary History of the American Revolution* (New York: W.W. Norton, 1967).

Gribbin, William, *The Church Is Militant: The War of 1812 and American Religion* (New Haven: Yale University Press, 1973).

Hall, Mark David, *The Political and Legal Philosophy of James Wilson, 1742–1798* (Columbia: University of Missouri Press, 1957).

Hall, Verna M., *Christian History of the Constitution* (San Francisco: Foundation for American Christian Education, 1962, 1979).

Hamilton, Alexander, *Selected Writings and Speeches of Alexander Hamilton*, edited by Morton J. Frisch (Washington, D.C.: AEI Press, 1985).

Hanke, Lewis, *All Mankind Is One* (Dekalb: Northern Illinois University Press, 1974).

——, *Aristotle and the American Indians* (Bloomington: Indiana University Press, 1970).

Hanley, Thomas O'Brien, *Charles Carroll of Carrollton: The Making of a Revolutionary Gentleman* (Chicago: Loyola University Press, 1982).

——, *Revolutionary Statesman: Charles Carroll and the War* (Chicago: Loyola University Press, 1983).

Hart, D. G., "The Failure of American Religious History," *The Journal of the Historical Society* (Boston University) vol. 1, no. 1 (Spring 2000).

Hartz, Louis, *The Liberal Tradition in America: An Interpretation of American Political Thought since the Revolution* (New York: Harcourt, Brace, 1955).

Hawke, David Freeman, *Benjamin Rush: Revolutionary Gadfly* (Indianapolis: Bobbs-Merrill, 1971).

Heimert, Alan and Perry Miller, eds., *The Great Awakening* (New York: Bobbs-Merrill, 1967).

History Book Club, *The Spark of Independence* (New York: History Book Club, 1997), especially created to accompany Pauline Maier's *American Scripture*.

Hittinger, Russell, "What Really Happened in the Casey Decision," *Crisis*, September 1992.

Hofstadter, Richard, ed., *Ten Major Issues in American Politics* (London: Oxford University Press, 1968).

Hoffman, Ronald, *Princes of Ireland, Planters of Maryland, A Carroll Saga 1500–1782* (Chapel Hill: University of North Carolina Press, 2000).

Hooker, Richard, *Ecclesiastical Polity* (Great Britain: Carcanet Press, 1990).

Hughes, William H., *Souvenir Volume: Three Great Events in the History of the Catholic Church in the United States* (New York: Arno Press, 1978).

Hutson, James, *Forgotten Features of the Founding: The Recovery of Religious Themes in the Early American Republic* (Lanham, MD: Lexington Books, 2003)

——, "The Great Doctrine of Retribution: The Founders' Views on the Social Utility of Religion," presented to the John Courtney Murray Seminar at the American Enterprise Institute, 6 June 2000 (unpublished paper, on file with author).

——, " 'Nursing Fathers': The Model for Church-States Relations in America from James I to Jefferson" (unpublished paper, on file with author).

——, *Religion and the Founding of the American Republic* (Washington, D.C.: Library of Congress, 1998).

——, ed., *Religion and the New Republic: Faith in the Founding of America* (Lanham, MD: Rowman & Littlefield, 2000).

Hyneman, Charles and Donald Lutz, eds., *American Political Writing During the Founding Era: 1760–1805*, 2 vols. (Indianapolis: Liberty Fund, 1983).

Jaffa, Harry V., *The Crisis of the House Divided: An Interpretation of the Issues in the Lincoln-Douglas Debates* (Chicago: University of Chicago Press, 1959).

——, *A New Birth of Freedom : Abraham Lincoln and the Coming of the Civil War* (Lanham, MD: Rowman & Littlefield, 2000).

Jefferson, Thomas, *The Jefferson Bible*, introduced by Douglas Lurton (New York: Henry Holt, 1995).

——, *Jefferson: Writings*, Merrill D. Peterson, ed. (New York: Library of America, 1984).

——, *The Life and Selected Writings of Thomas Jefferson* (Adrienne Koch and William Peden, eds., (New York: Modern Library, 1972).

John Paul II, *Fides et Ratio*, September 14, 1998, in *Origins*, vol. 28, no. 19 (October 22, 1998), pp. 317-348.

Kammen, Michael, *The Origins of the American Constitution* (New York: Viking Penguin, 1986).

Kesler, Charles R., ed., *Saving the Revolution* (New York: Free Press, 1987).

Kirk, Russell, *The Conservative Constitution* (Washington, D.C.: Regnery Gateway, 1990).

——, *The Roots of the American Order* (Washington: Regnery Gateway, 1991).

Koch, Adrienne, and William Peden, eds., *The Life and Selected Writings of Thomas Jefferson* (New York: Modern Library, 1972).

Kurland, Philip B. and Ralph Lerner, eds., *The Founders' Constitution* (Chicago: The University of Chicago Press, 1987).

Landes, David, *The Wealth and Poverty of Nations* (New York: Norton, 1998).

Lathrop, Rose Hawthorne, *Selected Writings of Rose Hawthorne Lathrop* (in the series *Sources of American Spirituality*), Diana Culbertson, O.P., ed. (New York: Paulist Press, 1993).

Lerner, Ralph, *The Thinking Revolutionary* (Ithaca: Cornell University Press, 1987).

Lewis, R.W. B., *The American Adam: Innocence, Tragedy, and Tradition in the Nineteenth Century* (Chicago: The University of Chicago, Phoenix Books, 1958).

The Library of America, *The American Revolution*, contents selected and notes written by John Rhodehamel (New York: Literary Classics of the United States, 2001).

Locke, John, *Essays on the Law of Nature*, ed. W. von Leyden (Oxford: Clarendon Press, 1954).

——, *Two Treatises of Government* (New York: The New American Library, 1963).

Long, Hamilton Albert, *The American Ideal of 1776: The Twelve Basic American Principles* (Philadelphia: Your Heritage Books, 1976).

Lossing, Benson, *Lives of the Signers of the Declaration of Independence* (Aledo: Wallbuilders Press, 1998).

Lutz, Donald S., *Colonial Origins of the American Constitution* (Indianapolis: Liberty Fund, 1998).

——, *The Origins of American Constitutionalism* (Baton Rouge: Louisiana State University Press, 1988).

——, "The Relative Influence of European Writers on Late Eighteenth-Century American Political Thought," *The American Political Science Review*, vol. 78 (1983) pp. 185-197.

Madison, James, Alexander Hamilton, and John Jay, *The Federalist Papers* (New York: New America Library, 1961).

Madison, James, "Memorial and Remonstrance against Religious Assessments," in *The Founders' Constitution*, vol. 5, ed. Philip B. Kurland and Ralph Lerner (Chicago: University of Chicago Press, 1987).

——, *Notes of Debates in the Federal Convention of 1787* (New York: W.W. Norton, 1987).

Mahoney, Daniel J., "Tocqueville's Democracy," *The Weekly Standard*, October 23, 2000.

Maier, Pauline, *American Scripture: Making the Declaration of Independence* (New York: Knopf, 1997).

Main, Jackson Turner, *The Anti-Federalists: Critics of the Constitution 1781–1788* (New York: W.W. Norton, 1961).

Maline, Julian L., Wilfred M. Mallon, et al., eds., *The Prose and Poetry of America* (Syracuse, NY: The L.W. Singer Company, 1949).

Maritain, Jacques, *Christianity and Democracy* (San Francisco: Ignatius Press, 1986).

——, *Creative Intuition in Art and Poetry*, Bollinger Series (New York: Pantheon Books, 1953).

——, *Existence and the Existent*, Lewis Galantiere and Gerald Phelan, trans. (New York: Image Books, 1956).

——, *Man and the State* (Chicago: University of Chicago Press, 1951).

——, *The Person and the Common Good*, trans. John J. Fitzgerald (New York: Charles Scribner's Sons, 1947).

——, *Reflections on America* (New York: Scribner's, 1958).

——, *Scholasticism and Politics* (New York: The Macmillan Company, 1990).

Marshall, James V., *The United States Manual of Biography and History* (Philadelphia: James B. Smith & Co., 1856).

Marshall, Terence E., "A French-American Dialogue: The Problem of Human Rights for Constitutional Government," in Hancock, Ralph & L. Lambert, eds., *The Legacy of the French Revolution* (Lanham, MD: Rowman & Littlefield, 1996).

Marty, Martin, *Pilgrims in Their Own Land, 500 Years of Religion in America* (Boston: Little, Brown, 1984).

Matthews, Richard K., *If Men Were Angels: James Madison and the Heartless Empire of Reason* (Lawrence, KS: University Press of Kansas, 1995).

Mayer, David N., *The Constitutional Thought of Thomas Jefferson* (Charlottesville: University of Virginia Press, 1994).

McCaughey, Elizabeth P., *From Loyalist to Founding Father: The Political Odyssey of William Samuel Johnson* (New York: Columbia University Press, 1980).

McCoy, Drew R., *The Last of the Fathers: James Madison and the Republican Legacy* (New York: Cambridge University Press, 1989).

McCullough, David, *John Adams* (New York: Simon & Schuster, 2001).

McDonald, Forrest, *Novus Ordo Seclorum: The Intellectual Origins of the Constitution* (Lawrence, KS: University Press of Kansas, 1985).

——, *The Presidency of George Washington* (Lawrence, KS: University Press of Kansas, 1988).

——, *The Presidency of Thomas Jefferson* (Lawrence, KS: University Press of Kansas, 1988).

McLean, Edward B., ed., *An Uncertain Legacy: Essays on the Pursuit of Liberty* (Wilmington, DE: Intercollegiate Studies Institute, 1997).

McWilliams, Wilson Carey, *The Idea of Fraternity in America* (Berkeley: University of California Press, 1973).

Miller, John C., *Sam Adams: Pioneer In Propaganda* (Stanford: Stanford University Press, 1960).

Miller, Perry, and Thomas H. Johnson, eds., *The Puritans* (New York: Harper & Row, 1968).

Miller, Perry, ed., *The American Puritans* (New York: Anchor Books, 1956).

——, ed., *The American Puritans: Their Prose and Poetry*, Morningside ed. (New York : Columbia University Press, 1982).

——, ed., *The American Transcendentalists: Their Prose and Poetry* (New York: Doubleday Anchor, 1957).

——, *Errand into the Wilderness* (New York: Harper Torch Books, 1964).

Miller, William Lee, *The Business of May Next* (Charlottesville: University of Virginia Press, 1992).

Morgan, Edmund, ed., *Puritan Political Ideas* (Indianapolis: Bobbs-Merrill, 1965).

Morris, Dan and Inez, *Who Was Who in American Politics* (New York: Hawthorn Books, 1974).

Morris, Richard B., *The Forging of the Union 1781–1789* (New York: Harper & Row, 1987).

——, *Witnesses at the Creation: Hamilton, Madison, Jay, and the Constitution* (New York: Signet Books, 1986).

—— and Robert Ferris, *The Signers* (Arlington: Interpretive Publications, 1982).

Morrison, Jeffrey Hays, "John Witherspoon and 'The Public Interest of Religion,'" *Journal of Church and State*, vol. 4 (Summer 1999).

Muñoz, V. Phillip, "Religion and the Social Compact: James Madison's Principle of Religious 'Non-Cognizance'" (draft of a doctoral dissertation for Claremont Graduate School, on file with the author).

Murray, John Courtney, S.J., *We Hold These Truths; Catholic Reflections on the American Proposition* (New York: Sheed & Ward, 1960).

The National Archives and Record Administration (www.nara.gov).

Niebuhr, Reinhold, *The Irony of American History* (New York: Charles Scribner's Sons, 1952).

——, *Man's Nature and His Communities: Essays on the Dynamics and Enigmas of Man's Personal and Social Existence* (New York: Scribner's, 1965).

Niemcewicz, Julian Ursyn and Metchie J. E. Budka, eds., *Under their Vine and Fig Tree: Travels through America in 1797–1799, 1805* (New Jersey: The Grassman Publishing Co., 1965).

Nolan, Hugh, ed., *Pastoral Letters of the United States Catholic Bishops*, vol. I: *1792–1940* (Washington, D.C.: United States Catholic Conference, 1983).

Noonan, John T., Jr., *The Lustre of Our Country* (Berkeley: University of California Press, 1998).

Novak, Michael, "American Founding Principles, Current Practices," in *The Catholic Ethic and the Spirit of Capitalism* (New York: Free Press, 1993).

——, "The Federalist and Tocqueville on Self-Interest," in *Free Persons and the Common Good* (Lanham, MD: Madison Books, 1989).

——, *God's Country: Taking the Declaration Seriously* (Washington, D.C.: AEI Press, 2000).

——, "How to Make a Republic Work," *The Kansas Journal of Law and Public Policy*, vol. 2, no. 1 (Spring 1992).

——, "The Influence of Judaism and Christianity on the Founding," in *Religion and the New Republic* (Lanham, MD: Rowman & Littlefield, 2000).

——, "The New Order of Ages," in *Free Persons and the Common Good* (Lanham, MD: Madison Books, 1989).

——, "St. Thomas in Motion," *Downside Review*, vol. 78 (1960).

——, "Thomas Aquinas, The First Whig," in *This Hemisphere of Liberty* (Washington, D.C.: The AEI Press, 1992).

—— and Brian Anderson, eds., *On Cultivating Liberty: Reflections on Moral Ecology by Michael Novak* (Lanham, MD: Rowman & Littlefield, 1999).

Oberholtze, Ellis Paxson, *Robert Morris: Patriot and Financier* (New York: Macmillan, 1903).

O'Brien, Conor Cruise, *The Long Affair: Thomas Jefferson and the French Revolution, 1785–1800* (Chicago: University of Chicago Press, 1996).

Padover, Saul K., *Thomas Jefferson and the Foundations of American Freedom* (New York: Van Nostrand Reinhold Company, 1965).

Paine, Thomas, *Thomas Paine: Complete Writings*, ed. Eric Foner (New York: Library of America: 1995).

Pangle, Thomas L., *The Spirit of Modern Republicanism: The Moral Vision of the American Founders and the Philosophy of Locke* (Chicago: University of Chicago Press, 1988).

Parish, Helen Rand, ed., and Francis Patrick Sullivan, S.J., trans., *The Only Way* (Mahwah, NJ: Paulist Press, 1992).

Parkes, Henry Bamford, *The American Experience* (New York: Random House Vintage, 1959).

Parrington, Vernon, *Main Currents in American Thought* (New York: Harcourt, Brace & Company, 1927).

Parsons, Wilfred, S.J., *The First Freedom: Considerations on Church and State in the United States* (New York: The Declan X. McMullen Company, 1948).

Penn, William, *Fundamental Constitutions of Pennsylvania* (Philadelphia: The Historial Society of Pennsylvania, 1682).

——, *Some Fruits of Solitude*, in *Reflections and Maxims Relating to the Conduct of Life* (Bedford, MA: Applewood Books, 1996).

Perkins, John, "A Well-Wisher to Mankind," in Charles S. Hyneman and Donald S. Lutz, eds., *American Political Writing During the Founding Era: 1760–1805* (Indianapolis: Liberty Press, 1983).

Peterson, Merrill D., ed., *Jefferson: Writings* (New York: Library of America, 1984).

Pezzimenti, Rocco, *The Open Society and its Friends* (Rome: Millennium Editrice, 1997).

Poore, Benjamin Perley, *The Federal and State Constitutions, Colonial Charters, and other Organizing Laws of the United States* (Washington, D.C.: Government Printing Office, 1878).

Ramsay, David, *The History of the American Revolution* (Indianapolis: Liberty Classics, 1990).

Reeves, Richard, *American Journey: Traveling with Tocqueville in Search of Democracy in America* (New York: Simon & Schuster, 1982).

Rhodehamel, John, ed., *The American Revolution* (New York: Literary Classics of the United States, 2001).

Rorty, Richard, *Achieving Our Country: Leftist Thought in Twentieth-Century America* (Cambridge: Harvard University Press, 2000).

Rosen, Gary, *American Compact: James Madison and the Problem of Founding* (Lawrence, KS: University Press of Kansas, 1999).

Rosen, Stanley, *The Ancients and the Moderns: Rethinking Modernity* (New Haven: Yale University Press, 1989).

Rossiter, Clinton, *1787: The Grand Convention* (New York: The Macmillan Company, 1966).

——, *The First American Revolution: The American Colonies on the Eve of Independence* (New York: Harcourt, Brace, 1956).

——, *Seedtime of the Republic: The Origin of the American Tradition of Political Liberty* (New York: Harcourt, Brace, 1953).

Rowland, Kate Mason, ed., *The Life and Correspondence of Charles Carroll of Carrollton, 1737–1832*, 2 vols. (New York, 1898).

Rutland, Robert A., *George Mason, Reluctant Statesman* (Baton Rouge: Lousiana State University Press, 1989).

——, *James Madison and the American Nation* (New York: Simon & Schuster, 1994).

Safire, William, *Scandalmonger* (New York: Simon & Schuster, 2000).

Sandoz, Ellis, ed., *Political Sermons of the American Founding Era: 1730–1805* (Indianapolis: Liberty Press, 1991).

Schindler, David, *Heart of the World, Center of the Church* (Grand Rapids: Eerdmans, 1996).

Schleifer, James. T., *The Making of Tocqueville's Democracy in America* (Indianapolis: Liberty Fund, 2000).

Schwarz, Barry, *George Washington: The Making of an American Symbol* (New York: The Free Press, 1987).

Secor, Robert, general editor, *Pennsylvania 1776* (University Park: Penn State University Press, 1975).

Shain, Barry A., *The Myth of American Individualism* (New Jersey: Princeton University Press, 1994).

Sharp, James Roger, *American Politics in the Early Republic: The New Nation in Crisis* (New Haven: Yale University Press, 1993).

Sheehan, Colleen A. and Gary L. McDowell, eds., *Friends of the Constitution: Writings of the "Other" Federalists, 1787–1788* (Indianapolis: Liberty Fund, 1998).

Sheldon, Garrett Ward, *The Political Philosophy of Thomas Jefferson* (Baltimore: Johns Hopkins University Press, 1991).

Sidney, Algernon, *Discourses Concerning Government* (Indianapolis: Liberty Fund, 1996).

Smith, Charles Page, *James Wilson: Founding Father* (Chapel Hill: North Carolina University Press, 1956).

Spalding, Matthew and Patrick Garrity, *A Sacred Union of Citizens* (New York: Rowman & Littlefield, 1996).

Stedman, W. David and LaVaugn G. Lewis, *Our Ageless Constitution* (Asheboro, NC: W. David Stedman Associates, 1987).

St. John, Jeffrey, *A Child of Fortune: A Correspondence Report* (Ottawa, IL: Jameson Books, 1990).

——, *Constitutional Journal* (Ottawa, IL: Jameson Books, 1987).

——, *Forge of Union, Anvil of Liberty: A Correspondence Report* (Ottawa, IL: Jameson Books, 1992).

Storing, Herbert, ed., *The Anti-Federalist* (Chicago: University of Chicago Press, 1985).

Story, Joseph, *The Constitution of the United States* (Lake Bluff, IL.: Regnery Gateway, 1986).

Strauss, Leo, *Natural Right and History* (Chicago: University of Chicago Press, 1953).

——, *What Is Political Philosophy?* (Chicago: University of Chicago Pres, 1988).

Taylor, George Rogers, *Hamilton and the National Debt* (Boston: D.C. Heath, 1950).

Thompson, C. Bradley, *John Adams and the Spirit of Liberty* (Lawrence, KS: University Press of Kansas, 1998).

Thucydides, *The Peloponnesian Wars* (New York: Modern Library, 1951).

Tierney, Brian, *The Idea of Natural Rights* (Atlanta: Scholar Press, 1997).

Tocqueville, Alexis de, *Democracy in America* (New York: Anchor Books, 1969).

——, *Democracy in America*, trans. George Lawrence and ed. J. P. Mayer (New York: Anchor Books, 1969).

——, *Democracy in America*, trans. and ed. Harvey C. Mansfield and Delba Winthrop (Chicago: University of Chicago Press, 2000).

——, *The Old Régime and the French Revolution* (New York: Vintage Books, 1955).

Trenchard, John, and Thomas Gordon, *Cato's Letters*, ed. Ronald Hamowy (Indianapolis: Liberty Fund, 1995).

Tyler, Moses Coit, *Patrick Henry* (New York: Frederick Ungar, 1898).

Umbreit, Kenneth, *Founding Fathers: Men Who Shaped Our Tradition* (Port Washington, NY: Kennikat Press, 1941).

Unger, Harlow Giles, *The Life and Times of Noah Webster an American Patriot* (New York: John Wiley & Sons, 1998).

Vetterli, Richard and Gary Bryner, *In Search of the Republic: Public Virtue and the Roots of American Government*, rev. ed. (Lanham, MD: Rowman & Littlefield, 1996).

Walling, Karl-Friedrich, *Republican Empire: Alexander Hamilton on War and Free Government* (Lawrence, KS: Kansas University Press, 1999).

Walsh, James J., *The Education of the Founding Fathers of the Republic; Scholasticism in the Colonial Colleges; A Neglected Chapter in the History of American Education* (New York: Fordham University Press, 1935).

Warner, W. Lloyd, *The Family of God: A Symbolic Study of Christian Life in America* (New Haven: Yale University Press, 1961).

Warren, Mercy Otis, *History of the Rise, Progress and Termination of the American Revolution* (Indianapolis: LibertyClassic, 1988).

Weisheipl, James A., O.P., *Friar Thomas D'Aquino: His Life, Thought and Works* (Garden City, NY: Doubleday & Company, 1974).

Wertenbaker, Thomas Jefferson, *The Puritan Oligarchy* (New York: Scribner, 1970).

West, Tom, "John Locke, Philosopher of the Founding *And Why We Should Be Glad He Was*" (unpublished paper for the John Courtney Murray lecture), October 4, 2000.

——, *Vindicating the Founders: Race, Sex, Class, and Justice in the Origins of America* (Lanham, MD: Rowman & Littlefield, 1997).

White, Morton, *Philosophy, The Federalist, and the Constitution* (New York: Oxford University Press, 1987).

Will, A. S., *Life of Cardinal Gibbons, Archbishop of Baltimore*, 2 vols. (New York: E. P. Dutton & Company, 1922).

Will, George F., *Statecraft as Soulcraft* (New York: Simon & Schuster, 1983).

Wills, Garry, *Explaining America* (New York: Doubleday & Company, 1981).

Wilstach, Paul, ed., *Correspondence of John Adams and Thomas Jefferson 1812–1826* (Indianapolis: The Bobbs-Merrill Company, 1925).

Witte, John, Jr., "A Most Mild and Equitable Experiment," in *Religion and the New Republic* (Lanham, MD: Rowman & Littlefield, 2000).

——, *Religion and the American Constitutional Experiment* (Boulder, CO: Westview Press, 2000).

Wood, Gordon S., *The Radicalism of the American Revolution* (New York: Knopf, 1992).

Yarbrough, Jean M., *American Virtues: Thomas Jefferson on the Character of a Free People* (Lawrence, KS: Kansas University Press, 1998).

Yates, Christopher S., *Alexander Hamilton: How the Mighty Are Redeemed* (Washington, D.C.: Family Research Council, 2000).

Zahniser, Marvin R., *Charles Cotesworth Pinckney: Founding Father* (Chapel Hill, NC: University of North Carolina Press, 1967).

Zuckert, Michael P., "Founder of the Natural Rights Republic," in Thomas S. Engeman, ed., *Thomas Jefferson and the Politics of Nature* (Notre Dame: Notre Dame University Press, 2000).

——, *The Natural Rights Republic* (Notre Dame: University of Notre Dame Press, 1996).

——, *Natural Rights and the New Republicanism* (Princeton: Princeton University Press, 1994).

INDEX